A Taste of Astrology

ALFRED A. KNOPF   NEW YORK   1988

A TASTE OF ASTROLOGY

by LUCY ASH

This Is a Borzoi Book Published by Alfred A. Knopf, Inc.

Copyright ©1987, 1988 by Lucy Ash

Portions of this text were originally published in Gourmet magazine.

Library of Congress Cataloging-in-Publication Data

Ash, Lucy.
    A taste of astrology.

    Includes index.
    1. Cookery.   2. Astrology.   I. Title.
TX652.A83   1988   64.5   88-45209
ISBN 0-394-55667-4

Manufactured in the United States of America

*To my wonderful mother, Dulcie Ommanney,
for her help and inspiration*

ACKNOWLEDGMENTS

I'm grateful to Judith Jones and Toula Polygalaktos at Knopf for believing in me and in this book. Thanks also to Amanda Marshall, Kate Kilroy, and Pat Hay, for pushing me to start this project; my bank manager, Ron Coles, for his patience; Mary Scott, China, and Assam, for their help in the kitchen; Bob Cross, for being my artistic alter ego; and others who have offered practical help and support.

CONTENTS

Introduction   *ix*

Aries   3

Taurus   29

Gemini   53

Cancer   75

Leo   101

Virgo   123

Libra   149

Scorpio   173

Sagittarius   197

Capricorn   221

Aquarius   247

Pisces   273

Index   297

INTRODUCTION

Food is a completely individual experience. What may be ambrosia to one person can be distasteful to another. Moreover, eating need never be dull; the varying nature of food is also one of its great attractions, not only because of the differences in taste and texture, but also because of the associations we have with food.

Memories are often triggered by a taste or smell, and they will help to color our enjoyment or lack of it. Taramosalata may remind us of blissful days spent on a Greek island, or of a bad holiday experience. Strawberries we invariably associate with good times—that first taste, maybe at an early summer picnic, of those berries whose scarlet juices represent the changing season, the heat of the summer to come. Shapes and colors of food also suggest images. For instance, I can't look at macaroni without seeing the horns of the sea goat, or at soft peaks of meringue or lightly beaten cream without imagining the foamy white waves of the Mediterranean where Venus was born.

Food and mythology have always been entwined. Scallops, like oysters, are said to have aphrodisiac qualities, and eating them can be a very sensual experience. So it makes sense that in mythology scallop shells should signify passionate love. Remember also that Venus, the Roman goddess of love, was carried across the ocean on such a shell. Food is so rich in symbolism that you need only bite into an apple to have all sorts of associations float into your mind—Snow White, the Garden of Eden, or some vivid memory of childhood.

The connection of astrology with food also works by association. Garlic, for example, is ruled by the fiery planet Mars because it too has a fiery nature. Oranges relate to the Sun and thus to Leo (the sign of the zodiac that it rules) because of their shape and color and sweet taste. Birds are linked to Venus, the goddess whose love encourages man to rise above the earth, and sensual fruits and curved mousses reflect her soft beauty.

So we have mythology and astrology working together when we try to understand the relationship between food and people. The ancient Greeks and Romans attributed the names of their gods to the planets according to the different natures of the gods. For example, the planet Mars, which rules the hot and fiery sign of Aries, is named after the Roman god of war, whose spirited nature is embodied in this sign, while Venus is named after the Roman goddess of love, whose sensual and gracious nature is reflected in the signs of Taurus and Libra.

As a painter, I have always been interested in symbolism and how it relates to color. I have worked on a series of paintings exploring this subject and I have come to feel that the colors of the zodiac should run as a rainbow—that in doing so, they make good symbolic sense. Aries is hot and fiery like its color, scarlet; Taurus is earthy like the orange-red soil; while, farther around the zodiac, Capricorns have a tendency to suffer the "indigo" blues.

If a separate color shines through each sign, it suggests that those born under different signs will have varying natures and thus will relate to food in different ways. While the earthy Taurean will enjoy being wined and dined on practical and substantial delights, a Gemini will be more at home with foods that are fun and novel.

Think how satisfying it could be for you, as host or hostess, to plan the menu for dinner around the personalities of your guests. All you need to do is find out the Sun sign of each person and then use astrology as your guide in devising a meal that will leave everyone charmed.

Have you ever invited a Gemini to dinner, served him a fiery curry, and then wondered why he spent all evening talking and hardly touched a bite? Geminis may like the sound of their own voices, but they may not be so wild about hot spicy food.

I should mention that your guests may not be typical of their signs, that exceptions to the rule are always possible—there are bound to be a few Geminis who are partial to curries. The Sun is not the whole picture in astrology (even though it is the best guide); there are nine other planets (for convenience, in astrology, the Sun is referred to as a planet) that influence our likes and dislikes.

But the awareness of differences, even the delight we find in learning about ourselves—why we are drawn to certain foods and why we cook the way we do—can make the thrice-daily act of preparing meals so much more fun and satisfying.

Alas! What various tastes in food,
Divide the human brotherhood!
Birds in their little nests agree
With Chinamen, but not with me.
Colonials like their oysters hot,
Their omelettes heavy—I do not.
—H. Belloc

A Taste of Astrology

ARIES

MARCH 21–APRIL 20

Rules the first house, the house of self-awareness

RULING PLANET
Mars
Υ

ELEMENT
Fire
Υ

QUALITIES
Cardinal, active
Υ

CHARACTERISTICS
Adventurous, assertive, creative, enterprising,
enthusiastic, impulsive
Υ

OPPOSITE SIGN
Libra
Υ

BODY AREA
Head
Υ

GEMSTONE
Ruby
Υ

COLOR
Scarlet
Υ

FLAVOR
Astringent, burning, pungent,
spicy, stimulating
Υ

METAL
Iron
Υ

FAUNA
Lamb, shark, spring chicken
Υ

FLORA
Blackberries, capers, coffee, garlic, leeks, onions, peppers, pineapple, radishes, rhubarb
Υ

HERBS AND SPICES
Cayenne, chilies, chili powder, chives,
curry powder, ginger, horseradish,
mustard, pepper
Υ

CELL SALT
Potassium phosphate (Kali. Phos.), found
in apples, beets, carrots, cauliflower, celery,
lemons, lentils, onions, radishes, spinach,
tomatoes, walnuts, watercress
Υ

ARIES THE COOK

If the Arian ever gets a chance to stop and exchange a few words, he or she is likely to invite you to dinner, because this sign of the zodiac is impulsive and remarkably gregarious and will love to give dinner parties. Warmhearted and generous, Aries likes to entertain in grand style.

This is a fire sign, full of forcefulness and passion, and Aries burns scarlet red with extravagant energy. It is an assertive and occasionally reckless sign of the zodiac, and for these reasons it is advisable to avoid the Arian's kitchen; if the smell of pungent spices is not enough to keep you at bay, then perhaps the resounding clang of pots and pans flying in different directions may be.

Arians love to cook spontaneously and to experiment; having an impressive capacity for creative thought (indicated by the ram's horns), this sign of the zodiac will experience a great sense of freedom in the kitchen. As cooks, they also possess a strong desire for knowledge and will forge ahead undaunted by the awesome task of interpreting a complicated recipe. Being very quick-witted people who like immediate results, they will invariably spot a faster approach, which they will carry through effectively and rapidly, leaving critics submissive.

Limited attention spans are often a trait with this sign of the zodiac, and Arians will be more likely to cook using approximations than carefully measured amounts. Fortunately this is not a sign that is easily daunted by failures—they are quickly forgotten and fresh ideas and inventions are introduced.

In Aries we see the mirror image of its ruling planet, Mars, the Roman god of war. The leader and conqueror of men and the disperser of misgivings, doubt, and fear makes Arians capable of sweeping aside obstacles and tackling almost any dish, from the most complicated curry to a simple kebab. There is no knowing what to expect in this household, but whatever it is, it won't have been cooked halfheartedly, because Aries will have put plenty of energy and thought into the creation. The food is more than likely to be colorful both to the eye and to the mouth, with firm shapes, sharp angles, and pungent flavors. The dishes will be stimulating by their nature and variety, and there will be plenty—all qualities that suggest the strength and vitality of Mars and the fiery essence of this sign.

Arians are unlikely to be mean with their food and drink, and will probably over-cater since they enjoy spending money, especially on things of pleasure. They also like to impress, so extravagant foods such as asparagus are a strong possibility and maybe even champagne, although they would probably prefer good red wines.

What makes Aries an efficient cook is a desire to be second to none. That, combined with a creative mind, makes this sign of the zodiac passionate, ambitious, and forceful in the kitchen. Don't offer any advice, because this headstrong sign always knows best. And visit their households when you are feeling strong, because you will be bombarded by punchy conversation and even punchier food.

RECIPES FOR ARIES

MENU SUGGESTIONS FOR ARIES

First Courses

A Mélange of Seafood in White
   Wine Sauce
Garlic Mushrooms
Hummus
Maria's Sardines on Fried Bread
Gazpacho
Steamed Asparagus with Hollandaise
Kidneys in Pastry Shells

Main Courses

Singapore Sole
Spaghetti with Tuna Fish and Olives
Chili con Carne
Lamb Kebabs
Cheese and Onion Tart
Spring Chicken
Spiced Fish

Side Dishes

Minted Cucumber and Radish Salad
Garlic Bread
Mixed Spiced Vegetables

Desserts

Queen of Puddings
Blackberry Cream
Ginger Cheesecake
Rhubarb Pie
Steamed Ginger Pudding
Coffee-Marshmallow Mousse

A Mélange of Seafood in White Wine Sauce
Chili con Carne
Ginger Cheesecake
♈

Garlic Mushrooms
Spaghetti with Tuna Fish and Olives
Rhubarb Pie
♈

Hummus
Lamb Kebabs
Steamed Ginger Pudding
♈

Maria's Sardines on Fried Bread
Cheese and Onion Tart
Blackberry Cream
♈

Gazpacho
Singapore Sole
Coffee-Marshmallow Mousse
♈

Steamed Asparagus with Hollandaise
Spring Chicken
Blackberry Cream
♈

Kidneys in Pastry Shells
Spiced Fish
Queen of Puddings

ARIES THE GUEST

Aries is a cardinal sign of the zodiac, indicating a nature that is active and outgoing; it is the hot cry of spring, representing new beginnings, and as its color scarlet suggests, the burning energy of fire. Persuade these fireballs to stand still for a moment, invite them to dinner, and they will respond with eagerness. You are bound to have a stimulating evening; supreme conversationalists and extremely quick-witted (indicated by Aries' rulership of the head), Arians make good guests and they will give their all to make your dinner party a success.

Like the ram that symbolizes this sign of the zodiac, Arians command a headstrong and impulsive nature that longs for action and adventure. What they won't enjoy is a dull evening, with no intellectual stimulation, so it might be wise to invite along a few other fire signs, or an airy intellectual sign such as an Aquarian, so they can exchange new thoughts and fresh ideas. Not that this sign of the zodiac is happy just talking concepts; doers and achievers, they would rather be out in the world putting their ideas in motion. It's important that they feel that your party is where the action is.

Don't bother feeding people under this sign delicate intricacies—the subtlety would pass them by. This outgoing guest will have firm ideas about his or her likes and dislikes and will prefer foods with strong pungent flavors rather than sweet seductive tastes, despite a keen palate (which comes from Aries' rulership of the head and face). Arians will be fond of diversity, so dine them on many varied dishes—perhaps a selection of curries or a flambé, to appeal to the fiery nature and strong warmth of feeling that Arians possess (it will also help to hold their attention).

Food is not the most important thing to this sign of the zodiac, but Arians do have hearty appetites, mainly because they burn up so much energy with zestful living, and for this reason it is a good idea to feed them foods rich in protein. Perhaps Chili con Carne or a fish dish or foods that include their cell salt, potassium phosphate, which helps to restore their mental vigor. Bright colors and hot spicy dishes will also attract them, but don't worry if none of these foods is on your menu, because those born under this sign of the zodiac will probably be starving by the time they arrive; they won't have had a chance to stop for a snack all day and will be delighted with whatever you choose to give them.

A Mélange of Seafood in White Wine Sauce

This delicious appetizer is rich in protein and iodine and should act as a restorative for the zestful Arian. Serve with thin slices of whole wheat bread and butter. *Serves 4*

1/2 lb squid

3/4 lb monkfish

1 1/2 lb mussels

4 cloves garlic, peeled and chopped

1 cup (8 oz) dry white wine

2 medium egg yolks

4 Tb (2 oz) heavy or double cream

2 tsp cornstarch

2 Tb chopped fresh parsley

Salt and black pepper

2 Tb olive oil

Cut the tentacles and head off the squid and then clean out the body; remove the cartilage and peel off the translucent outer membrane. Then wash the tentacles and the body in cold water. Chop the tentacles and slice the body into rings of about 1/2 inch across. Remove any skin from the monkfish, rinse it under cold water, then cut it off the bone and into bite-size pieces. Pat seafood dry with a paper towel.

Scrub the mussels clean in a basin of cold water. If any mussels are open when you have finished, throw them out. Place the garlic and wine in a medium-size saucepan, cover, and bring the wine to a boil. Simmer for 5 minutes, then add the mussels, cover, and cook for 5 minutes, until the mussel shells have steamed open. Remove the pan from the heat, transfer the mussels to a bowl, and strain the mussel liquor through cheesecloth or muslin, reserving 1/2 cup (4 ounces).

In the top of a double boiler, mix the egg yolks with the cream and whisk in the cornstarch, place over barely simmering water, and stir in the reserved mussel liquor. Continue to stir until the mixture thickens, then mix in the parsley, season to taste with salt and pepper, and remove from the heat. Cover with a lid and leave over hot water while you cook the remaining seafood.

Heat the olive oil in a frying pan and over moderate heat sauté the squid and monkfish, turning several times, for about 8 minutes, or until the monkfish is just cooked through. Season, and arrange equal amounts of the seafood on 4 plates with the mussels, then pour over the sauce and serve hot.

Garlic Mushrooms

The strong hot taste of the garlic sauce beautifully complements the succulent mushrooms, as well as providing remarkable healing qualities. Garlic purifies the blood and is a good remedy for many ailments; it acts as a stimulant, and for these reasons is ruled by the hot, fiery planet Mars. Spanish in origin, this dish goes particularly well with a young white Rioja and a crusty white loaf. *Serves 2*

Garlic sauce
>   3 cloves garlic, peeled and pushed through a press
>   2 Tb chopped fresh parsley
>   Pinch of salt
>   3 Tb (1¹/2 oz) olive oil
>
>   ¹/2 lb button mushrooms, wiped clean
>   3 Tb (1¹/2 oz) olive oil
>   Freshly ground black pepper

Preheat the broiler.

In a small bowl, mix the garlic with the parsley and salt, then work in the olive oil until the sauce is mixed thoroughly. Turn the sauce into a small glass bowl.

Cover the broiling rack with foil, and arrange the mushrooms on top. Sprinkle them with 2 tablespoons of olive oil, and season with black pepper. Set the rack 3 inches below the broiler, and let the mushrooms cook for 5 minutes. Turn the mushrooms, sprinkle them with the remaining oil, and cook an additional 5 minutes. Arrange them on a warmed serving dish and serve immediately with the sauce.

Hummus

A nourishing dish that is thought to increase virility, combining the influence of the two planets that represent human love: chick-peas for Venus, garlic for Mars. Serve as the Greeks do, sprinkled with paprika, and garnished with black olives and rounds of hot pita bread. *Serves 4*

>   ¹/2 cup (4 oz; 125g) dried chick-peas
>   6 Tb (3 oz) olive oil
>   6 Tb (3 oz) tahini
>   6 Tb (3 oz) lemon juice
>   6 Tb (3 oz) water
>   2 cloves garlic, peeled
>   2 Tb chopped fresh parsley
>   Salt and black pepper

Garnishes
>   Paprika
>   Black olives

In a medium-size bowl, soak the chick-peas overnight with 2–3 inches of cold water to cover. Drain and transfer them to a medium-size saucepan with 2–3 inches of water to cover. Bring them to a boil, cover, and simmer for 2¹/2–3 hours, or until the beans are tender. Drain the chick-peas and transfer them to a food processor or blender with all the other ingredients (apart from the garnishes), and purée until the mixture is well blended but still has a slightly rough texture. Season to taste with black pepper, turn into a shallow dish, sprinkle paprika on top, decorate with olives, and serve.

Maria's Sardines on Fried Bread

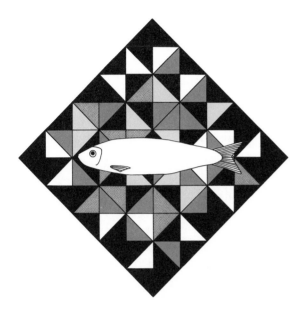

in 1 tablespoon of capers, the curry powder, and lemon juice.

Remove the crusts from the bread and cut each slice into 4 triangles. Heat 3 tablespoons of the oil in a large frying pan, and over high heat, sauté the bread in batches (you don't want to crowd the pan) for about 1–2 minutes on each side, or until golden brown. Transfer to paper towels to drain, then remove to a dish and keep warm.

Lower the heat to moderate and turn the sardine mixture into the frying pan, pressing it flat with a spatula. After 1–2 minutes, turn it and cook 1–2 minutes longer, taking care not to brown the sardines. Season generously with black pepper, remove from the heat, and spread a little of the sardine mixture on each piece of bread and serve.

Sardines on fried bread is a fittingly quick and easy dish to prepare for this overly busy sign of the zodiac. Spanish in origin, it should be served with a smoky Rioja to complement its special taste. Garnish with a caper in the center of each piece of bread. *Serves 6*

> *Three 4-oz (120-g) cans of sardines*
> *Capers*
> *1 Tb curry powder*
> *1 Tb lemon juice*
> *Six ¼-inch slices of whole wheat or white bread*
> *6 Tb (3 oz) olive oil*
> *Freshly ground black pepper*

Empty the sardines and their oil into a medium-size bowl and mash them well with a fork. Mix

Gazpacho

This chilled, fresh-tasting soup, attributed to Aries for its color and clean taste, is ideal for a hot summer day; it is also very easy to prepare. Tomatoes, a fruit of the Sun, are especially nutritious since they contain the Aries' cell salt, potassium phosphate, which is beneficial for this sign of the zodiac because it helps to repair its often exhausted nervous system. *Serves 4 to 6*

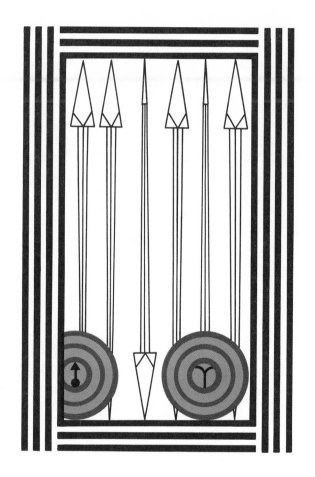

1/2 green pepper
1 small onion, peeled and chopped
1 large cucumber, peeled and chopped
4 cups (1 1/2 lb) peeled and chopped tomatoes
2 cloves garlic, peeled
1 cup (3 ribs) chopped celery
2 Tb olive oil
2 Tb lemon juice
1 Tb horseradish
Salt and black pepper to taste

Garnishes
  Ice cubes
  1 ripe avocado, peeled, pitted, and chopped
  Cayenne

Remove the seeds and the white membrane from the pepper, then place all the ingredients except the garnishes in a food processor or blender and purée. Pour into a soup tureen and chill for a few hours before serving. To serve, stir in a handful of ice cubes, scatter the chopped avocado on top, and sprinkle with a little cayenne.

Steamed Asparagus with Hollandaise

Here the asparagus symbolizes the warriors' sacred spears, the fine-pointed lines of the asparagus enchanting Arians because of their direct approach in life. Enjoy this luxurious vegetable during May and June when it is most available, and serve it with finger bowls, since it is traditionally eaten with fingers. *Serves 4*

2 lb asparagus, or 6–8 spears per person

Hollandaise sauce
    8 Tb (4 oz; 115 g) butter
    3 medium egg yolks
    2 Tb lemon juice
    Salt to taste
    Pinch of cayenne

Rinse the asparagus in cold water, peel the stalks, lightly near the top and quite deeply as you reach the stem, and cut off any woody ends that remain. Place it in the top of a steamer, over boiling water, and cover. Steam the asparagus for 5–10 minutes, or until the stems are tender when pierced with a knife. When the asparagus is nearly ready, make the hollandaise sauce.

In a saucepan gently melt the butter, until it is just bubbling. Mix the egg yolks with the lemon juice, salt, and cayenne for a few seconds in a food processor or blender. Then, with the food processor or blender running at high speed, very slowly pour in the hot butter through the funnel, and blend for a few minutes until the sauce is light and fluffy and has thickened.

Alternatively, make the sauce in the top of a double boiler. First melt the butter in a saucepan over gentle heat. Remove the pan from the heat and pour the butter into a jug. Then place the egg yolks in the top of a double boiler over barely simmering water and thoroughly whisk until they have thickened slightly and are smooth. Whisk in the lemon juice, salt, and cayenne and very slowly pour in the butter, whisking as you pour. Continue to whisk for 1–2 minutes, until the sauce has thickened but is light and fluffy. Remove the pan from the heat, but leave the sauce over hot water unless you are serving it immediately.

When the asparagus is cooked, arrange it in equal portions on 4 plates, pour the hollandaise into a bowl, and serve.

Kidneys in Pastry Shells

A decorative dish that is rich in iron and very nourishing, ideal for replenishing the Arian's exhausted energy. Its distinctive but unusual taste should also make this a favorite with this sign of the zodiac. Make the pastry quickly and lightly so that it does not get warm—the secret to good pastry. *Serves 4*

Shortcrust pastry (to line 10-inch pie pan)
    1½ cups (8 oz; 225 g) flour
    ¼ tsp salt
    8 Tb (4 oz; 115 g) butter
    3–4 Tb cold water

Filling
    6 lamb kidneys
    2 Tb butter
    1 tsp red currant jelly
    3 Tb (1½ oz) dry sherry
    2 tsp flour
    Salt and black pepper
    6 Tb cottage cheese
    2 tsp chopped fresh chives

    Trimmed watercress for garnish

First prepare the pastry. Place the flour and salt in a large bowl. Cut in the butter and with your fingertips work the flour and butter together until the mixture has the consistency of coarse bread crumbs. Pour in the water, tossing with a fork, until it is mixed in. Alternatively, you can make this pastry in a food processor. First mix the flour, salt, and butter; then add the water through the feed tube and process until a dough forms. Shape the dough into a ball, wrap it in plastic wrap, and refrigerate for about 20–30 minutes.

While the dough is chilling, prepare the kidneys. Remove any fat surrounding the kidneys and then peel off the thin translucent membrane. Cut the kidneys in half lengthwise and snip out the white core. Slice each kidney half into four pieces, and set aside. Then grease four 4-inch tart pans.

Preheat the oven to 425°F (220°C; gas 7).

Divide the pastry into four equal pieces and roll out on a floured board to about ⅛-inch thickness. Ease the rounds of dough into the tart pans and trim the edges. Prick the bottoms and sides with a fork and bake for 15–20 minutes, or until golden.

While the pastry is cooking, prepare the filling. In a medium-size frying pan, melt the butter over moderate heat, then add the kidneys and cook for 1–2 minutes on each side, turning occasionally. Transfer the kidneys to a plate. Turn the heat to low, then mix in the red currant jelly and sherry. Stir in the flour until you have a smooth paste, and simmer for a few minutes until the flour has cooked. Return the kidneys and any juices to the pan, coat them in the sauce, and season to taste with salt and black pepper. Remove the pan from the heat.

In a small bowl, mix the cottage cheese with the chives and divide the mixture equally among the 4 pastry shells to cover the bottoms. Then place the kidney mixture on top, garnish each tart with a small bunch of watercress in the center, and serve.

MAIN COURSES

Singapore Sole

Mercurial yellow, Singapore Sole suggests a food rich in goodness for the mind. Full of Eastern promise, this dish will appeal to the Arian's spirit of adventure. Serve garnished with watercress and with a bowl of hot rice. *Serves 2*

1 lb (2–4 fillets) of lemon sole, flounder, or plaice
3 Tb flour
1/2 medium pineapple
3 Tb (1 1/2 oz) sunflower or vegetable oil
1 medium onion, peeled and finely chopped
1-inch piece of gingerroot, peeled and minced
6 anchovy fillets, coarsely chopped
1/2 tsp chili powder
1 tsp turmeric
Finely grated rind of 1 lemon
Finely grated rind of 1 orange
1/4 cup (2 oz) fresh orange juice
Salt and black pepper
Trimmed watercress for garnish

Parsnip sauce
2 1/4 cups (3/4 lb) peeled and chopped parsnips
2 Tb fresh lemon juice
6 Tb (3 oz) light or single cream
1 tsp brown sugar
Salt and black pepper

Roll the fillets in the flour, shake off any excess, and set aside. Using a sharp knife, remove the skin and woody eyes from the pineapple. Halve it lengthwise and cut out the center core. Then cut the flesh into bite-size pieces and set aside.

Heat 1 1/2 tablespoons oil in a large frying pan, over moderate heat, and sauté the onion and ginger for 5 minutes, stirring occasionally.

Mix in the pineapple, anchovies, spices, and lemon and orange rinds, pour over the orange juice, and stir thoroughly. Reduce the heat, season to taste with salt and black pepper, and simmer for 10 minutes, stirring occasionally. While the pan is simmering, prepare the sauce.

Place the parsnips in a pan with about 2 inches of boiling water. Cover, and simmer for 10 minutes, or until they are tender. Then drain and place them in a food processor or blender with lemon juice, cream, and brown sugar. Purée until smooth, season to taste with salt and black pepper, and set aside.

Place the pineapple and onion mixture on a plate and keep warm. Heat the remaining oil in the same frying pan over moderate heat, cook the fish for 5 minutes on each side, and season with salt and black pepper. While the fish is cooking, transfer the parsnip sauce to a saucepan, heat it through, then pour it over the bottom of a warmed serving dish. Arrange the fish over the sauce, then distribute the pineapple-onion mixture on top, garnish with watercress, and serve hot.

Spaghetti with Tuna Fish and Olives

The olives give this spaghetti dish its soft, rich flavor. It makes a good family dish, unusual enough also for a dinner party. Serve with a mixed salad, plenty of garlic bread (see page 20), and some Chianti wine. *Serves 4*

1 cup (about 4½ oz; 125 g) green olives

1 green pepper

½ red pepper

2 Tb olive oil

2 medium onions, peeled and sliced

5 cloves garlic, peeled and chopped

1 Tb tomato paste

1 cup (3 ribs) finely chopped celery

One 28-oz (395-g) can Italian tomatoes

1 lb spaghetti

Two 7-oz (200-g) cans tuna fish, drained and flaked

Dash of Tabasco

¼ tsp dried basil, or ½ tsp chopped fresh

Salt and freshly ground black pepper

2 Tb butter

4 Tb grated Parmesan

Pit and slice the olives. Halve the green pepper lengthwise, remove the seeds, stalk, and whitish membrane from both peppers, and then chop them. Heat the oil in a large frying pan over moderately high heat, and sauté the onions for 5 minutes, or until they are a light golden. Lower the heat to moderate and mix in the garlic, tomato paste, olives, red and green pepper, and celery. Stir-fry 1–2 minutes and then mix in the tomatoes. Simmer 15–20 minutes, stirring occasionally.

When the tomato mixture is nearly ready, cook the spaghetti in a large pan of boiling salted water for 10–15 minutes, or until it is cooked *al dente.*

Meanwhile add the tuna fish, Tabasco, and basil to the tomato mixture, season to taste with salt and black pepper, and cook for 5 minutes more, stirring occasionally. Drain the spaghetti when it has cooked, and transfer it to a warmed serving dish. Toss it in the butter, pour the sauce over the middle, sprinkle the Parmesan cheese over, and serve.

Chili con Carne

Chili con Carne is a quick-to-do dish that is ideal for parties; its spirited nature mirrors that of the red-hot planet Mars (which rules Aries). The Sun is exalted in Aries, and here the Sun-ruled tomatoes benefit this sign of the zodiac, containing their cell salt, potassium phosphate, which helps to relieve nervous headaches and exhaustion, often common Arian complaints. Serve this dish with a mixed green salad, brown rice, whole wheat Italian bread, and plenty of red wine. *Serves 4 to 6*

> *1 cup (7 oz; 200 g) dried red kidney beans*
> *1 large red pepper*
> *2 Tb olive oil*
> *2 medium onions, peeled and chopped*
> *4 cloves garlic, peeled and finely chopped*
> *Salt and black pepper to taste*
> *1 lb ground beef (chuck)*
> *1 Tb flour*
> *2 tsp chili powder*
> *1 tsp ground cumin*
> *2 Tb tomato paste*
> *One 28-oz (395-g) can Italian tomatoes*

Soak the kidney beans overnight in a bowl with 2 inches of cold water to cover.

Drain the beans and transfer them to a large saucepan, with a few inches of water to cover, bring them to a boil, then reduce the heat, cover, and simmer for 1½–2 hours, or until the beans are firm but tender.

Preheat the oven to 350°F (180°C; gas 4).

Cut the red pepper in half lengthwise, remove the seeds, stalk, and whitish membrane, and cut it across into thin slices. In a large frying pan, heat the oil over high heat and sauté the onions, garlic, and red pepper for 5 minutes, stirring continuously. Season to taste with salt and black pepper and transfer to an ovenproof casserole.

Add the meat to the saucepan and over high heat cook for 5 minutes, stirring and turning so it browns lightly and evenly (it should have a crumbly texture). Sprinkle the flour and spices over the meat, season to taste with salt and black pepper, and mix well before stirring in the tomato paste and tomatoes. Turn the meat mixture into the casserole. Drain the cooked beans and mix them into the casserole so that the meat and vegetables are evenly distributed. Check the seasoning, cover, and place the casserole in the oven for 40 minutes. Serve hot.

Lamb Kebabs

Lamb Kebabs make a perfect Arian meal, and the unusual combination of fruit and meats are a pleasant and easy change. It is also an ideal dish for the barbecue—a festivity this fiery sign will love. Serve the kebabs on a bed of rice with Minted Cucumber and Radish Salad (see page 20) and hot crusty garlic bread (see page 20). *Serves 4*

Marinade

> 6 Tb (3 oz) sunflower oil
>
> 3 Tb (1½ oz) red wine vinegar
>
> 1 tsp Dijon mustard
>
> 1 tsp superfine or castor sugar
>
> 1 clove garlic, peeled and pushed
>> through a press
>
> Salt and black pepper to taste
>
> 1 lb lamb, cut from the leg
>
> 8 lamb kidneys
>
> ½ medium pineapple
>
> 16 medium mushrooms, wiped clean
>
> 1 Granny Smith or tart apple
>
> 16 small white onions, peeled
>
> Pinch of ground ginger
>
> Salt and black pepper to taste

In a small bowl or jar, mix together all the marinade ingredients. Remove any surrounding fat from the lamb and cut the meat into sixteen 1½-inch cubes. Remove any fat surrounding the kidneys and peel off the thin translucent membrane. Cut them in half crosswise and snip out the white core. Arrange the kidneys and lamb cubes in a shallow dish, pour the marinade over, and leave them to stand for about an hour, while you prepare the rest of the ingredients.

Using a sharp knife, pare the skin from the pineapple, cut out the woody eyes, slice it in half lengthwise, remove the core, and then cut it into 12 pieces. Break off the mushroom stems. Quarter the apple, remove the core, and cut it into 12 slices.

Preheat the broiler. Arrange the meat, fruit, and vegetables evenly among four 16-inch skewers, sprinkle them with the ground ginger, and season to taste with salt and pepper. Place the kebabs on the broiler rack 3 inches from the heat, pour over a little of the marinade, and cook, turning and pouring a little of the marinade over every 2–3 minutes, for 15–20 minutes, until the kebabs are browned and the meat is cooked.

Cheese and Onion Tart

Cheese and Onion Tart can be served hot or cold, as a main course with a green salad and new potatoes, or in small slices as a starter. It also makes an ideal picnic dish. The Mars-ruled onions help to stimulate the appetite and also contain Aries' cell salt, potassium phosphate. Serve sprinkled with cayenne—a spice of Mars and a good digestive. *Serves 4*

Whole wheat pastry
>   1¹/2 cups (8 oz) whole wheat flour
>   ¹/4 tsp salt
>   8 Tb (4 oz; 115 g) butter
>   3–4 Tb (1¹/2–2 oz) cold water

Filling
>   2 Tb sunflower oil
>   1 lb Spanish onions, peeled and sliced
>   4 cloves garlic, peeled and pushed through a press
>   4 medium eggs
>   2 Tb light or single cream
>   2 tsp Dijon mustard
>   2 cups (4 oz) grated Cheddar cheese
>   Salt and black pepper to taste
>   Cayenne for garnish

Place the flour and the salt in a large bowl and cut in the butter. Mix lightly, using your fingertips to work the butter and flour together, until the mixture has the consistency of bread crumbs. Pour in the water, mixing with a fork, until the dough forms a soft ball. Or, alternatively, you can make this pastry in a food processor. First mix the flour, salt, and butter together until the mixture resembles coarse bread crumbs, then add the water through the funnel. Mix dough and shape into one round piece. Wrap it in plastic wrap and refrigerate for 20–30 minutes while you prepare the onions.

Heat the oil in a medium-size frying pan over low heat; very gently sauté the onions and garlic for 40–60 minutes, stirring occasionally until they are soft and well cooked.

Preheat the oven to 425°F (220°C; gas 7).

While the onions are cooking, roll out the pastry on a floured board 2 inches larger than the pie pan, and then ease it into the pan (this will be enough pastry for a 9- or 10-inch pie pan), crimp the edges and prick the bottom with a fork, then bake it for 10 minutes. Remove the pastry shell from the oven and lower the heat to 350°F (180°C; gas 4).

In a large mixing bowl beat the eggs with the cream and mustard. Stir in the onions and cheese and season generously. Turn into the pastry shell and bake for 30–35 minutes, or until a knife comes out clean when plunged into the center. Sprinkle with cayenne and serve.

Spring Chicken

Attributed here because Aries is the sign of the spring equinox, when the new year bursts forth with its fresh energy, Spring Chicken is full of the goodness of young root vegetables. Serve with a crusty loaf and a young French wine. (One chicken would be too meager for four people, so if you have any left over, use it for Asparagus and Chicken Salad, page 202.) *Serves 4*

Giblets from 1 chicken

1 small onion, peeled and quartered

2 ribs of celery, cut into 2-inch pieces

Bouquet garni

2¼ cups (18 oz) water

3 Tb (1½ oz) olive oil

Two 2–2½-lb chickens

5 cloves garlic, peeled and quartered

2 cups (16 oz) medium-dry white wine

1 lb baby carrots, scraped

1 lb new potatoes, scrubbed clean

Salt and black pepper

8 scallions or spring onions,
chopped into 1½-inch lengths

1 lb snow peas, topped and tailed, with any
strings removed

To make the stock, place the giblets in a saucepan with the onion, celery, and bouquet garni, and cover with the water. Bring to a boil and spoon off any scum from the surface; cover and simmer for 1½–2 hours. When the stock is nearly ready, prepare the chicken.

Preheat the oven to 400°F (200°C; gas 6).

Heat the oil in an ovenproof casserole over fairly high heat, and sear the chickens, one at a time so you don't crowd the pan, turning so they brown evenly, for about 5 minutes each. Put both chickens back in the casserole. Add the garlic for the last minute, so it just browns lightly. Strain the stock and pour 2 cups of it and the wine over the chicken. Add the carrots and potatoes, cover, and bring to a boil, then place in the preheated oven for 40 minutes. Remove the casserole and season to taste with salt and black pepper. Add the chopped scallions and the snow peas. Cover, and return to the oven for 20 minutes longer, or until the chicken is cooked.

To serve, remove the chicken to a board, and carve it. Then arrange it on a warmed serving dish and serve, surrounded with the vegetables.

Spiced Fish

An exotic fish dish that is not hard to make but is deliciously different. Its spiciness is just right for this most fiery of fire signs. Here an exciting taste is combined with the purifying and cleansing properties of the Martial spices. Serve this dish with Mixed Spiced Vegetables (see page 21), rice, and a cold beer or white wine. *Serves 4*

> 2 lb (4 thick) shark, cod, or haddock steaks, skinned and boned
>
> 4 Tb (2 oz) lemon juice
>
> 3 Tb (1½ oz) sunflower or vegetable oil
>
> 2 small onions, peeled and chopped
>
> 2 Tb flour
>
> 1 cup plain yogurt
>
> 1 Tb tomato paste
>
> ½ lb tomatoes, peeled and chopped
>
> ¼ cup golden raisins or sultanas, washed
>
> 4 cloves garlic, peeled and pushed through a press
>
> 2 tsp ground coriander
>
> 2 tsp ground turmeric
>
> 1 tsp ground cumin
>
> 1 tsp ground ginger
>
> 1 tsp dried thyme, or 2 tsp chopped fresh
>
> ½ tsp chili powder
>
> Salt and black pepper
>
> 1 Tb chopped fresh parsley
>
> 1 Tb butter

Preheat the oven to 375°F (190°C; gas 5).

Place the fish in a shallow dish, in one layer. Pour the lemon juice over and marinate while you prepare the sauce.

Heat the oil in a large frying pan over moderate heat, and sauté the onions for 5 minutes. Stir the flour into the pan so it absorbs the oil, and gradually pour in the yogurt. Stir until you have a smooth paste and then add the tomato paste, tomatoes, raisins, garlic, and spices. Season to taste with salt and black pepper, lower the heat slightly, and simmer for 5 minutes, stirring occasionally. Remove the pan from the heat and mix in the parsley.

Drain the fish and arrange it in one layer in an ovenproof dish, pour the sauce over, cover with foil, and bake for 30 minutes. Pour the sauce back into the frying pan. Cover the fish and keep it warm. The sauce will now be fairly liquid, so you will need to reduce it to a thicker consistency. Place the frying pan over high heat, and boil the sauce for 4–5 minutes, stirring constantly, until the sauce has thickened. Remove from the heat and immediately swirl in the butter, stirring until it is thoroughly blended. Arrange the fish on a warmed serving dish, pour the sauce over, and serve hot.

Minted Cucumber and Radish Salad

A refreshing salad that makes a delicious accompaniment to most dishes. For a quick and nouring lunch, try this with Hummus (see page 8), a Red, White, and Black Salad (page 108), and plenty of hot pita bread. *Serves 4*

1 cup (6 oz) or a bunch of radishes

6–8 scallions or spring onions

1 clove garlic, peeled and pushed through a press

1 cup chopped cucumber (1/2 cucumber)

1/2 cup (2 3/4 oz; 80 g) washed golden raisins or sultanas

3 Tb chopped fresh parsley

1 Tb dried mint, or 2 Tb chopped fresh

1/2 cup (4 oz) plain yogurt

Salt and black pepper

Wash the radishes, pat them dry, and cut off the tops and thin root. Slice them crosswise. Chop the scallions (you should have about 1/2 cup). In a mixing bowl, combine the next six ingredients, mix thoroughly, and season to taste with salt and black pepper. Turn into a glass serving bowl and serve.

Garlic Bread

Garlic bread is an excellent accompaniment to a great many dishes and is best served hot from the oven. *Serves 4*

4 Tb (2 oz; 60 g) soft butter

3 cloves garlic, peeled and pushed through a press

1 Tb finely chopped fresh parsley

1 long, thin loaf French or Italian bread, about 16 inches long

Preheat the oven to 400°F (200°C; gas 6).

In a small bowl cream together the butter, garlic, and parsley. Slice the bread diagonally across about every 2 inches to within 1/4 inch of the base. Spread a little of the butter mixture on each slice, wrap the bread in foil, and bake it for 10–15 minutes, until it is hot and crunchy. Unwrap and serve.

Mixed Spiced Vegetables

A delicious way of serving vegetables: the spicy creamy sauce gives this dish its hot but delicate flavor and makes it an ideal accompaniment to a curry dish, relating directly to the creative fire embodied in this sign of the zodiac. Alternatively, serve this for two people as a light lunch or supper dish with rice or mashed potatoes and plenty of cold beer. *Serves 4*

1 small cauliflower

1/2 lb (2 medium) parsnips

3 Tb corn or vegetable oil

2 small onions, peeled and chopped

1 clove garlic, peeled and finely chopped

1-inch piece of gingerroot, peeled and
    finely chopped

1 Granny Smith apple

1/2 lb peas, shelled (1/2 cup)

Salt and black pepper

1 Tb butter

1 Tb flour

1/2 tsp ground cumin

1/2 tsp ground coriander

1/2 tsp ground turmeric

1/2 tsp cayenne

1/4 tsp chili powder

1 tsp brown sugar

2 Tb water

1 cup (8 oz) plain yogurt

Break the cauliflower into bite-size florets. Peel the parsnips and cut them into 3/4-inch cubes. Place both vegetables in a pan with about 2 inches of salted boiling water, cover, and simmer for 2 minutes. Drain and set aside. Heat the oil in a large saucepan, and mix in the onions, garlic, and ginger. Cook them over moderate heat for 5 minutes, stirring occasionally. Add the cauliflower and parsnips, mix well, cover, reduce the heat slightly, and let them sweat for about 3 minutes. Peel, core, and chop the apple into 1/2-inch cubes and add them and the peas to the saucepan with the other vegetables. Season to taste with salt and black pepper and give everything a good stir. Cover, and leave to cook for a few minutes while you make the sauce.

In a separate saucepan, melt the butter over low to moderate heat, stir in the flour, and cook together for 2 minutes. Then, in a small glass or jar, mix the spices and sugar with the water and pour into the roux. Mix well, then stir in the yogurt and cook gently for a few minutes. Pour the sauce over the vegetables, thoroughly mix, then turn into a warmed serving dish and serve.

Queen of Puddings

Queen of Puddings is a traditional English dessert, which is suitably regal for this commanding sign of the zodiac. Topped with soft meringue and full of the goodness of fresh fruits and whole wheat bread, it makes a family favorite or even an impressive dinner-party dish. *Serves 4–6*

> 1 cup (8 oz) milk
> 1 cup (8 oz) light or single cream
> 1 Tb butter
> 1¾ cups (3 oz) soft whole wheat bread crumbs
> 3 Tb brown sugar
> Finely grated rind of 1 lemon
> Finely grated rind of 1 orange
> 3 large eggs, separated
> 4 Tb (2 oz) raspberry or blackberry jam
> 2 Tb superfine or castor sugar
> 2 Tb confectioners or icing sugar

Preheat the oven to 350°F (180°C; gas 4).

Pour the milk and cream into a saucepan with the butter, and, over gentle heat, bring them nearly to a simmer. Do not boil. While the milk and cream are warming through, place the bread crumbs, brown sugar, and lemon and orange rinds in a medium-size bowl, and pour the milk and cream over. Leave to soak for 30 minutes, then mix in the egg yolks. Turn the mixture into a buttered shallow baking dish (a glass dish looks good since it shows the layers of the pudding), and bake for 30–35 minutes. When a knife plunged into the center comes out clean, the pudding is cooked. Remove it from the oven and spread the jam over while it is still hot. In a mixing bowl, beat the egg whites, gradually adding the remaining sugars, until they form peaks. Spread over the pudding so it is evenly covered and return it to the oven for 10 minutes more to brown the meringue topping. Serve hot.

Blackberry Cream

A luxuriously musky-scented dish, which indicates that Nicholas Culpeper (the famous seventeenth-century astrologer-physician) was right when he stated that blackberries are a fruit of Venus in Aries. Appropriately, all planets with thorns and prickles are ruled by the spirited planet Mars (or the sign of the zodiac that shares its characteristics). Serve this delectable dish in tall glasses, topped with a spoonful of whipped cream and accompanied by ladyfingers. *Serves 4*

> 6 Tb (3 oz) superfine or castor sugar
>
> 1/4 cup plus 2 Tb (3 oz) water
>
> 1 Tb lemon juice
>
> 1½ pints (1 lb) blackberries, hulled and
>   rinsed in cold water
>
> 1½ tsp gelatin

Custard

> 3 medium egg yolks
>
> 2 Tb brown sugar
>
> 1 cup (8 oz) light or single cream

Place the sugar, 1/4 cup of the water, lemon juice, and berries in a medium-size saucepan, and bring to a simmer. Cover, and cook gently over low heat for 10 minutes, or until tender. While the blackberries are cooking, place the remaining 2 tablespoons cold water in a medium-size bowl, sprinkle over the gelatin, and leave it to soak for 5 minutes. Remove the blackberries from the burner and, using the back of a spoon, push them and their juice through a sieve into a bowl. Return the blackberry purée to the saucepan and bring it to the boiling point. Immediately pour it over the gelatin mixture, stirring continuously, until the gelatin has completely dissolved. Set aside while you make the custard.

In the top of a double boiler mix together the egg yolks and brown sugar, then stir in the cream, and place over barely simmering water. Stir until the mixture thickens, then remove it from the heat. Allow the custard to cool slightly, then mix it thoroughly with the blackberry purée. Turn into individual glass dishes or a glass bowl and leave to chill and thicken for a few hours or overnight before serving.

Ginger Cheesecake

This protein-packed dessert is a cheesecake with a difference—a delicious way to replace some of the energy expended by an Arian. Accompany it with a smoky red Rioja. *Serves 6*

Crumb crust

1¾ cups (8 oz; 225 g) crushed gingersnaps

2 tsp ground ginger

⅓ cup melted butter

Filling

3 Tb (1½ oz) lemon juice

1 Tb plus ½ tsp gelatin

2 medium eggs, separated

½ cup (4 oz; 115 g) superfine or castor sugar

2 cups (1 lb) cream cheese

¼ cup (2 oz) boiling water

½ cup (4 oz) heavy or double cream

3–4 pieces of stem ginger in syrup or candied ginger, sliced for garnish

In a mixing bowl, thoroughly combine the gingersnaps, ground ginger, and butter. Pack them into a 10-inch pie pan to form a crumb crust, then chill while you make the filling.

Pour the lemon juice into a small bowl, sprinkle the gelatin over, and leave it to soak for a few minutes. In a large bowl or food processor, thoroughly mix the egg yolks, sugar, and cream cheese. Pour the boiling water over the gelatin, and stir until it has completely dissolved, then blend it thoroughly into the cheese mixture. In a separate bowl, beat the cream until stiff and fold it into the cheese mixture. In a fresh bowl, with clean beaters, beat the egg whites until they form peaks. Using a metal spoon, fold the beaten whites into the cheesecake mixture, then pour into the crumb crust. Chill for a few hours or overnight, then decorate with the stem ginger and serve.

Rhubarb Pie

The delightful piquant flavor of this pie makes this a charming way to end a meal. Serve it with some whipped cream and a sweet white dessert wine. *Serves 4 to 6*

Pastry

2¼ cups (11 oz; 315 g) flour

¼ tsp salt

2 Tb superfine or castor sugar

Grated rind of 1 orange

12 Tb (6 oz; 170 g) butter

4–5 Tb (2–2½ oz) fresh orange juice

Filling

1½ lb rhubarb, ends and leaves removed

2 Tb gin

1 cup (6 oz) light brown sugar

2 tsp superfine or castor sugar

Place the flour, salt, superfine sugar, and orange rind in a large bowl, and cut in the butter. Mix lightly, then, with your fingertips, work the flour and butter together until the mixture has the consistency of bread crumbs. Pour in the orange juice, mixing with a fork until the juice is all absorbed. Or alternatively, you can make this pastry in a food processor. First mix the flour, salt, sugar, orange rind, and butter together until the mixture resembles bread crumbs, then add the orange juice through the funnel. Blend to a dough, remove, and shape into one round ball. Wrap it in plastic wrap and leave to chill for 20–30 minutes.

Preheat the oven to 400°F (200°C; gas 6).

While the pastry is chilling, wash the rhubarb and cut it into 2-inch pieces. Place it in a medium-size saucepan with the gin and brown sugar, bring it to a simmer, cover, and let it cook very gently for 15–20 minutes. Now roll half the pastry out on a floured board and line an 8-inch pie pan with it. Thoroughly drain the rhubarb and set aside to cool, then turn it into the pastry shell. Roll out the remaining pastry, cover the rhubarb with it, crimp the edges, and then cut two 2-inch slits in the top so that steam can escape. Cook the pie in a hot oven for 30–35 minutes and serve it hot with the top sprinkled with superfine sugar.

Steamed Ginger Pudding

Light and moist, this pudding suggests the heat of the Sun (the Sun is exalted in Aries), with its golden color and firm round shape. It is perfect served with a syrupy sauce and a jug of light cream. *Serves 6*

> 3 Tb (85 g) rinsed and finely chopped stem
>   ginger in syrup, or candied ginger
>   wiped clean
> ¾ cup (3½ oz; 105 g) flour
> 1 tsp baking powder
> 6 Tb (3 oz; 85 g) superfine or castor sugar
> Pinch of salt
> 2 tsp ground ginger
> 4 Tb (2 oz; 60 g) soft butter
> 2 large eggs
> 2 Tb milk

Sauce
> 6 Tb (3 oz) corn or golden syrup
> 2 tsp lemon juice
> 1 Tb water

Pat the stem ginger dry with a paper towel. Put all the other pudding ingredients in a mixing bowl or food processor. Beat (or if using a processor, blend) until thoroughly mixed and then fold in the stem ginger. Mix well and turn the batter into a greased 1½-quart pudding mold. Cut a piece of wax paper to lie on top of the pudding and just touch the edges of the mold. Take a large piece of foil, fold a pleat in the center, and lay it over the pudding mold with 3 inches to spare all around. Wrap tightly around the mold and secure with a piece of string. Fill the bottom of a steamer three-fourths full of water and bring it to a simmer. Place the pudding in the top of the steamer over the water. Cover, and steam for 2–2½ hours, checking occasionally to see that the water has not evaporated.

When the pudding is nearly ready make the sauce. Place the syrup, lemon juice, and water in a small saucepan over low heat and stir for 3–4 minutes, until the syrup has melted. Take care not to boil. When the pudding is cooked, turn it out onto a serving dish. Pour the hot sauce into a small jug and serve.

Coffee-Marshmallow Mousse

Coffee-Marshmallow Mousse is a good dish for Arians because of the qualities coffee has as a stimulant and energizer. It is a smooth and creamy dessert that is effortless to make and can be prepared well in advance. It is a scrumptious end to a meal. *Serves 6*

3 cups (9 oz; 250 g) marshmallows

1¹/₂ cups (12 oz) strong coffee

1¹/₂ cups (12 oz) heavy or double cream

1 Tb coarsely grated semisweet chocolate

Cut the marshmallows into pieces and place them in a saucepan, then add the coffee and, over low heat, gently warm through without boiling (or the marshmallows will not set and the coffee will lose its flavor). Stir occasionally until the marshmallows have melted. Turn the mixture into a bowl and chill for 2–3 hours, or until it has thickened. Now beat it until it is well mixed. In a separate bowl, beat the cream until it is stiff, add to the coffee-marshmallow mixture, and beat well. Turn the mousse into a glass serving dish and chill for 30 minutes, or until you wish to serve it, sprinkled with grated chocolate.

TAURUS

APRIL 21–MAY 21

Rules the second house, the house of finance and possessions

RULING PLANET
Venus
♉

ELEMENT
Earth
♉

QUALITIES
Fixed, passive
♉

CHARACTERISTICS
Cautious, determined, gracious, harmonious, masterful, sensual
♉

OPPOSITE SIGN
Scorpio
♉

BODY AREA
Neck, throat
♉

GEMSTONE
Diamond, emerald
♉

COLOR
Orange-red
♉

FLAVOR
Sweet, delicately savory
♉

METAL
Copper
♉

FAUNA
Beef, chicken, lamb, scallops
♉

FLORA
Apples, beans, bread, cherries, chick-peas, gooseberries, grapes, kiwi fruit, lentils, peaches, pears, plums, root vegetables, wheat
♉

HERBS AND SPICES
Coriander, mint, nutmeg, thyme
♉

CELL SALT
Sulphate of soda (Nat. Sulph.), found in beets, cabbage, cucumber, onions, radishes, spinach
♉

TAURUS THE COOK

If you're lucky enough to be invited to dine with a Taurean, don't say no! This sign of the zodiac has the common sense, calmness, and love of food necessary to make a good cook. Great gourmets and chefs, such as James Beard, are born under this sign.

Don't go expecting anything too exotic or diverse, because Taureans believe that it is the simple things on earth that equal excellence; they are concerned with the tangible aspects of life, and since food is such a necessity it is very important to them. This is an earth sign, full of the practicality of earth, and reflecting the physical side of life. It represents the red-orange soil, soft and nourishing, and it is this influence that shines through Taurus.

Taureans understand method, order, and reason, like the earth and its changing seasons, and they possess the feeling of ease that comes from being in harmony with nature. Taureans know better than to cut corners or rush a work of beauty, instinctively realizing that excellence takes time and can't be hurried; they probably won't want to hurry anyway because cooking is something that gives them great pleasure. This sign of the zodiac will happily spend hours in the kitchen, inspired by love of family and friends, and will enjoy creating practical and substantial delights rather than frivolous dishes. A nourishing soup or pie that reflects their sensible outlook on life will quite possibly be on the menu, or a beef dish that symbolizes the sign of the bull.

The Taurean's kitchen will be a place of welcome; it will be well organized and quite safe to visit. This sign of the zodiac makes cooking look easy. Patiently understanding and following a recipe, Taureans have the persistence and determination necessary for culinary success along with a naturally physical and intuitive response to food.

The homes of Taureans will also reflect the nature of their ruling planet, Venus, the Roman goddess of love, and they will enjoy entertaining with graciousness. They are born home lovers, and their households will be attractive and comfortable, the influence of Venus bringing a softness and love of sensuality and tranquility. The food that this sign cooks will not only taste good, but look good. Presentation is important, and the soft curves and gentle rhythms of Venus will be in evidence. Soft voluptuous fruits and sensual delights will be among the Taureans' favorite dishes, but they will be treated with the simplicity of nature.

If you are wined and dined by a Taurean, don't expect champagne; a full-bodied red wine, reflecting the solidity and strong foundations of character, is more likely. Taurus rules the second house of the zodiac, which is concerned with finance and material possessions, making this sign quite sensible with money. However, Taureans' interest is more for what money can buy than the power it accumulates in the bank. Venus, their ruling planet, governs the festive and social aspects of life, bringing a love of giving and entertaining, and Taureans will spend freely on things of pleasure, such as food and drink. An evening with a Taurean is likely to be a physical and sensual one, given over to pleasures of the flesh, and it will be best to visit when you are feeling hungry.

RECIPES FOR TAURUS

First Courses

Avocado, Kiwi Fruit, and Radicchio Salad
Chicken Liver Pâté
Curried Parsnip Soup
Potato Gnocchi
Baked Spinach Creams
Mixed Bean Vinaigrette
Pear, Cress, and Chicken Salad

Main Courses

Moussaka
Halibut with Peanuts and Grapes
Spring Stew
Fish Pie
Fillet Steak with Scallop and
    Mushroom Sauce
Bean Salad with Lemon and
    Yogurt Dressing
Chicken with Asparagus

Side Dishes

Carrots with Coriander
Puréed Rutabagas

Desserts

Chocolate Charlotte
Nelly's Shape
Plum Tart
Cherry Ice Cream with Cherry Brandy
Gooseberry Crumble
Toasted Apple Brûlée

MENU SUGGESTIONS FOR TAURUS

Chicken Liver Pâté
Fish Pie
Toasted Apple Brûlée

♉

Potato Gnocchi
Halibut with Peanuts and Grapes
Chocolate Charlotte

♉

Avocado, Kiwi Fruit, and Radicchio Salad
Chicken with Asparagus
Cherry Ice Cream with Cherry Brandy

♉

Mixed Bean Vinaigrette
Moussaka
Nelly's Shape

♉

Curried Parsnip Soup
Bean Salad with Lemon and Yogurt Dressing
Plum Tart

♉

Baked Spinach Creams
Fillet Steak with Scallop and
    Mushroom Sauce
Gooseberry Crumble

♉

Pear, Cress, and Chicken Salad
Spring Stew
Plum Tart

TAURUS THE GUEST

Listen for the Taurean—he or she is probably singing a romantic melody in the back garden. You will probably need to tempt them to venture out and dine, since they will be perfectly happy tending to the flowers and birds, but it shouldn't be too difficult—eating is one of the things Taureans like to do best.

Taurus is a fixed sign, making people of this sign determined and masterful. It reflects a happy and hopeful time of year, when spring is emerald green and seems as if it will stay that way forever. In the same way, this sign of the zodiac is rich in character, possessing strong feelings. A friendship with a Taurean should be long and lasting, even if you are not such a good cook! Invite Taureans to dinner and they will bring the joys of spring with them, being courteous and gracious visitors who will be only too delighted to eat all you place before them.

Taurus is the emerald forest—rich, fertile, and warm, suggesting an ability to get on with other guests and a special compatibility with other earth and water signs. Taureans long for a harmonious existence and love the comfort and pleasure that food can bring; they like to feel secure, and eating is a good way of achieving this. Like the bull that symbolizes this sign of the zodiac, Taureans have an earthy nature, giving them a strong sense of reality and a feeling of harmony that comes from being in tune with the earth and nature. Feed your Taurean guests earthy delights such as Moussaka or a Spring Stew, and they couldn't be happier. It's the good-quality but simple things in life that appeal to this sign of the zodiac.

The right atmosphere is also important since Taureans are sensitive to their surroundings. A few flowers and soft candlelight will help to make them feel most at home, and perhaps some gentle music in the distance to appeal to the romantic in them. Highly decorative foods are not for this sign, so don't spend endless hours in the kitchen working on elaborate details. What the Taurean will most appreciate is the simple beauty that nature herself provides, such as a plum tart where the full round shapes of the plums are a work of art, not the frilly extras that are manmade and contrived. Feed them foods of love—Chocolate Charlotte, for instance—and the rays of Venus will shine through and reveal the soft sensual side of the bull's nature.

Experiment cautiously; although Taureans are fond of good food, sudden change is not for them (being a fixed earth sign). Feed them an old favorite; stress delicately savory foods, maybe a fish pie or foods that contain their cell salt, sulphate of soda. Soft fruits—the pink and green colors of Venus—are also a good idea, and give them plenty of courses, because Taureans like to leave the table well grounded.

Avocado, Kiwi Fruit, and Radicchio Salad

Here fruits the colors of Venus make an exotic starter, combining sensual pale reds and greens to offer an irresistible combination of tastes. Enchantingly easy to prepare, this dish is an ideal way to begin a dinner party and should be served with thin slices of whole wheat bread and butter and a chilled white Frascati wine. *Serves 6*

Dressing

> 6 Tb (3 oz) sunflower oil
> 3 Tb (1½ oz) wine vinegar
> 2 tsp Dijon mustard
> 2 tsp superfine or castor sugar
> Salt and black pepper to taste

Salad

> 1 head of radicchio
> 3 ripe avocados, peeled and pitted
> 1 Tb lemon juice
> 3 kiwi fruit
> Salt and black pepper

Mix the dressing ingredients in a small bowl or jar. Break off radicchio leaves, rinse them in cold water, and dry. Arrange the raddichio leaves over the base of a large shallow serving dish. Slice the avocados thinly lengthwise and arrange the slices over the radicchio. Sprinkle with lemon juice to prevent the flesh from discoloring. Peel the kiwi fruit and slice it thinly crosswise. Arrange the slices decoratively on top of the avocado and pour the dressing over. Season to taste with salt and black pepper and serve.

Chicken Liver Pâté

This rich silky starter suggests the fertile soil that Taurus, the most earthy sign of the zodiac, symbolizes. Serve Chicken Liver Pâté as an appetizer to a light main dish (perhaps a vegetarian or fish dish), and accompany it with rounds of hot toast and butter and a fruity red wine. *Serves 4 to 6*

> 1 lb chicken livers
> 4 Tb (2 oz; 60 g) butter
> 1 small onion, peeled and thinly sliced
> 2 cloves garlic, peeled and pushed through a press
> 2 bay leaves
> ½ tsp mixed dried Provençal herbs
> 3 Tb (1½ oz) heavy or double cream
> 2 Tb brandy
> Salt and freshly ground black pepper

Trim any skin or veins from the livers. In a medium-size frying pan, melt the butter over low heat, add the onion, garlic, and bay leaves, and sauté gently for about 8 minutes, stirring occasionally. Increase the heat to medium-high, add the chicken livers and mixed herbs, and sauté for 2–3 minutes, turning until the livers have cooked but are still slightly pink in the center. Remove the pan from the heat, discard the bay leaves, and in a food processor or blender purée all the contents of the pan with the cream and brandy until very smooth. Season to taste with salt and black pepper, turn into 2 small dishes, and chill slightly before serving.

Curried Parsnip Soup

A pale cream-colored soup, warming like a ray of sunlight with the delicate aroma and subtle taste of parsnips, is a very delicious way to begin a meal. *Serves 4 to 6*

> 4 Tb (2 oz; 60 g) butter
> 1 lb parsnips, peeled and chopped
> 1 medium potato, peeled and chopped
> 2 medium onions, peeled and finely chopped
> 1 clove garlic, peeled and pushed through a press
> 1 bay leaf
> Salt
> 2 cups (16 oz) chicken stock
> 1½ cups (12 oz) milk
> 1 tsp curry powder
> Pinch of nutmeg
> Black pepper
> ½ cup (4 oz) light or single cream

Garnishes
> 1 Tb coarsely chopped Italian parsley
> 4–6 warmed rolls

Place the butter in a large saucepan and melt it over moderately low heat. Mix in all the vegetables and the bay leaf and season with a little salt. Cover, and let the vegetables sweat for 15 minutes, stirring occasionally. Stir in the chicken stock, milk, curry powder, and nutmeg. Cover and simmer for 20 minutes, until the vegetables are tender, and season to taste with additional salt and black pepper. Remove from the heat. Discard the bay leaf, turn the soup into a food processor or blender, and purée. Return the soup to the pan, place it over low heat, and warm through. Mix in the cream and check the seasoning. Turn into a warmed soup tureen, garnish with parsley, and serve with warmed rolls.

Potato Gnocchi

Potato Gnocchi makes a tasty and inexpensive appetizer, showing how the simple things in life are so often the best. Serve this traditional Roman dish hot from the oven with some Italian wine. *Serves 4*

> *1 lb potatoes*
> *Salt*
> *1/2 cup (1 oz; 30 g) grated Cheddar cheese*
> *4 Tb (2 oz; 60 g) butter*
> *3/4 cup (4 oz; 115 g) flour*
> *1 medium egg, lightly beaten*
> *Black pepper*
> *Pinch of grated nutmeg*
> *2 Tb (1 oz; 30 g) grated Parmesan*

Preheat the oven to 425°F (220°C; gas 7).

Peel, wash, and quarter the potatoes, then place in a saucepan and just cover with water. Add a pinch of salt, cover, and cook for 15–20 minutes, or until tender. Remove from the heat, drain, and return the potatoes to the pan. Mash until smooth, and if necessary place over very low heat to cook off any excess water. Then while they are still hot, mix with the Cheddar cheese and 2 tablespoons of butter. Add the flour and egg, and season to taste with salt, black pepper, and nutmeg. Turn the mixture onto a floured board and roll it into a sausage. Then slice it into 1/2-inch rounds and arrange the slices in a single layer in a greased ovenproof dish. Dot generously with the remaining 2 tablespoons of butter and sprinkle the Parmesan over with a little more salt and black pepper. Cook in a hot oven for 20–25 minutes, until the top is golden and bubbling, and serve immediately.

Baked Spinach Creams

Dark velvety green, Spinach Creams highlight the earthy vibration and green pulse of vegetable life, and suggest the warm moist rays of Venus, which shine through Taurus. Unusual and rich in taste, this dish is full of goodness for this sign of the zodiac, containing their cell salt, sulphate of soda, as well as plenty of iron. Serve this delicious starter accompanied by a full-bodied red wine. *Serves 4*

> *1 lb spinach*
> *Salt*
> *3 Tb (1 1/2 oz; 45 g) butter*
> *Three 1/2-inch slices of whole wheat bread,*
> *   from a medium loaf*
> *1/4 cup (2 oz) olive oil*
> *2 cloves garlic, peeled and pushed through a press*
> *3/4 cup (6 oz) heavy or double cream*
> *Freshly ground black pepper*
> *2 Tb freshly grated Parmesan*
> *1/4 tsp cayenne*

Preheat the oven to 280°F (140°C; gas 1).

Wash the spinach in several changes of cold water and remove any tough stems. Put the leaves in a saucepan with a pinch of salt (no water because spinach is full of moisture), cover, bring to a simmer, and cook gently for 5–8 minutes, or until the spinach is tender. Drain. Turn the heat to low, gently melt 2 tablespoons of the butter in the saucepan, then mix in the spinach and sauté for 5 minutes, stirring occasionally. While the spinach is cooking, prepare the bread.

Remove the crusts from the bread and cut it into 1/2-inch squares. Then heat the oil in a large

BAKED SPINACH CREAMS, CONTINUED

Mixed Bean Vinaigrette

frying pan over high heat, and sauté the garlic and bread cubes for 1–2 minutes on each side, or until a dark golden. Remove from the heat.

Turn the spinach into a food processor or blender with the cream, and purée. Season to taste with salt and black pepper, then transfer to a bowl. Thoroughly mix with the bread cubes and garlic and then spoon equal amounts of the mixture into four ramekin dishes. Sprinkle the Parmesan cheese and cayenne over. Dot the top of each ramekin with the remaining butter and bake for 10–15 minutes, until the top is bubbling and the spinach creams are hot through. Serve hot.

Soft and sweet, these Venus-ruled beans make a healthy and practical change and can be made with ease the night before a dinner party. An ideal dish for Taureans, who instinctively like to have things well organized, enabling them to enjoy the pleasures that the evening will bring. Serve this delightful dish with thin slices of whole wheat bread and butter. *Serves 4*

> *1/2 lb (225 g) green beans, trimmed*
> *1/2 lb (225 g) shelled lima or broad beans*
> *Salt*

Vinaigrette
> *4 Tb (2 oz) sunflower oil*
> *2 Tb red wine vinegar*
> *1 tsp superfine or castor sugar*
> *1 tsp Dijon mustard*
> *1/2 tsp finely chopped fresh mint, or 1/4 tsp dried*

Place both kinds of beans in a saucepan, just cover with water, add a pinch of salt, partially cover, and bring to a boil. Simmer for 6–10 minutes, or until the beans are tender.

While the beans are cooking, mix together all the vinaigrette ingredients. Drain the beans when cooked. Arrange them in a shallow serving dish, with the green beans lying across the center and the lima beans in a row on each side. Pour the vinaigrette over while the beans are still hot. Cover with plastic wrap and leave to chill before serving.

Pear, Cress, and Chicken Salad

Sweet and savory tastes live in harmony in this delectable salad, making an enticing start to a meal or even a light lunch dish for two. Serve it with hot rolls and a chilled dry white wine. *Serves 4*

   3 cups (3 oz; 85 g) or 1 bunch watercress
   3 ripe Comice pears
   1¼ cups (6 oz; 180 g) shredded cooked chicken
   ½ cup (2 oz; 60 g) chopped shelled walnuts
   ⅓ cup (3 oz) mayonnaise (see page 59)
   Salt and black pepper

Remove two-thirds of the watercress stems and break the watercress into florets. Peel and core the pears and cut them into ¾-inch cubes. In a mixing bowl, combine all the ingredients and season to taste with salt and black pepper. Arrange on individual plates or in a salad bowl and serve.

Moussaka

Scrumptious and wholesome, this traditional dish of Greece goes particularly well with Greek Salad (see page 266) and a bottle of Greek red wine such as Demestica. The tenderness of the lamb suggests the tenderness and softness of Venus; the many layers of the dish, the depth of feeling and strength of character that this sign possesses. If you're entertaining, make Moussaka the night before—it will improve in flavor and save time in the kitchen. *Serves 6*

   1½ lb eggplant or aubergine
   Salt
   Olive oil
   2 medium onions, peeled and finely chopped
   4 cloves garlic, peeled and pushed through a press
   1 Tb tomato paste
   1 lb ground lamb
   ½ cup (4 oz) red wine
   Freshly ground black pepper
   2 lb potatoes, peeled, cooked, and sliced
   1 lb tomatoes, peeled and chopped
   ¼ tsp dried thyme, or ½ tsp chopped fresh

Béchamel sauce
   2 Tb butter
   2 Tb flour
   1½ cups (12 oz) milk
   1 tsp Dijon mustard
   Pinch of cinnamon
   Salt and black pepper
   ½ cup (2 oz; 60 g) freshly grated Parmesan

Cut the eggplant crosswise into ½-inch slices, then lay the slices on a plate lined with a paper

MOUSSAKA, CONTINUED

towel. Sprinkle with 1 teaspoon salt and leave them to sweat for 15 minutes, then turn them over. Sprinkle the other sides with 1 teaspoon salt and leave to sweat for 15 minutes longer. Meanwhile prepare the onions and lamb.

Place 2 tablespoons of olive oil in a large frying pan over moderate heat, add the onions and garlic, and sauté, stirring occasionally, for 8 minutes. Mix in the tomato paste, meat, and wine, stirring and turning to break up any lumps in the meat. Simmer for 15–20 minutes, or until the liquid has cooked off and the meat has browned. Season to taste with salt and black pepper, remove the pan from the heat, and spread the mixture evenly over the bottom of a 2½-quart (3¾–4–Imperial pint) ovenproof dish and set aside.

Cook the potatoes in two batches so you don't crowd the pan. Add 2 tablespoons oil to the frying pan and return it to a fairly high heat. When the oil is hot, add half of the sliced potatoes, and sauté for a few minutes on each side, until golden. Lay them on a paper towel to remove any excess oil, and cook the remaining potatoes in the same way. Then arrange all the potato slices over the meat.

Place 4 tablespoons of oil in a large sauce-pan over moderate heat, pat the eggplant slices dry with paper towels, and add them to the pan, turning them in the oil. Add the tomatoes, stirring well so they are thoroughly mixed in, cover, and simmer for 30–40 minutes, turning occasionally. Season to taste with black pepper and thyme (you probably won't need any salt). When the eggplant is tender, spread the mixture evenly over the potatoes and meat.

Preheat the oven to 350°F (180°C; gas 4).

To make the sauce: Melt the butter in a sauce-pan over moderate heat, and stir in the flour. Cook together for 2 minutes, stirring constantly, and then gradually pour in the milk, stirring until you have a smooth sauce. Bring to a boil and simmer for a few minutes. Remove from the heat, stir in the mustard and cinnamon, and season to taste with salt and black pepper. Pour the sauce over the eggplant and tomatoes. Sprinkle the cheese over and bake for 35–40 minutes, or until golden brown and bubbling.

Halibut with Peanuts and Grapes

Blissfully easy to make, this dish is unusual enough for a special occasion, and combines fish rich in iodine, which Taureans have a tendency to lack, with pale soft grapes of Venus and protein-rich nuts. Serve it with a green salad, boiled new potatoes, and a very chilled bottle of white wine. *Serves 2*

3/4 cup (4 oz; 115 g) green seedless grapes

4 Tb (2 oz) ground nut or corn oil

1/2 cup (2 oz; 60 g) finely chopped raw peanuts

1/2 tsp ground coriander

1 lb or 2 fillets of halibut, haddock, or cod from the thick end of fish, skinned

2–3 Tb flour

Salt and black pepper

1/4 cup (1 oz; 30 g) roughly chopped raw peanuts

Rinse the grapes in cold water, pat them dry, and halve lengthwise. Place 2 tablespoons of oil in a medium-size frying pan, over moderate heat, then add the finely chopped peanuts, coriander, and grapes, and turn them in the oil. Cook, turning, for 2 minutes, then transfer to a bowl and keep warm. Rinse the fish in cold water and pat dry. On a wooden board or plate roll the fish in the flour. Heat the remaining oil in the same frying pan over moderately high heat. Add the fish and sauté for 5 minutes on each side, and season to taste with salt and black pepper.

While the fish is cooking, preheat the broiler and arrange the roughly chopped nuts in a thin layer on a piece of foil on a rack. Place 2 inches from the broiler element. Toast them for 30 seconds, then remove from the heat. When the fish is cooked, transfer the fillets to a warmed serving dish. Spoon the grape and nut mixture over, sprinkle the toasted nuts on top, and serve.

Spring Stew

A nutritious and extremely tasty supper or lunch dish for the family-minded Taurean, whose sign of the zodiac evokes the fruitfulness of springtime. This stew is full of the goodness of fresh spring vegetables and tender lamb. Serve hot from the oven with a hot crusty loaf and a young French red wine. *Serves 4*

> 5 Tb whole wheat flour
>
> 1 tsp dry mustard
>
> Salt and freshly ground black pepper
>
> 1½ lb shoulder of lamb
>
> 2 Tb sunflower or vegetable oil
>
> 4 Tb (2 oz; 60 g) butter
>
> ½ lb small white onions, peeled
>
> 3 cloves garlic, peeled and chopped
>
> 1 cup (8 oz) red wine
>
> 1 lb Jerusalem artichokes, peeled and rinsed in cold water
>
> 3 ribs of celery, ends and strings removed
>
> 2 bay leaves
>
> 4-inch sprig of fresh rosemary, or 1 tsp dried
>
> 3 cups (24 oz) water
>
> 1 lb small new potatoes, scrubbed and rinsed in cold water
>
> ½ lb baby turnips, peeled, rinsed in cold water, and quartered
>
> ½ lb baby carrots, tops removed, scrubbed in cold water
>
> ¾ lb tomatoes, peeled and quartered
>
> ½ lb lima or broad beans, shelled
>
> ¾ tsp dried mint, or 1½ tsp chopped fresh

Preheat the oven to 325°F (165°C; gas 3).

Mix 3 tablespoons of the flour with the dry

mustard, ½ teaspoon of salt, and ¼ teaspoon of freshly ground black pepper. Cut the meat into 1¼-inch cubes, removing any excess fat and gristle, then roll it in the flour. Shake off any excess. Heat the oil and 2 tablespoons of the butter in a large frying pan over high heat and quickly brown the meat, on all sides, to seal in the juices. Do this in two or three batches so you do not crowd the pan. Transfer the meat once it has browned to a large casserole. Lower the heat to moderate and then add the onions and garlic to the pan. Sauté for 2 minutes, turning occasionally, then transfer to the casserole.

Add the remaining butter to the pan, stir it around until it melts, and then mix in the remaining flour, cook for 2 minutes, stirring constantly, then add the wine and continue to stir until you have a smooth paste. Transfer the wine

Fish Pie

sauce to the casserole. Cut the Jerusalem artichokes into 1-inch cubes and the celery into 3-inch pieces. Add them to the casserole with the bay leaves, rosemary, water, and all the other vegetables except the beans. Season to taste with salt and black pepper, cover, and cook in a slow oven for 1 hour 40 minutes. Remove the casserole from the oven, add the lima beans and mint, and check the seasoning, then cook 20 minutes longer. Serve hot.

This fish pie is delicious enough for a special occasion as well as making an excellent family dish that can go a long way. Vary the amount of potato and cheese topping according to the size of your baking dish and the number of people you wish to feed, and serve it with a mixed green salad or peas, a loaf of hot bread, and plenty of chilled white Burgundy wine. *Serves 6*

> *4¹/₂ cups (3 lb) potatoes, peeled and cubed*
> *6 scallops*
> *1¹/₂ lb cod or haddock*
> *¹/₂ Spanish onion, peeled and finely chopped*
> *1 tsp fennel seed*
> *2¹/₂ cups (1 Imperial pint) milk*
> *2 cups (¹/₂ lb) raw shrimp, peeled*
> *³/₄ lb tomatoes, peeled and chopped*
> *3 Tb cornstarch dissolved in 3 Tb cold milk*
> *Salt and black pepper*
> *3 Tb (1¹/₂ oz; 45 g) butter*
> *1 cup (2 oz) grated Cheddar cheese*

Place the potatoes in a saucepan and just cover with cold salted water. Bring to a boil, cover, and boil gently for 20 minutes, or until tender. While the potatoes are cooking, prepare the fish.

Rinse the scallops in cold water, pat them dry with a paper towel, and cut them in half. If you have king scallops (scallops with an orange roe) separate the roe from the rest of the scallop with a sharp knife and set aside. Then place the scallops, cod, onion, fennel seed, and milk in a large shallow pan. (This should be enough milk to just cover the fish.) Bring to a simmer, and gently poach for 10 minutes. Remove the fish

FISH PIE, CONTINUED

and scallops to a plate or wooden board. Add the shrimp, tomatoes, and any scallop roe to the pan, and poach for 3 minutes, or until the shrimp turn pink. Remove the pan from the heat and with a perforated spoon transfer the shrimp, tomatoes, and roe to a bowl. Whisk the cornstarch mixture into the poaching liquid, return to the heat, and stir constantly until you have a smooth sauce. Simmer for a few minutes, stirring occasionally, and then remove from the heat.

Skin and bone the fish and break it into largish pieces. Then gently mix all the ingredients together in a large bowl (except for the potatoes, butter, and cheese). Season to taste with salt and black pepper and turn into a buttered 2½-quart (4–Imperial pint) ovenproof serving dish.

Preheat the oven to 400°F (200°C; gas 6).

When the potatoes have cooked, drain them and return to the pan they were cooked in over very low heat. Add ⅔ cup (5 oz) milk and the butter, and mash until smooth and all the liquid has cooked off. Season to taste with salt and black pepper. Spread the potato evenly over the fish mixture and sprinkle the cheese over the top. Bake for 20–30 minutes, or until the top is golden and bubbling and the pie is hot through. Serve hot.

Fillet Steak with Scallop and Mushroom Sauce

Aphrodite, the Greek goddess of love, was born from the ocean and carried across it on a scallop shell, its two halves joined together so tightly that they symbolized passionate love. Appropriately, this is a dish for the romantic Taurean, who embodies the qualities of this goddess. Serve this tender delight with Puréed Rutabagas (see page 46) or potatoes, green beans, and a delicious red wine. *Serves 2*

> 4 large scallops
> ½ cup (4 oz) dry white wine
> Butter
> Two 2-inch-thick fillet steaks or filet mignon
> 4 scallions or spring onions, finely chopped
> ½ lb (225 g) mushrooms, wiped clean
>   and thinly sliced
> Salt and black pepper
> 2 tsp cornstarch
> 3 Tb (1½ oz) heavy or double cream
> 1 Tb finely chopped fresh parsley
> Pinch of paprika

Preheat the broiler.

Rinse the scallops in cold water, pat them dry with a paper towel, and then cut them in half. If you have king scallops (scallops with an orange roe) separate the roe with a sharp knife and set it aside. Pour the wine into a small saucepan, place it over moderate heat, and bring to a simmer. Reduce heat to low, add the scallops, and poach very gently for 8 minutes (add the roe to the pan after 6 minutes). Remove from the heat, reserve the liquor, and transfer the scallops to a plate.

Prepare the steaks. Place 1 teaspoon of butter on the center of each steak and arrange them on the broiler rack. Place the rack so the steaks are 3 inches below the broiler element. Cook for 6–10 minutes, depending on whether you like your steak rare or well done. While the steak is cooking, continue to prepare the sauce.

Over a low heat, melt 1 tablespoon of butter in a frying pan, add the scallions and mushrooms, and sauté for 5 minutes. Season to taste with salt and black pepper and then whisk in the cornstarch. Slowly stir in the scallop liquor and simmer for a few minutes, until you have a smooth sauce. (Keep over low heat and stir occasionally while the steaks are cooking.)

Then turn the steaks over, place 1 teaspoon of butter on the center of each, and cook 6–10 minutes longer. When the steaks are nearly ready, return the scallops to the sauce. Warm them through, stir in the cream and parsley, and season to taste with salt and black pepper. Arrange the steaks on a warmed serving dish, spoon the sauce over, sprinkle with paprika, and serve.

Bean Salad with Lemon and Yogurt Dressing

Delicate and exquisitely subtle, this creamy, protein-rich salad makes an excellent lunch dish. Serve it with a whole wheat Italian bread, a selection of cheeses, and plenty of red wine.
Serves 3 to 4

> ½ cup (4 oz; 125 g) dried chick-peas
> ½ cup (3½ oz; 100 g) red kidney beans
> ½ cup (4 oz; 115 g) flageolets, or small white beans or pea beans

Lemon and yogurt dressing

> 1 cup (8 oz) plain yogurt
> 3 large egg yolks
> 1 Tb lemon juice
> ½ tsp dried mustard
> ¼ tsp dried thyme, or ½ tsp chopped fresh
> Salt and black pepper

Garnishes

> 2 Tb pitted, chopped green olives
> 3 scallions or spring onions, chopped
> 1 Tb chopped fresh parsley

Soak the beans overnight in separate bowls, with 2 inches of water to cover. Then drain and turn into three separate pans. Cover with 2–3 inches of water. Bring the chick-peas to a boil, cover, and simmer for 2–3 hours, or until tender. After about 45 minutes bring the red beans to a boil, then lower the heat, cover, and simmer for 1½–2 hours, or until the beans are tender. Flageolets take less time to cook, so leave them until the red beans have been simmering for about an hour. Then bring the flageolets to a boil, cover, and simmer for 45–50 minutes, or until tender.

When the beans are nearly tender make the dressing. In the top of a double boiler mix the yogurt with the egg yolks, lemon juice, mustard, and thyme. Place over simmering water and stir for 10–15 minutes, or until the mixture thickens into a custard. Season to taste with salt and pepper and remove from the heat.

Drain the beans. Turn them into a salad bowl, pour the yogurt dressing over, and thoroughly mix. Garnish with chopped olives, scallions, and parsley, and toss before serving.

Chicken with Asparagus

This is an ideal dish for the early summer months when fresh asparagus is in abundance, its delicate taste and color making a very special dish when served with rice and Carrots with Coriander (see page 46) and a very chilled French white wine. *Serves 4*

4 chicken breasts, boned and skinned

1 bay leaf

¾ cup (6 oz) dry white wine

¾ cup (6 oz) water

Salt and black pepper to taste

1 lb asparagus

½ cup (4 oz) light or single cream

3 Tb butter

2 cloves garlic, peeled and pushed through a press

½ lb mushrooms, wiped clean and thinly sliced

2 Tb flour

Trimmed watercress for garnish

Preheat the oven to 375°F (190°C; gas 5).

Arrange the chicken breasts, with the bay leaf, in an ovenproof dish. In a saucepan bring the wine and water to a simmer. Pour over the chicken, season with salt and black pepper, and then cover with foil. Poach the chicken in the oven for 20 minutes, or until cooked.

While the chicken is cooking, rinse the asparagus in cold water, peel the stalks, lightly near the top and quite deeply as you reach the stem, and cut off any woody ends that remain. Divide it into two equal parts, and place half in the top of a steamer over boiling water, and cover. Steam the asparagus for 5–10 minutes, or until the stems are tender when pierced with a knife. (Reserve the steamer and water to cook the remaining asparagus later.) Place the cooked asparagus in a food processor or blender with the cream and purée. Set aside while you prepare the mushrooms.

Over moderately low heat, melt the butter in a large frying pan. Then mix in the garlic and mushrooms, and sauté for about 12 minutes, stirring and turning occasionally.

When the chicken has cooked, drain it, reserving 1 cup (8 oz) of its juices. Transfer the chicken breasts to a serving dish, cover with foil, and keep warm while you finish the sauce. Stir the flour into the mushroom juices and cook together for 2 minutes, stirring constantly. Then gradually add the juices from the chicken, and stir until you have a smooth sauce. Simmer gently for a few minutes, reduce the heat, and mix in the creamed asparagus. Season to taste with salt and black pepper. While the sauce is warming through, cook the remaining asparagus in the same way as you cooked the first half. Uncover the chicken breasts, remove the bay leaf, pour the sauce over, arrange the asparagus spears on top, and garnish with small clusters of watercress. Serve hot.

Carrots with Coriander

Carrots evoke the red-orange of the Sun that warms the Earth, and this light, spicy dish is perfect for the physical Taurean. Sweet and aromatic, Carrots with Coriander makes a good accompaniment to most meat and fish dishes. *Serves 4*

> 1/2 cup (2 oz; 60 g) golden raisins or sultanas
> 1 1/2 lb carrots
> 2 Tb olive oil
> 2 cloves garlic, peeled and pushed through a press
> 2 tsp brown sugar
> 1 tsp ground coriander
> 1/4 tsp ground cumin
> 1/4 tsp ground ginger
> Salt and black pepper
> 1/4 cup plain yogurt

Place the raisins in a small bowl, cover with boiling water, and leave to soak while you prepare the carrots. Top and tail the carrots and peel or scrub them in cold water, depending on their age. Slice them crosswise into 1/4-inch pieces and place them in a pan with 2 inches of boiling salted water. Cover, and boil for 3 minutes. Drain the carrots, and set aside for a moment. Add the olive oil to the pan. Place over low heat and mix in the garlic and carrots, cover, and let them sweat for 1 minute. Drain the raisins and stir them into the carrots with the sugar, spices, and salt and pepper to taste. Cook, covered, for 10 minutes, stirring occasionally. Then remove the pan from the heat, mix in the yogurt, turn into a warmed serving dish, and serve.

Puréed Rutabagas

Full of earthy goodness, Puréed Rutabagas make a delicious accompaniment to lamb, beef, and turkey dishes during the winter and early months of spring. *Serves 4*

> 1 1/2 lb rutabagas or swedes
> 2 Tb butter
> 4 Tb (2 oz) light or single cream
> 1 tsp lemon juice
> 2 tsp brown sugar
> Pinch of nutmeg
> Salt and freshly ground black pepper

Cut off the top and roots of the rutabagas and then peel. Rinse in cold water and then chop into 1-inch cubes. Place the rutabagas in a pan of boiling salted water to cover, cover, and boil for 30 minutes, or until tender. Drain and combine with the butter, cream, lemon juice, brown sugar, and nutmeg. Mash with a potato masher or turn into a food processor and purée. (If you are using a food processor, leave a bit of texture to the rutabagas.) Season to taste with salt and black pepper, turn into a warmed vegetable dish, and serve.

Chocolate Charlotte

Taureans will be inspired by the density and shapely rhythm of this dark chocolate food of love. Make this dish in advance and serve it with a jug of light cream for a truly delectable end to a meal. *Serves 4 to 6*

18 ladyfingers
1/4 cup (2 oz) Cointreau
1/2 cup (2 oz; 60 g) cocoa
1/2 cup (3 oz; 85 g) light brown sugar
6 medium egg yolks
2 1/2 cups (1 Imperial pint) milk
3 Tb fresh orange juice
1 Tb plus 1/2 tsp gelatin
1 Tb butter
A few drops of vanilla
1/2 cup (1 1/2 oz; 45 g) toasted slivered almonds
5/8 cup (5 oz) light or single cream

Lay the ladyfingers in a shallow dish, pour the Cointreau over, and let them soak. In a mixing bowl, mix the cocoa, sugar, and egg yolks together, and beat in half the milk, until the mixture is smooth and evenly blended. Line the edges of a 5-cup (2–Imperial pint) mold with the ladyfingers. Pour the orange juice into a large bowl, sprinkle the gelatin over, and leave it to soak while you make the custard.

Turn the chocolate mixture into the top of a double boiler, place over barely simmering water, and then stir in the rest of the milk. Stir continuously until the mixture thickens to a custard. Remove from the heat and immediately pour over the softened gelatin, stirring so that the gelatin becomes thoroughly mixed in. Blend in the butter, vanilla, and almonds, and stir in the light cream. Turn into the mold and chill for a few hours or overnight, until the charlotte has set. Trim any protruding ends off the ladyfingers and unmold onto a serving dish by dipping the mold in and immediately out of very hot water.

Nelly's Shape

The sensual and seductive taste of this dessert should satisfy the Taurean's love of things both sweet and pleasurable, its pale soft topping suggesting the foamy waves of the sea from which Venus was born. Simple and quick to make, Nelly's Shape makes a good dish for a lunch or dinner party. *Serves 6*

2¹/2 cups (1 Imperial pint) milk
1 Tb plus ¹/2 tsp gelatin
4 medium eggs, separated
¹/2 cup (3 oz; 85 g) light brown sugar
1 Tb sweet sherry
2 Tb marmalade
¹/2 cup (4 oz) heavy or double cream
¹/2 cup (1¹/2 oz; 45 g) toasted slivered almonds

Place 3 tablespoons of milk in a large bowl, and sprinkle the gelatin over. Let it soak while you make the custard.

Mix the egg yolks with the sugar in the top of a double boiler. Place over barely simmering water and mix in the remaining milk. Stir continuously until the mixture thickens into a custard. Remove from the heat and immediately pour over the softened gelatin, stirring so the gelatin becomes thoroughly mixed in. Mix in the sherry and leave the mixture to chill for 20–30 minutes.

Beat the egg whites until they form soft peaks and fold them into the custard, using a metal spoon. Turn into a glass serving dish and chill for several hours. The custard will separate, leaving a foamy top and a jelly bottom.

Place the marmalade in a small saucepan and warm it very gently over low heat. Then spread it evenly over the top of the pudding. Turn the cream into a bowl and beat it stiff. Spread the cream evenly over the layer of marmalade, then sprinkle the nuts over, and serve.

Plum Tart

A soft, beautiful dish that will appeal to the esthetic in Taurus. Plum tart is particularly delicious served with whipped cream or a thick custard and a sweet white dessert wine.
Serves 6

Pastry

    1½ cups (8 oz; 225 g) flour

    2 Tb superfine or castor sugar

    Pinch of salt

    Pinch of cinnamon

    *10 Tb (5 oz; 140 g) vegetable shortening
        or butter*

    3–4 Tb cold milk

Filling

    2 lb ripe plums

    ¾ cup (4 oz; 115 g) brown sugar

    ½ cup (4 oz; 115 g) cream cheese

    2 tsp cornstarch

    2 Tb Kirsch

Place the flour, superfine sugar, salt, and cinnamon in a large bowl and cut in the shortening or butter. Mix lightly, and with your fingertips work the flour and fat together until the mixture has the consistency of bread crumbs. Make a well in the center and fill it with the milk. Then catch the edges of the flour mixture with a fork until the milk is mixed in. Mix to a dough and shape into one round piece. Wrap in plastic wrap and leave to chill for 20–30 minutes.

Preheat the oven to 400°F (200°C; gas 6).

On a floured board, roll the pastry out to line a 10-inch pie pan. Ease the pastry into the pan, and trim and crimp the edges. Prick the bottom and sides with a fork and bake for 20 minutes. Remove the pastry from the oven and let it cool. While it is cooling, prepare the plums.

Rinse the plums in cold water, cut them in half using a sharp knife, and remove their pits. Place the plums in a saucepan with the brown sugar over low heat. (They are moist enough not to need any water.) Cover, and simmer gently for 10 minutes. Remove the pan from the heat and, using a slotted spoon, remove the plums to a bowl (set the pan and the juices aside).

Spread the cream cheese evenly over the bottom of the pastry and arrange the plums over. Whisk the cornstarch into the plum juices and return the pan to the heat, stirring continuously until the mixture thickens. Let it simmer for a few minutes, stirring occasionally, then remove from the heat, stir in the Kirsch and pour over the plums, using a pastry brush to spread the mixture evenly. Chill until the glaze has set, and serve.

Cherry Ice Cream with Cherry Brandy

Homemade ice cream is an ideal dish to have on hand in the freezer for surprise visitors, and it is unexpectedly easy to make. But if you don't have time to make the cherry ice cream, use this topping to transform ordinary vanilla ice cream into a special dinner party dish. *Serves 4*

Ice cream

1½ cups (12 oz) milk

1 vanilla bean

3 medium egg yolks

⅓ cup (2½ oz; 75 g) superfine or castor sugar

1 cup (10 oz; 285 g) pitted Morello cherries, drained if canned, or cooked if fresh

⅔ cup (2 oz; 60 g) marshmallows

1¼ cups (10 oz) heavy or double cream

Pinch of salt

Topping

½ cup (4 oz) heavy or double cream

½ cup (4 oz) cherry brandy

¼ cup (1 oz; 30 g) toasted slivered almonds

Place the milk and vanilla bean in a saucepan and bring to the simmering point. Remove from the heat and leave to cool for 15 minutes, so that the vanilla bean can infuse. Remove the vanilla bean, and in the top of a double boiler, mix the egg yolks with the sugar. Place over barely simmering water and pour in the milk. Stir until the mixture has thickened to a custard, then remove from the heat and turn into a bowl. Allow the custard to cool while you prepare the cherries and marshmallows.

Place half the cherries in a food processor or blender and purée. Roughly chop the remaining cherries. Then mix all the cherries into the custard. Cut the marshmallows into pieces (an easy way is with kitchen scissors), and mix them into the custard. Turn the heavy cream into a bowl and beat until stiff, then fold it into the custard mixture with a pinch of salt. Turn into an ice tray, and chill in the freezer for 2 hours, or until it is half frozen. (If you have an ice cream maker, make the ice cream following the manufacturer's directions.) Remove the ice cream from the freezer and whisk it with a fork so that the crystallized edges are mixed into the center. Return to the freezer and leave at least 3 hours or overnight before serving. Remove the ice cream from the freezer and place in the refrigerator a few hours before you wish to serve it so it can soften. Whip the cream for the topping, and in a small saucepan warm the cherry brandy. Place a few scoops of ice cream in each bowl, cover with a spoonful of whipped cream and 2 tablespoons of cherry brandy. Sprinkle the nuts over, and serve.

Gooseberry Crumble

Simple to make, gooseberry crumble makes an inexpensive family dish that is perfect served with whipped cream or custard. If fresh gooseberries are not available, use good canned gooseberries. Just drain and turn them into an ovenproof dish and top with crumble. *Serves 4 to 6*

> 1¹/2 lb gooseberries
> ³/4 cup (5 oz; 150 g) granulated sugar
> 1 Tb water

Topping
> ³/4 cup (3¹/2 oz; 105 g) whole wheat flour
> ⁵/8 cup (2 oz) oatmeal
> 6 Tb (3 oz; 85 g) soft butter
> 6 Tb (3 oz; 85 g) demerara or raw sugar
> Pinch of salt
> Pinch of nutmeg

Preheat the oven to 350°F (180°C; gas 4).

Top and tail the gooseberries, and rinse them in cold water. Place them in a saucepan with the granulated sugar and water over low heat, and bring to a simmer. Cover, and cook very gently for 10 minutes, or until tender. While the gooseberries are cooking, make the crumble topping.

Place the flour, oatmeal, butter, 4 tablespoons of the demerara sugar, salt, and nutmeg in a large bowl and thoroughly mix. Spoon the gooseberries into a fairly shallow 1-quart (1¹/2–2-Imperial pint) ovenproof dish and cover with an even layer of crumble. Sprinkle the remaining sugar evenly over, and bake for 30–40 minutes, or until the topping is golden brown and the fruit is hot through. Serve warm.

Toasted Apple Brûlée

Apples belong to Venus on account of the mythological references to love and because of the story of the fall of Adam and Eve from the Garden of Eden. Cut crosswise an apple reveals the five-pointed star of Venus. *Serves 4*

> 2 lb cooking apples
> 5¹/2–6 Tb (2¹/2–3 oz) butter
> ³/4 cup (3 oz; 85 g) brown sugar
> ¹/4 tsp cinnamon
> 2 Tb medium-sweet cider or water
> Pinch of salt
> 2¹/2–3 slices white bread
> 2 Tb (1 oz; 30 g) superfine or castor sugar
> ¹/4 tsp vanilla

Peel, core, and slice the apples, then place them in a saucepan with 3 tablespoons of butter, the brown sugar, cinnamon, cider, and salt. Cover and simmer for 10–15 minutes, stirring occasionally, until the apples are soft. Uncover and boil over high heat for 2–3 minutes, stirring constantly, to reduce some of the liquid. Purée in a food processor or blender, then turn into a shallow 1-quart (1¹/2–2-Imperial pint) ovenproof dish.

Cut the crusts off the bread and butter generously (about 1 tablespoon for each slice). Cut each slice into 4 triangles and fit them closely together over the top of the apple purée. (The amount of bread and butter needed will vary slightly according to the size of the dish.) Sprinkle with superfine sugar, then dot with vanilla. Place about 3¹/2 inches below the broiler and cook for about 7 minutes, or until the sugar has melted. Remove from the heat and cool for about 15 minutes. Serve with a jug of heavy cream.

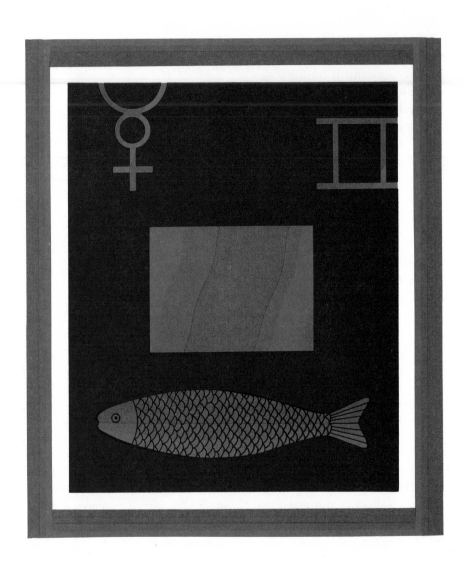

GEMINI

MAY 22–JUNE 21

Rules the third house, the house of sisters, brothers, and cousins

RULING PLANET
Mercury
♊

ELEMENT
Air
♊

QUALITIES
Mutable, active
♊

CHARACTERISTICS
Agile, changeable, clever, eloquent, expressive,
mental, versatile
♊

OPPOSITE SIGN
Sagittarius
♊

BODY AREA
Hands, arms, lungs
♊

GEMSTONE
Opal, beryl
♊

COLOR
Orange
♊

FLAVOR
Sharp, savory, mixed
♊

METAL
Mercury
♊

FAUNA
Fish, hare, poussin
♊

FLORA
Apricots, capers, carrots, coffee, fennel, globe artichokes, hazelnuts, lemons, mushrooms
♊

HERBS AND SPICES
Aniseed, caraway, dill, fennel seed, licorice,
mace, marjoram, parsley
♊

CELL SALT
Potassium chloride (Kali. Mur.), found in
fresh fruits and vegetables such as asparagus,
beets, carrots, celery, green beans, oranges,
pineapple, sweet corn, tomatoes
♊

GEMINI THE COOK

Geminis never get much time to sit down and eat a meal, or if they do, they are probably so busy talking that they don't stop long enough to eat much. People of this sign of the zodiac like to live in a constant whirl of excitement, and spend their lives darting from one place to the next, if not physically then with the help of the telephone.

This is an air sign, which indicates a nature that loves to communicate, idealize, and intellectualize. Geminis are mentally very sharp people (ruled by Mercury, the planet of the mind), who will apply pure reason to their work in the kitchen. They have an intellectual rather than physical response to food. They will reason out their failures rather than throw a tantrum, and they can work with an emotional detachment that you wouldn't find in a fire sign.

Actually, you will be lucky if your Gemini friends have had much of a chance to cook you that wonderful meal they promised, and they may well resort to a Japanese takeout instead. Not that they would let on that they hadn't really cooked it; this sign of the zodiac is the trickster who has the ability to escape awkward situations with the greatest ease. It's also quite possible that they did cook it, because Geminis are such speedy workers (this is suggested by the swiftness of Mercury's flight), and what should take hours, a Gemini can rustle up in moments as if by magic.

The Gemini's kitchen will be full of pots bubbling with exotic ingredients, a whirlwind of activity, full of people and action that would give any other sign a nervous breakdown. Geminis like to live on their nerves (Mercury rules the nervous system), and are capable of controlling many simultaneous happenings.

Left to its own devices this sign of the zodiac would probably just grab a quick snack, but this is not often possible. Gemini, as well as being an air sign, rules brothers, sisters, and cousins, and Gemini homes are likely to be full of people needing food and drink. Actually, Geminis are in their element surrounded by friends and family, since they love to communicate, and always have plenty to say.

In the right mood this sign of the zodiac is quite capable of spending an entire day in the kitchen, experimenting with new dishes from different parts of the world (Mercury rules short-distance travel). And because the familiar will bore their tireless, inquiring minds, you are unlikely to get the same meal twice in this household. A failure is a possibility in their quest for novelty, but they are quick to learn and also very good with their hands (Gemini rules the hands). As a result they can make excellent cooks—the kind who will spend hours perfecting the smallest detail until they become technically very skilled.

Although this sign of the zodiac possesses a sharp business sense, Geminis like to spend money, particularly on fun things, and can be quite extravagant. If it's champagne that matches the mood of the moment, they will quite happily buy it, but more often a very chilled white wine, or a sparkling wine, is the right complement to the sharp and clean-tasting food that appeals to them. Don't miss an evening with a Gemini—it should have a touch of magic and be lighthearted and good fun.

RECIPES FOR GEMINI

First Courses

Carrot, Cashew Nut, and Dill Soup
Mushrooms Montreal
Black-and-White Salad
Salad Saint-Tropez
Globe Artichokes with Hollandaise
Stuffed Tomatoes
Smoked Haddock Mousse

Main Courses

Asparagus Soufflé
Roast Poussin with Fennel
Sweet-and-Sour Fish
Poached Skate with Capers and Lemon
Hamburgers with Cheese and Nuts
Shrimp Fricassee
Pork Costoletta

Side Dishes

Fennel in Cheese Sauce
Zucchini all'Uovo

Desserts

Zabaglione
Lemon Lovely
Coffee-Hazelnut Charlotte
Strawberry Cream Cake
Orange Cream
Apricot Fool

MENU SUGGESTIONS FOR GEMINI

Mushrooms Montreal
Sweet-and-Sour Fish
Lemon Lovely

♊

Black-and-White Salad
Pork Costoletta
Zabaglione

♊

Smoked Haddock Mousse
Hamburgers with Cheese and Nuts
Strawberry Cream Cake

♊

Stuffed Tomatoes
Poached Skate with Capers and Lemon
Apricot Fool

♊

Carrot, Cashew Nut, and Dill Soup
Roast Poussin with Fennel
Coffee-Hazelnut Charlotte

♊

Globe Artichokes with Hollandaise
Shrimp Fricassee
Orange Cream

♊

Salad Saint-Tropez
Asparagus Soufflé
Orange Cream

GEMINI THE GUEST

It's hard to find that elusive Gemini when you want to; Geminis have a tendency to be in more than one place at the same time. But if you do manage to track him or her down, it should be worthwhile—they make delightful dinner guests, extremely social, and, if they wish to, they can charm the birds off the trees.

Don't invite a Gemini if it's a quiet evening you have in mind, because this sign of the zodiac has the gift of many tongues. It is ruled by the planet Mercury (the winged messenger of the gods), who bestows a quick and agile mind, and a suggestion of duality since Mercury has two forms—that of a graceful boy and the child of fearful gods. Geminis are lively talkers, who are more concerned with intellectual pursuits than physical. Not that this will make them unappreciative of your hard labors in the kitchen; they love to be invited out to dine, even if it is more for social reasons than for a pure love of food.

They will enjoy an evening full of surprises, so if you want the conversation to flow, invite along a fellow air sign, who will share their desire to communicate, or a fire sign—perhaps a Leo—who has a similar zest for life.

What this sign of the zodiac will appreciate most is change, so don't bore them with that same old dish; they would rather have a new exciting failure than yesterday's meal disguised. If you want a bit of peace and quiet, feed them ethereal foods, such as a soufflé or a white meat or fish dish to appeal to their airy intellectual nature. Or perhaps a jelly or mousse that trembles like their element, air. And give them variety: little snacks they can eat with their fingers (Gemini rules the hands), canapés of caviar and smoked salmon, or a fun food like a hamburger.

Gemini is a mutable sign of the zodiac, suggesting a changeable and versatile nature with a tendency to act according to the mood of the moment. Its duality is depicted in its symbol of the heavenly twins, Castor and Pollux, making this sign capable of unexpected behavior and a duality in life; they have the subtlety and knowledge of maturity combined with the capriciousness of a child. Your Gemini's favorite food might have been fish last week, but today it's going to be something completely different. Match changeable moods and their duality with a sweet-and-sour dish or a food of contrasting colors, such as a Black-and-White Salad.

If an earthy stew is in the oven, don't despair; your Gemini guests won't let on that the thought doesn't thrill them—anyway, they are probably too busy talking to even notice. Geminis are born with natural good manners, sensitivity, and charm, and they will conceal their dislike so well you will never know it existed. So don't worry if your "airy" visitor leaves not having touched a bite all evening. It doesn't mean they've had a bad time; it's just that they've been captivated by the busy atmosphere around them. Anyway, they will like to breeze out the same way they breezed in.

Carrot, Cashew Nut, and Dill Soup

Carrot soup makes an ideal lunch dish or starter for a dinner party. Pale orange, the color of Gemini, it suggests the energy of the Sun (Mercury is the closest planet to the Sun), and can make a warming dish for a cold evening. Good for the brain and sight, since dill helps to strengthen the brain and carrots are rich in vitamin A, its different taste will delight the novelty-curious Gemini. Serve this satisfying creamy soup hot with hot rolls. *Serves 4*

> 1½ lb carrots
> 4 Tb corn or vegetable oil
> 1 medium onion, peeled and chopped
> 1 clove garlic, peeled and pushed through a press
> ¾ cup (3 oz; 85 g) finely chopped
>   raw cashew nuts
> 1 tsp ground dill
> 1 tsp brown sugar
> 2 cups (16 oz) milk
> 2 cups (16 oz) water
> Salt and freshly ground black pepper
> Plain yogurt

Peel the carrots and rinse them in cold water. Chop them crosswise into ½-inch pieces. Heat the oil in a saucepan and add the onion and garlic. Sauté over moderate heat for 2 minutes, then mix in the carrots, nuts, dill, and sugar, and turn them in the oil. Lower the heat, cover, and let them sweat for 10 minutes, stirring occasionally. Then pour the milk and water over, and season to taste with salt and black pepper. Cover, and simmer for 20 minutes, or until the carrots are tender, stirring occasionally. Remove from the heat. (Don't worry about any scum on the surface; it will blend out.) Turn into a food processor or blender and purée until smooth. Return the soup to the pan and heat through. Adjust seasoning. Remove from the heat, spoon into soup bowls, and float a tablespoon of yogurt on top of each bowl. Serve immediately.

Mushrooms Montreal

An easy-to-prepare dish for the quicksilver Gemini that combines the foods of Mercury—parsley and mushrooms—with a creamy coating. Because of their associations with death, mushrooms are an appropriate food for the god whose duty was to conduct the souls of the dead to the underworld. Rich in minerals and vitamins, parsley helps relieve nervous conditions (often a Gemini complaint) and soothes the stomach. Serve this delicious starter with a very chilled white wine and thin slices of whole wheat bread and butter. *Serves 4 to 6*

> 4 scallions or spring onions
> 1/2 cup (4 oz) light or single cream
> 2 Tb lemon juice
> 2 Tb chopped fresh parsley
> 1 lb mushrooms, peeled, stems trimmed, and thinly sliced
> Salt and black pepper

Chop the scallions finely crosswise. Then, in a mixing bowl, whisk together the cream, lemon juice, and parsley. Lightly but thoroughly mix in the mushrooms and scallions. Season to taste with salt and black pepper, turn into a serving dish or salad bowl, and serve at once or leave it in a cool place for a few hours so that the mushrooms can absorb the flavor of the dressing.

Black-and-White Salad

A dual dish for the sign of the twins Castor and Pollux, which suggests the twin pillars at the entrance of the temple of wisdom, one dark and one light. *Serves 4 to 6*

> 1 lb new potatoes
> 1 cup (5 oz; 140 g) black grapes
> 1 cup (5 oz; 140 g) cooked, shelled mussels
> 1 clove garlic, peeled and pushed through a press
> 4–5 Tb Mayonnaise (recipe follows)
> Salt and black pepper

Garnish
> Thin slices of whole wheat bread and butter

Scrub the potatoes and place them in a pan of boiling salted water. Cover, and boil gently for 15–20 minutes, or until the potatoes are tender when pierced with a knife. Drain and leave them to cool slightly. Halve and pit the grapes. Slice the potatoes, and turn all the ingredients into a mixing bowl. Mix gently but thoroughly. Season to taste with salt and black pepper. Turn into a serving dish or arrange on individual plates, and serve accompanied by a plate of whole wheat bread and butter.

Mayonnaise

Makes 2 cups (16 ounces)

2 large egg yolks
1 tsp superfine or castor sugar
1/2 tsp dry mustard
*1 1/2 cups (12 oz) olive oil (or a mixture
    of olive and sunflower oils)*
1 1/2 Tb lemon juice
Salt and black pepper

Place the egg yolks, sugar, and mustard in a
bowl (set it on a towel to prevent it from moving)
and beat thoroughly. Very slowly, drop by drop
to begin with, beat in the oil until the mixture
starts to thicken. Then beat in the rest of the oil
in a thin, steady stream. When the mayonnaise
is thick, mix in the lemon juice. Season to taste
with salt and black pepper. Refrigerate until you
need it.

TO MAKE MAYONNAISE IN A FOOD PROCESSOR:
*Use 1 medium egg yolk and 1 medium whole
egg (instead of 2 large egg yolks). Blend all the
ingredients except the oil. With the food processor running, add the oil, drop by drop at first,
then in a thin steady stream, until the mixture is
thick. Season to taste.*

Salad Saint-Tropez

A sophisticated salad that makes a delectable first course for four or lunch dish for two, and can be accompanied by a chilled rosé wine. It's so good it's hard to follow, except perhaps with a light soufflé. *Serves 4*

> *1/2 lb (225 g) dandelion or young spinach leaves,*
> *long stems and rough leaves discarded*
> *2 Tb olive oil*
> *6 thick slices (6 oz; 180 g) streaky bacon*
> *1 clove garlic, peeled and pushed through a press*
> *2 scallions or spring onions*
> *1 ripe avocado*
> *1 Tb fresh lemon juice*
> *1 Tb toasted sesame seeds*
> *Freshly ground black pepper*

Warm a large bowl for the salad. Wash and dry the dandelion or spinach leaves. Heat the oil in a frying pan over high heat. When it is hot reduce the heat to moderately high. Add the bacon and garlic, and, turning frequently, sauté for about 8 minutes, or until the bacon is just crisp. While the bacon is cooking, chop the scallions crosswise and set aside. Cut the avocado in half lengthwise, remove pit, and lay cutside down on a plate or wooden board. Then, using a sharp knife, pierce the skin down the center from top to bottom and peel it off. Slice thinly lengthwise and sprinkle the avocado with the lemon juice. Then arrange the dandelion or spinach leaves in the warm bowl, cover with the avocado slices, and scatter the bacon over, along with the pan juices. Sprinkle the scallions and sesame seeds over, season to taste with black pepper, then toss and serve.

Globe Artichokes with Hollandaise

Artichokes are attributed to Gemini because they are regarded as a food rich in goodness for the brain—probably due to the phosphorus they contain and to their complex structure and the short sharp lines of the leaves. Also the leaves must be eaten with the hands, which are ruled by Gemini. Serve with finger bowls and a large plate for the discarded leaves. *Serves 4*

> *4 globe artichokes*
> *1 large clove garlic, peeled*
> *Hollandaise (see page 11)*

Rinse the artichokes in cold water. Trim the stalks so they can stand upright, and remove any tough outer leaves from the bottom. Cut about 1/2 inch off the top leaves and arrange the artichokes in the top of a steamer. Place over boiling water, with a clove of garlic in the water, cover, and steam for about 30 minutes, depending on the size of the artichokes, until they are tender when the bottoms are pierced with a knife. When the artichokes are nearly ready, make the hollandaise. Then arrange the artichokes on four plates and serve hot with the hollandaise.

Stuffed Tomatoes

Stuffed tomatoes make an attractive and interesting light lunch dish served with a tossed green salad and potato salad, or as a starter on their own. The variation and delightful blend of ingredients will appeal to one so fond of the variety of life, and tomatoes are beneficial to this sign of the zodiac since they contain Gemini's cell salt, potassium chloride (which helps to regulate the fibrin in the body and prevent coughs, colds, and inflammatory illnesses). Complement this dish by serving it with a fruity red wine. *Serves 4*

4 large ripe tomatoes

2 Tb butter

1 large onion, peeled and finely chopped

2 cloves garlic, peeled and pushed through a press

6 thick slices (6 oz; 180 g) bacon, finely chopped

1 tsp tomato paste

1 cup (4 oz; 115 g) finely chopped mushrooms

1/4 tsp dried marjoram, or 1/2 tsp chopped fresh

1 cup (2 oz; 60 g) soft whole wheat bread crumbs

Salt and black pepper

1 1/2 Tb chopped fresh parsley

1/2 cup (1 oz) grated Cheddar cheese

4 Tb olive oil

4 circles of whole wheat bread, 4 inches in diameter, 1/2 inch thick

Preheat the oven to 375°F (190°C; gas 5), and grease a baking tray.

Slice the tops off the tomatoes and discard them. Then scoop out the flesh, discard the seeds, and set aside. Melt the butter in a frying pan over low heat, add the onion, garlic, and bacon, and sauté for 10 minutes, turning occasionally. Mix in the tomato paste, mushrooms, marjoram, bread crumbs, and tomato flesh, increase the heat to moderate, and cook, turning, for 10 minutes longer (toward the end of the cooking, if necessary, increase the heat slightly to reduce any excess liquid from the tomatoes). Season to taste with salt and black pepper and remove from the heat. Mix in 1 tablespoon of parsley and spoon equal amounts of the mixture into the tomato shells. Sprinkle the cheese and remaining parsley over the tops and place on the baking tray. Cook for 10 minutes. While the tomatoes are cooking, place the olive oil in a frying pan over high heat, then add the bread and sauté for 1–2 minutes on each side, or until golden brown. Remove the bread to a paper towel to drain. Then place 1 round of bread on each plate, set a tomato on top, and serve.

Smoked Haddock Mousse

Given here because of the contrasting color of the pale yellow (the color of Mercury) with the black-blue of caviar, this mousse conjures up a picture of a black sea and light golden sand, and suggests the dual nature of Gemini. Serve with rounds of hot toast and a cold champagne or white wine. *Serves 6 to 8*

> 4 scallions or spring onions
> 1 lb smoked haddock
> 2 cups (16 oz) milk
> Black pepper
> 1 tsp fennel seeds
> 2 Tb fresh lemon juice
> 1 Tb plus 1/2 tsp gelatin
> 1/2 cup (4 oz) heavy or double cream
> 3 medium eggs, hard-boiled, peeled,
>   and sliced across
> Salt to taste
> 3 Tb black caviar or Danish lumpfish caviar

Chop the scallions. Arrange the fish in a shallow pan just large enough to hold it in one layer. Pour the milk over and add a few twists of freshly ground black pepper, the fennel seeds, and scallions. Place the pan over moderate heat and simmer the fish very gently for 8 minutes. While the fish is cooking place the lemon juice in a bowl. Sprinkle the gelatin over and let it soak for a few minutes. When the fish has cooked, remove it to a wooden board or plate and let it cool. Return the milk to the heat, and when it is just simmering, pour it over the softened gelatin. Stir continuously until it is thoroughly mixed in, then refrigerate. Skin, bone, and flake the fish. In a medium-size bowl, beat the cream stiff and fold in the fish and eggs. Gently but thoroughly mix in the gelatin-and-milk mixture and season to taste with salt and black pepper (not too much salt, because the fish is salty). Turn into a 5-cup (2–Imperial pint) mold and chill for several hours or overnight, until set. Turn the mousse out onto a serving dish. To unmold, dip the mold in and immediately out of very hot water. Spread the caviar evenly over the top and serve.

Asparagus Soufflé

Asparagus (most available during the month of Gemini) flecks this light and airy soufflé green, making a tempting delicacy for this talkative and airy sign of the zodiac. Serve it hot from the oven with boiled new potatoes, a mixed salad, and a very cold Alsatian wine. *Serves 3 to 4*

> 1 lb fresh asparagus
> 3 Tb (1½ oz) light or single cream
> 2 Tb butter
> 2 Tb flour
> 1 cup (8 oz) milk
> 1 Tb lemon juice
> 1 cup (2 oz; 60 g) grated Cheddar cheese
> Salt and black pepper
> 4 large eggs, separated, the yolks lightly beaten

Preheat the oven to 375°F (190°C; gas 5), and butter a 1½-quart soufflé dish.

Rinse the asparagus in cold water, peel the stalks, lightly near the top and quite deeply as you reach the stem, and cut off any woody ends that remain. Place it in the top of a steamer over boiling water, and cover. Steam for 5–10 minutes, or until the stems are tender when pierced with a knife. Then turn into a food processor or blender and purée with the cream.

Place the butter in a saucepan and melt it over gentle heat. Mix in the flour and, stirring continuously, cook for 2 minutes. Stir in the milk and whisk until you have a smooth sauce. Bring to a boil and simmer for a few minutes, stirring occasionally. Remove from the heat, mix in the lemon juice and cheese, and season to taste with salt and black pepper. Turn into a large bowl and mix with the egg yolks and puréed asparagus. Then, in a separate bowl, beat the egg whites until they are stiff and, using a metal spoon, fold them into the asparagus mixture. Turn into the prepared soufflé dish, and bake for 35 minutes, or until the soufflé has risen and cooked through. Serve immediately.

Roast Poussin with Fennel

The two poussins are a reminder of the heavenly twins Castor and Pollux, who symbolize this sign of the zodiac. In this recipe they are delicately flavored with the licorice taste of fennel, making an unusual dish that is delightful served with broccoli and Hollandaise (see page 11) and roast potatoes. If poussins or squab are unavailable, you could use Rock Cornish hens, cooking them 15 minutes longer, or a small chicken, roasting it in a moderate oven for about 20 minutes per pound. *Serves 2*

Stuffing

>   2 scallions or spring onions
>   Grated rind of 1 lemon
>   1½ cups (3 oz; 85 g) soft whole wheat
>   bread crumbs
>   1 medium egg
>   2 tsp dried tarragon, or 4 tsp chopped fresh
>   1 tsp fennel seed
>   1 Tb soft butter
>
>   Two 14–16-oz (400–450-g) poussins or
>   squab, cleaned
>   6 oz (180 g) fennel (1 small head)
>   2 Tb soft butter
>   2 Tb lemon juice
>   Salt and black pepper to taste

Preheat the oven to 400°F (200°C; gas 6).

Chop the scallions. In a mixing bowl, thoroughly blend all the stuffing ingredients. Divide the mixture in half and stuff the poussins. Fasten the body cavities with a skewer to hold the stuffing in, and truss to keep the birds intact. Remove any rough outer leaves from the fennel, trim the base and tops, and wash in cold water. Dry and slice thinly lengthwise. Then arrange the slices in a roasting pan just large enough to hold both birds. Set the birds on the fennel, and rub 1 tablespoon of butter over each of their skins. Pour the lemon juice over, and season with salt and black pepper. Roast for 30 minutes, or until the meat near the joints is no longer pink. Baste the birds every 15 minutes with the pan juices. When the birds are cooked, arrange them on two warmed plates, spoon around the fennel, and serve.

Sweet-and-Sour Fish

This is a dish to match the moods of the sweet and sour Gemini. Fish are attributed to Mercury because of their speed and changing, rainbowlike colors. They also have a reputation for being a food that's good for the brain. Serve this subtle Chinese meal with a bowl of noodles or rice, soy sauce, and Stir-fried Bean Sprouts (see page 291). *Serves 4*

Sweet-and-sour sauce

    6 Tb (3 oz) tomato ketchup

    6 Tb (3 oz) malt vinegar

    6 Tb (3 oz) water

    1½ Tb cornstarch

    2 Tb plus ¾ tsp superfine or castor sugar

    6 Tb flour

    ½ tsp salt

    ¼ tsp black pepper

    2 lb cod or haddock fillets, skinned and sliced across into 1-inch strips

    Corn or vegetable oil

    2 medium eggs, lightly beaten

In a bowl whisk together all the sweet-and-sour sauce ingredients. Then prepare the fish. Season the flour with the salt and pepper and turn it onto a large board or plate. Roll the fish in it. Film the bottom of a large frying pan with ⅛ inch of oil. Place the pan over high heat, and when the oil is very hot, lower the heat to moderately high. Place the eggs by the side of the frying pan, and dip the fish slices in them just before you add them to the pan (cook the fish in batches so you do not crowd the pan). Sauté for 3–5 minutes on each side. When the fish is cooked, remove it to a plate and keep warm. When all the fish is cooked, turn the sauce ingredients into a saucepan. Place over moderate heat, stir continuously, and when the sauce has thickened, let it simmer for a few minutes more to cook the cornstarch. Remove from the heat, turn into a small serving bowl, and serve immediately with the fish.

Poached Skate with Capers and Lemon

The wings of the skate recall the winged sandals and helmet of Mercury, the winged messenger of the gods. Serve this tempting dish with Fennel in Cheese Sauce (see page 69), boiled new potatoes, and a very cold dry white wine. *Serves 4*

> *2 lb (900 g) skate wing, cut into 4 equal pieces*
> *1 medium onion, peeled and cut into 8 pieces*
> *Juice of 2 lemons*
> *¼ tsp salt*
> *8 peppercorns*
> *1 bay leaf*

Sauce
> *4 Tb butter (2 oz; 60 g)*
> *Juice of 1 lemon*
> *1 Tb capers*
> *1 Tb chopped fresh parsley*
> *Salt and black pepper*

Rinse the skate in cold water and arrange it in a shallow pan, just large enough to hold it in one layer. Add the onion, lemon juice, salt, peppercorns, and bay leaf, and just cover the fish with cold water. Place over moderate heat, bring to a boil, and simmer gently for 10–15 minutes, or until the fish is just cooked.

While the fish is cooking, prepare the sauce. Melt the butter in a small pan over low heat. Turn off the heat and stir in the lemon juice, capers, and parsley. Season to taste with salt and black pepper. Then drain the fish thoroughly, remove the bay leaf, and arrange on a warm serving dish. Pour the sauce over and serve.

Hamburgers with Cheese and Nuts

Fun food, for the fun-loving Gemini, and a perfect dish for the barbecue during the hot summer months. Serve these hamburgers either in buns (Geminis love eating with their hands) or on their own with a green salad and garnishes, and plenty of cold beer or wine. *Serves 5*

2 lb medium-lean chopped meat
1 large onion, peeled and finely chopped
4 cloves garlic, peeled and pushed through a press
2 medium eggs
1 cup (2 oz; 60 g) soft whole wheat bread crumbs
1/2 cup (2 oz; 60 g) finely chopped mixed nuts
1 cup (2 oz; 60 g) grated Cheddar cheese
1 Tb tomato paste
1 tsp Dijon mustard
2 tsp dried marjoram, or 4 tsp chopped fresh
Pinch of nutmeg
Salt and black pepper to taste
10 burger buns with caraway seeds (warmed in the oven), optional

Garnishes
Thin slices of tomato
Thin slices of raw onion
Mustard
Thin slices of gherkin
Sweet pickle

Preheat the broiler.

In a large mixing bowl, gently but thoroughly mix all the burger ingredients. Then shape the mixture into about 10 burgers, approximately 3½ inches across by ¾ inch thick. Grease a broiler rack, arrange the burgers on it, and place the rack 3 inches below the broiler element. Broil the burgers for about 6–10 minutes on each side, depending on whether you like them rare or well done. Serve hot, either on buns or on their own, with a selection of garnishes.

Shrimp Fricassee

Shrimp Fricassee makes an excellent dinner-party dish that can easily be prepared ahead of time. Full of so many good things, it makes a substantial and delicious meal that needs to be accompanied by only a green salad and a cold white wine. It is ideal for social Geminis who will like to spend the evening chatting with their guests rather than being in the kitchen. *Serves 6*

1½ lb raw shrimp, peeled

Salt

3 ribs of celery

6 Tb (3 oz; 85 g) butter

2 medium onions, peeled and chopped

1 bay leaf

1 cup (8 oz; 225 g) long-grain white rice, washed

½ lb mushrooms, peeled and sliced

Black pepper

3 Tb flour

1 cup (8 oz) milk

½ cup (4 oz) light or single cream

2 Tb sherry

⅔ cup (2 oz; 60 g) toasted slivered almonds

½ cup (1 oz; 30 g) potato chips or crisps, broken into small pieces

Preheat the oven to 350°F (180°C; gas 4).

Bring 2 quarts (3 Imperial pints) salted water to a simmer, add the shrimp, and cook for 2–3 minutes, or until the shrimp turn pink. Drain and set aside while you prepare the vegetables.

Wash and dry the celery, remove the ends and strings, and chop it. Melt 3 tablespoons of butter in a fairly large saucepan over low heat, mix in the onion, celery, and bay leaf. Cover and cook gently, turning occasionally, for about 15 minutes, or until the celery is tender. While the celery and onion are cooking, prepare the rice. Bring to a boil 2 quarts of water with 1 teaspoon of salt. Add the rice and stir once. Simmer for 10–15 minutes, or until the rice is cooked *al dente*. Drain, and set aside. Stir the mushrooms into the celery-and-onion mixture, season to taste with salt and black pepper, and cook 8 minutes longer, or until the mushrooms are tender, then remove from the heat, discard the bay leaf, and set aside. Place the remaining butter in a saucepan over moderately low heat. When it has melted, mix in the flour. Stir continuously for 2 minutes and then gradually mix in the milk, and cream, stirring until you have a smooth sauce. Bring to a boil and simmer for a few minutes. Remove from the heat and mix in the sherry. In a large bowl combine all the ingredients, except for the chips, season to taste with salt and black pepper, and turn into a 2-quart ovenproof dish. Sprinkle the chips over so they cover the surface and bake for 20 minutes, or until the dish is hot through, and serve.

Pork Costoletta

This wonderful Roman food makes an excellent party dish or family meal. Serve it Italian-style with Zucchini all'Uovo (see page 70), a chilled white Italian wine such as a Frascati, and a tossed green salad or potato salad. *Serves 4*

> 1¼ lb loin of pork, trimmed of fat, boned, and
>   very thinly sliced
> Salt
> 6 medium eggs
> 2 Tb grated Parmesan
> Freshly ground black pepper
> ¾ cup (4 oz; 115 g) very fine dry bread crumbs
> Vegetable or sunflower oil

Garnish
> 1 lemon, cut into 4 wedges

Place the pork slices on a large plate or board and sprinkle with a little salt. In a bowl, beat the eggs with the Parmesan and season to taste with salt and black pepper. Cover a large plate or wooden board with the bread crumbs. Coat the pork slices with the bread crumbs so they have an even covering on each side. Pour enough oil into a large frying pan to fill ¼ inch, place over high heat, and when the oil starts to smoke, lower the heat to moderately high. Place the bowl of eggs by the side of the frying pan and dip the pork slices in the egg mixture just before you add them to the pan. Sauté the pork, in batches so you do not crowd the pan, for 5–7 minutes on each side. After you have cooked about half of the pork, change the oil and continue as before. Arrange the pork on a warmed serving dish and serve with wedges of lemon.

Fennel in Cheese Sauce

Fennel in Cheese Sauce makes an unusual side dish with a cheesy-licorice flavor that Geminis will love. Italian in origin, it is particularly good served hot with fish and chicken dishes, both favorites with this sign of the zodiac. *Serves 4*

> 1½ lb fennel

Cheese sauce
> 2 Tb butter
> 2 Tb flour
> 1 cup (8 oz) milk
> 1 cup (2 oz) grated Cheddar cheese
> 1 tsp Dijon mustard
> Salt and black pepper

Preheat the broiler.

Trim the tops and base off the fennel and remove any damaged outer leaves. Then cut lengthwise into ¾-inch slices. Rinse in cold water and pat dry with a paper towel. Place in a large pan with ½ inch of boiling salted water, cover, and simmer for about 15 minutes, or until tender. While the fennel is cooking, make the sauce.

Place a saucepan over moderately low heat and melt the butter, mix in the flour, and, stirring continuously, cook for 2 minutes. Gradually add the milk, stirring until you have a smooth sauce. Simmer for a few minutes, then mix in the cheese and mustard, cooking until the cheese has melted. Season to taste with salt and black pepper, and remove from the heat. Drain the fennel, arrange it in a broilerproof dish, and pour the sauce over. Place the top of the dish 2 inches from the broiler element and cook for 3–4 minutes, or until the top is golden brown and bubbling, then serve.

Zucchini all'Uovo

This is a tasty and different way of cooking zucchini—easy to do. It makes an excellent accompaniment to a variety of dishes, and is particularly good with Pork Costoletta (see page 69). *Serves 4*

1 lb zucchini or courgette
Salt
2 large eggs
Freshly ground black pepper
1/2 cup (2 1/2 oz; 70 g) flour
Vegetable or sunflower oil

Rinse the zucchini in cold water and dry them. Remove the ends and then slice them lengthwise into 1/8-inch thickness. Sprinkle them with a little salt and let them sweat for 15 minutes. In a small bowl beat the eggs and season to taste with salt and black pepper. Turn the flour onto a large plate or board. Pat the zucchini dry and turn them in the flour, so they are evenly coated on all sides. Film the bottom of a large frying pan with 1/8 inch of oil and place over high heat. When the oil starts to smoke, reduce the heat to moderately high. Place the bowl of egg by the side of the frying pan, and dip the zucchini slices in the egg just before you add them to the pan (cook in batches so you don't crowd the pan). Sauté for 3–4 minutes on each side, or until golden brown. Season to taste with salt and black pepper, then remove to a serving dish and keep warm. After you have cooked about half of the zucchini, change the oil and continue cooking in the same way. Arrange the zucchini on a serving dish and serve hot or cold.

Zabaglione

Zabaglione is a classic Italian dessert that is warm and rich, with a lightness and pale yellow color (the color of Mercury, Gemini's ruling planet) that should appeal to this intellectual, airy sign of the zodiac. *Serves 2*

4 large egg yolks
1 1/2 Tb superfine or castor sugar
1/3 cup (2 2/3 oz) Marsala (or use sweet sherry)

Warm two tall glasses.

Place the egg yolks and sugar in a mixing bowl and beat until pale yellow. Beat in the Marsala. Turn the mixture into the top of a double boiler and place over barely simmering water. Whisk until the mixture is frothy and has thickened; this will take about 10 minutes. Divide equally between the two glasses and serve.

Lemon Lovely

You can make Lemon Lovely easily the night before a dinner party. Sharp and light, it resembles a weightless cheesecake and is a delicious way to end a meal. The sharpness, color, and clean taste of the lemon implies a fruit of Mercury and suggests that this dish will be a favorite with this sign of the zodiac as well as the family. *Serves 6 to 8*

Crumb crust
   12 (6 oz) graham crackers or digestive biscuits
   6 Tb (3 oz) butter
   1/4 cup (2 oz) superfine or castor sugar
   1/2 tsp cinnamon

   2 Tb water
   1 Tb plus 1/2 tsp gelatin
   1 cup (8 oz) fresh lemon juice
   Grated rind of 1 lemon
   One 14 1/2-oz (410-g) can evaporated milk
   1/2 cup (4 oz) superfine or castor sugar

In a food processor or with a rolling pin, crush the graham crackers. Place the butter in a saucepan over low heat. Melt it gently and remove from the heat. Turn the crumbs into a bowl if you are not using a food processor and thoroughly mix with the sugar, cinnamon, and butter. Then press two-thirds of the crumb crust into the base of a 1 1/2-quart dish, approximately 8 by 9 inches, and leave to chill while you prepare the rest of the pudding.

   Place the water in a bowl and sprinkle the gelatin over. Let it soak for a few minutes. In a saucepan, heat the lemon juice with the rind until it reaches the simmering point, then pour it over the gelatin, and stir continuously so the gelatin is thoroughly mixed in. Refrigerate for about 1 hour, or until the mixture begins to thicken. Turn the evaporated milk into a bowl and beat it until it is light and fluffy. Beat in the sugar and lemon mixture, and pour the mixture evenly over the crumb crust. Leave to chill for a few hours or overnight, until set. Sprinkle the remaining crumb crust evenly over the top, and serve.

Coffee-Hazelnut Charlotte

Coffee-Hazelnut Charlotte makes a stimulating and delectable dessert, which should keep your Gemini guest quiet for a moment. The hazelnuts and trembling slender curves of this charlotte will appeal to their airy, mercurial nature—in ancient folklore the hazel was the tree of eloquence and wisdom. *Serves 6*

1/4 cup plus 2 Tb Tia Maria
1 Tb plus 1/2 tsp gelatin
2 cups (16 oz) strong black coffee
About 20 ladyfingers
1 1/4 cups (10 oz) heavy or double cream
1/2 cup (4 oz) superfine or castor sugar
1/2 cup (2 oz) chopped toasted hazelnuts
1/3 cup (1 1/2 oz; 45 g) coarsely grated
    milk chocolate

Place the 2 tablespoons of Tia Maria in a bowl and sprinkle the gelatin over. Let it soak for a few minutes. Place the coffee in a saucepan over low heat, and when it is very hot (do not let it boil) pour it over the softened gelatin. Stir continuously until the gelatin has completely dissolved. Refrigerate for about 1 hour, or until it is just beginning to set. Arrange the ladyfingers in one layer on the bottom of a shallow dish. Pour 1/4 cup (2 oz) of Tia Maria over and leave them to soak. Turn the cream into a bowl and beat until just stiff. Beat in the coffee mixture, sugar, hazelnuts, and the grated chocolate, except for 1 tablespoon. Then line the edges of a 7-cup (3–Imperial pint) glass bowl with the soaked ladyfingers. Turn the coffee mixture into the bowl and chill for a few hours, or until the charlotte has set. Then sprinkle the remaining chocolate over and serve.

Strawberry Cream Cake

Strawberries, the first of the summer fruits, signify the changing season of spring to summer, which is represented astrologically by the sign of Gemini. Strawberry Cream Cake makes a spectacular birthday cake or an end to a meal, and is delightfully extravagant served with champagne. *Serves 8 to 10*

    3 large eggs
    ³/4 cup (6 oz; 180 g) superfine or castor sugar
    Pinch of salt
    4 Tb cold water
    1¹/2 cups (8 oz) flour
    2 tsp baking powder

<u>Filling</u>
    2 cups (16 oz) heavy or double cream
    3 Tb superfine or castor sugar
    1¹/2 lb hulled strawberries

Butter and dust with flour two 8-inch cake tins. Preheat the oven to 350°F (180°C; gas 4).

In a mixing bowl, thoroughly beat the eggs until they thicken and become a very light color. Thoroughly beat in the sugar and salt, and then the water. In another mixing bowl, combine the flour with the baking powder and then fold them lightly into the egg mixture, until the mixture is well blended. Divide the mixture equally between the two cake tins and bake for 25–30 minutes, or until a knife plunged into the center of the cakes comes out clean. Remove from the oven and turn out onto cake racks and leave to cool.

While the cakes are cooling, prepare the filling. Pour the cream into a mixing bowl, beat it until it is stiff, and sweeten it. Slice three-fourths of the strawberries (you need to keep some whole for decoration). Then slice each cake in half and place one tier on a serving plate. Cover with a quarter of the whipped cream and then one-third of the sliced strawberries. Cover with a second layer of cake and then cream and strawberries. Continue this process until the last layer of cake is in place. For the top of the cake, cover with the remaining cream and arrange the whole strawberries over.

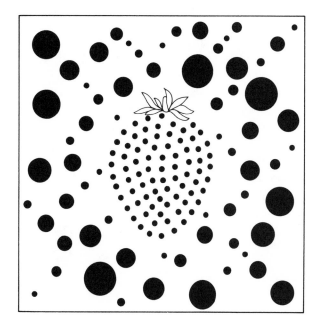

Orange Cream

Fruit the color of Gemini is layered with cream and flavored with Cointreau to make a refreshing dessert and one that is particularly beneficial for this sign of the zodiac, since oranges contain Gemini's cell salt, potassium chloride. *Serves 4 to 6*

> *5 medium-large oranges*
> *1 cup (8 oz) heavy or double cream*
> *3 Tb Cointreau or orange liqueur*
> *2 Tb superfine or castor sugar*
> *1 Tb (1/2 oz) grated semisweet chocolate*

Peel the oranges, divide them into segments, and remove the translucent skin and any pith. Pour the cream into a bowl and beat it until it is just stiff. Mix in the Cointreau and sugar. Then divide the oranges into three equal portions. Line the bottom of a 2½-cup (1–Imperial pint) glass bowl with one portion of the orange segments, and then cover with a third of the cream. Repeat this process until all the oranges and cream are used up. Sprinkle the chocolate over and chill before serving.

Apricot Fool

A fruit fool is a traditional English dessert that is usually made with either gooseberries or rhubarb, but is just as delicious with apricots. Served with sugar cookies, it makes a luxurious and simple dish for a dinner party. *Serves 4*

> *1 lb apricots*
> *4 Tb brown sugar*
> *1 Tb brandy*
> *1 cup (8 oz) heavy or double cream*
> *2 Tb superfine or castor sugar*

Rinse the apricots in cold water and pat them dry with a paper towel. Then slice them in half and remove the pits. Place in a saucepan over low heat with the brown sugar and brandy. When they begin to simmer, cover and cook for 10 minutes, or until the apricots are tender. Remove from the heat and turn into a food processor or blender, and purée. In a bowl beat the cream until it is just stiff. Then fold in the apricot purée and superfine sugar, and mix lightly. Turn into a glass bowl or individual glass dishes, and chill before serving.

CANCER

JUNE 22–JULY 23

Rules the fourth house, the house of the subconscious

RULING PLANET
The Moon
ତ

ELEMENT
Water
ତ

QUALITIES
Cardinal, passive
ତ

CHARACTERISTICS
Changeable, emotional, imaginative, inconstant,
receptive, reflective, sentimental, tenacious
ତ

OPPOSITE SIGN
Capricorn
ତ

BODY AREA
Breasts, stomach
ତ

GEMSTONE
Amber, moonstone
ତ

COLOR
Orange-yellow
ତ

FLAVOR
Strong, sweet
ତ

METAL
Silver
ତ

FAUNA
Crab, duck, pork, venison
ତ

FLORA
Cabbage, cucumber, dairy products, eggplant, lettuce, litchis, melon, pine nuts,
pomegranate, pumpkin, turnips, water chestnuts, watercress, zucchini
ତ

HERBS AND SPICES
Cloves, poppyseeds, sage, thyme
ତ

CELL SALT
Fluoride of lime (Calc. Fluor.), found in
protein foods such as cheese, eggs, rye,
dried fruits, seafood
ତ

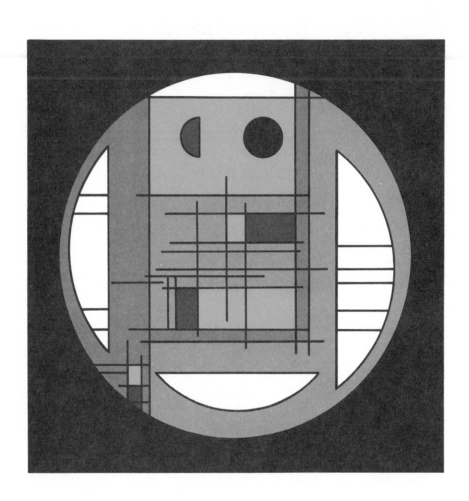

CANCER THE COOK

Cancerians love the kitchen, which is not surprising since the Moon, their ruling planet, represents the mother, the comforter and sustainer of life. For them the kitchen is the heart of the home, a place of animation, full of friends and family.

You will probably find them burrowing through their cupboards searching for that can of peas that they feel sure is in there somewhere. They are probably quite right, because this sign of the zodiac has a good memory (the Moon rules the memory), particularly where food is concerned. Cancerians' cupboards are likely to be full of all kinds of things, not only so they can find a quick snack any time of day or night but also because their tenacious nature likes to hoard things.

This is a water sign of the zodiac, suggesting an intuitive and imaginative nature that is ruled more by emotions and appetite than by logic. Cancerians are likely to cook instinctively, and with a lot of imagination rather than by the book. Although this approach could present problems, it tends not to, because they will take things stage by stage, tentatively adding ingredients until a genuine creation begins to take shape—fortunately, because this sign of the zodiac has a tendency to brood over mistakes, rather than gaily tossing them aside. A love of good food also indicates a good cook, and more than likely dinner with a Cancerian will be a gastronomic delight.

Cancer rules the fourth house of the zodiac. As well as being concerned with the mother and the home, it is also the sign of retirement and refreshment. Motivated by appetite and by material things (since the Moon is responsible for giving form and substance to things), a Cancerian host will be sensitive and receptive to your desires, and will probably have cooked you just what you like to eat.

So expect a delicious meal at a Cancerian's house, not only because people under this sign are top cooks, but also because the Moon is the planet of illusion, and even unlavish foods will taste as if they had been made for kings.

It's hard to say exactly what to expect in this changeable household—seafoods are likely to be a favorite, especially when they observe the motion of the Moon, the way cockles and mussels do, or a delicious spaghetti dish with a strong taste of the Mediterranean. Large, soft, and juicy fruits or vegetables, such as pumpkin or melons, are also favorites since they relate to their element of water. And wine should flow— after all, the Moon, their ruling planet, rules over all liquids, and this sign of the zodiac enjoys a drink. You might be offered white wine to match the white crescent of the Moon, or it could be red or rosé because there are three phases of the Moon. One thing certain is that the color and unpredictability of the evening will match the creative and colorful imagination that this sign possesses.

RECIPES FOR CANCER

First Courses

Chilled Consommé Maria
Melon, Cucumber, and Mango Salad
Egg Mousse
Stuffed Eggplant with Pine Nuts
Chicken Soup with Vermicelli
Seafood Pancakes
Celery Hearts with Mozzarella and
Tomato Sauce

Main Courses

Spaghetti with Mussels and Garlic
Roast Crab with Ginger and Scallions
Pork Pot with Hot Pepperoni
Beef and Apple Stew
Eggplant and Zucchini au Gratin
Roast Duck with Chili-Cherry Sauce
Chicken, Zucchini, and Shrimp Tart

Side Dishes

Sweet-and-Sour Red Cabbage
Quick-Fried Turnips with Soy Sauce
and Yogurt

Desserts

Chocolate Mousse
Pumpkin Pie
Baked Custard with Apricot Jam
and Cream
Lemon Snow with Custard
Layered Fruit Sponge Cake
Rhubarb Pudding with Strawberries

MENU SUGGESTIONS FOR CANCER

Melon, Cucumber, and Mango Salad
Pork Pot with Hot Pepperoni
Chocolate Mousse

ↄ

Chilled Consommé Maria
Chicken, Zucchini, and Shrimp Tart
Layered Fruit Sponge Cake

ↄ

Egg Mousse
Spaghetti with Mussels and Garlic
Lemon Snow with Custard

ↄ

Stuffed Eggplant with Pine Nuts
Beef and Apple Stew
Baked Custard with Apricot Jam and Cream

ↄ

Chicken Soup with Vermicelli
Eggplant and Zucchini au Gratin
Rhubarb Pudding with Strawberries

ↄ

Seafood Pancakes
Roast Duck with Chili-Cherry Sauce
Pumpkin Pie

ↄ

Celery Hearts with Mozzarella and
Tomato Sauce
Roast Crab with Ginger and Scallions
Rhubarb Pudding with Strawberries

CANCER THE GUEST

If you are going to entertain a Cancerian, the best way is to invite him or her home. This sign of the zodiac will be more motivated by the prospect of a good meal than anything else. Feed a Cancerian well and he will reveal the charming and entertaining side of his changeable nature.

That is, if your Cancerian friend doesn't phone and cancel at the last minute. This sign of the zodiac is a creature of the moment, and will want to be where he feels the limelight is (the Moon is the goddess of light). Cancerians are not very good at committing themselves, probably because they know their own nature better than anyone else does. So make sure you tell your Cancerian friend how good the food will be and what fun the guests are to make your invitation hard to resist.

Cancer is a cardinal sign of the zodiac, which implies an outgoing nature even though it has a passive and sympathetic side (indicated by its element of water). However, the waters of Cancer are waters of motion; they are the streams and bubbling brooks that create power and they are strong and forceful, suggesting a fieriness to this sign that goes with its season. Cancer, after all, is the sign that arrives with the summer solstice, and the promise of the joyous summer ahead energizes and revitalizes. So your dinner guest will be fun and outgoing—once you have persuaded him to dine.

The sign of Cancer is represented by a crab, and people born under this sign of the zodiac tend to conceal a sensitive and emotional nature beneath a hard exterior. They like to live harmonious lives and will retreat into their shells in times of discord or emotional upset. Their moods swing to extremes like the waxing and waning of the Moon, and you'll find a Cancerian has a tendency to be on a diet one day and be thoroughly enjoying food the next.

If this sign of the zodiac appears for dinner, be sure to cater well, because Cancerians have good appetites (the Moon is the planet that governs emotions, appetites, the stomach, and the absorption of food into the body). And those born under this sign will be happiest when they have eaten well. So it shouldn't be too difficult to please them, but if you are worried, bear in mind they like strong tastes. Try a crab dish on them to symbolize their sign, or a dish that will leave them feeling satisfied, such as pasta or a stew or a soup that absorbs quantities of liquid in the cooking process, since the Moon rules over all liquids. Messy foods are fine, so long as they taste good; Cancerians can be quite untidy, in the same way as their element, water, is uncontained and chaotic. And feed them a dessert, perhaps some pale yellow or white fruits such as litchis—for the white Moon goddess. The Moon also rules over sweet tastes (since it rules young children), and this sign won't want to miss a course.

Guests that Cancerians will be most compatible with tend to be other earth and water signs, although they could find a fire sign, such as a Sagittarian, quite stimulating company. Ask a Cancerian to dinner, and you could be inviting unpredictability—a person capable of many moods, and changeable like the Moon.

Chilled Consommé Maria

Black and white, Chilled Consommé Maria refers to the night and day and the journey the Moon goddess takes in her barge across the nocturnal sky at the end of each day and night. Rich and creamy, its soft texture relates to the soft parts of the body that Cancer rules over, and it should be followed by a light or refreshing main dish. *Serves 4*

> One 14½-oz (411-g) can of jellied consommé
> ¾ cup plus 2 Tb (8 oz; 225 g) cream cheese
> 2 cloves garlic, peeled and pushed through a press
> 1 tsp curry powder
> 4 Tb caviar or Danish lumpfish caviar

Set ½ cup (4 oz) of jellied consommé aside. Turn the remaining consommé into a mixing bowl or food processor and thoroughly mix with the cheese, garlic, and curry powder. Divide the mixture equally among 4 ramekin dishes and chill for about 1–1½ hours, or until set. Then spread 1 tablespoon of caviar evenly over the top of each dish. Pour the remaining consommé over the caviar, so each dish has an even covering. Chill for about 15 minutes, or until set, and serve.

Melon, Cucumber, and Mango Salad

Fruits of the Moon are combined to make an exotic and refreshing salad, which is ideal for a hot summer evening, and the sign of the zodiac that brings with it the heat of summer. Serve this unusual and easy-to-prepare starter with thin slices of whole wheat bread and butter. *Serves 6 to 8*

> 1 cantaloupe or honeydew melon (about 1½ lb; 675 g)
> ½ large cucumber
> 2 mangoes

Vinaigrette
> 4 Tb (2 oz) sunflower oil
> 2 Tb fresh lemon juice
> 1 tsp honey
> ½ tsp ground ginger
> Salt and black pepper to taste

Cut the melon in half lengthwise. Scoop out and discard the pips. Then scoop out the flesh in balls with a spoon or scoop. Place in a bowl. Peel the cucumber and remove the seeds (unless it is seedless), and cut it into ½-inch cubes. Peel the mangoes and cut the flesh off the pit in slices. Add the mango and cucumber to the melon. In a small bowl or jar thoroughly mix all the vinaigrette ingredients and pour over the fruits. Toss and leave to marinate and chill for 30 minutes. Serve either in individual tall glasses or bowls or in one large glass bowl.

Egg Mousse

Pale golden Egg Mousse suggests the light of the Moon, which illuminates the shadowy darkness of night, and makes a delightful way to begin a dinner party. Serve it with rounds of hot toasted rye bread and a cold white wine. *Serves 6 to 8*

3 Tb (1½ oz) dry sherry
1 Tb plus ½ tsp gelatin
One 2-oz (55-g) can anchovy fillets, drained
¼ cup (2 oz) milk

Béchamel sauce
2 Tb butter
2 Tb flour
1 cup (8 oz) milk

½ cup (4 oz) chicken stock
10 hard-boiled medium eggs
5 scallions or spring onions
3 Tb (1½ oz) lemon juice
½ cup (4 oz) heavy or double cream
Salt and black pepper to taste

Garnish
Trimmed watercress

Place the sherry in a bowl and sprinkle the gelatin over. Leave it to soften for a few minutes. Place the anchovy fillets in a small bowl, cover them with the milk, and leave them to soak while you prepare the béchamel sauce.

Place the butter in a saucepan over low heat. When it has melted, mix in the flour and cook together for 2 minutes, then mix in the milk and stir continuously until you have a smooth sauce. Bring to a boil, simmer for a few minutes, then remove from the heat, cover, and set aside. Turn the chicken stock into a saucepan and bring to a boil. Remove from the heat, pour over the softened gelatin, and stir continuously until the gelatin has completely dissolved. Peel and chop the eggs. Chop the scallions finely. In a mixing bowl or food processor thoroughly mix the béchamel with the gelatin mixture. (Turn this mixture into a bowl if it's not already in one.) Drain and chop the anchovies. Gently but thoroughly mix the eggs, scallions, anchovies, and lemon juice into the béchamel mixture. Turn the cream into a bowl and beat until it is stiff, then fold it into the egg mixture. Season to taste with salt and black pepper. Turn into a 5-cup mold and chill for several hours or overnight, until set. Then turn the mousse out onto a serving dish (to unmold, dip the mold in and immediately out of very hot water). Garnish with watercress and serve.

Stuffed Eggplant with Pine Nuts

A soft dark velvety case of eggplant encloses a deliciously textured filling and makes a tempting starter or lunch or supper dish served with a tossed mixed salad and a fruity red wine. *Serves 4*

> 2 medium eggplants or aubergines (about 9 oz;
>   250 g each)
> 3 Tb (1½ oz) olive oil
> 2 medium onions, peeled and finely chopped
> 4 cloves garlic, peeled and pushed through a press
> 2 ribs of celery, chopped
> 1 tsp ground cumin
> ½ tsp ground coriander
> ½ tsp turmeric
> ½ cup (2½ oz; 75 g) pine nuts
> 2 oz (60 g) mushrooms, peeled and well chopped
> Salt and black pepper
> 2 cups (4 oz; 115 g) grated Cheddar cheese
> 1 Tb chopped fresh parsley

Preheat the oven to 350°F (180°C; gas 4).

Rinse the eggplants in cold water. Trim the ends and place in a pan of boiling water. Cover and simmer for 10 minutes. Drain and refresh in cold water for a few minutes. Pat the eggplants dry with a paper towel and with a sharp knife cut the eggplants in half lengthwise. Cut out the flesh, leaving about ½ inch of shell. Chop the flesh and set aside. Heat the oil in a frying pan over moderate heat, mix in the onions, garlic, and celery, and sauté for 6 minutes. Add the chopped eggplant and spices, and cook 5 minutes more. Stir in the pine nuts and mushrooms, season to taste with salt and black pepper, and cook 5 minutes more. Remove from the heat and mix in

half of the cheese and the parsley. Divide the mixture into four equal portions and fill the eggplant shells with it. Sprinkle the remaining cheese evenly over the tops and arrange in a greased ovenproof dish. Cook in the oven for 20–30 minutes, or until the top is brown and bubbling and the shells are cooked. Serve hot.

Chicken Soup with Vermicelli

A clear and replenishing soup that suggests the reflective and inconstant waters of the Moon and the inner fluctuations of mood that this sign often experiences. Serve very hot, with a crusty bread. *Serves 8*

> *One 2¹/₂-lb stewing chicken, cleaned,*
> *   neck and feet removed, cut into 4 pieces,*
> *   the liver (and eggs, if a hen) reserved*
> *3 quarts (1³/₄ Imperial pints) water*
> *Salt and black pepper*
> *1 medium onion, peeled and cut into 8 pieces*
> *2 ribs of celery, chopped*
> *2 medium carrots, peeled and finely sliced*
> *1 turnip, about 8 oz (225 g), peeled and cut*
> *   into 16 pieces*
> *1 oz (30 g) vermicelli, broken into pieces*

Thoroughly wash the chicken. Skin it and place in a large saucepan. Cover with water and bring to a boil. Then pour off the water, set the chicken aside, and wipe the saucepan clean. Put the chicken back in the pan. Pour 3 quarts water over, season lightly with salt and black pepper, bring to a boil, and remove any scum from the surface. Cover, and simmer for 2 hours. Add the onion, cover, and simmer 30 minutes longer. Add the celery, carrots, and turnip, and simmer for 30 minutes. Remove from the heat to cool. Take the chicken out and bone it. (Discard the bones.) Flake the meat, cut the liver into bite-size pieces, and return the meats (and eggs, if you have any) to the broth. Bring the broth to a boil over moderately high heat, add the vermicelli, and cook until it is *al dente*. Correct the seasoning and serve.

Seafood Pancakes

These thin pancakes, which conceal a tasty mixture of fish, will appeal to the masked and mysterious side of the Cancerian, who when in need of refreshment and quiet will retire into his or her own protective shell. Deliciously different, Seafood Pancakes can be served as a first course or as a luncheon dish for four, with a green salad and a very chilled white wine. *Serves 10*

Pancakes

> *1 cup (5 oz; 140 g) flour*
> *Pinch of salt*
> *1 large egg, lightly beaten*
> *4 tsp sunflower oil*
> *1¹/₂ cups plus 1 Tb (12¹/₂ oz) milk*

Filling

> *¹/₂ lb (225 g) monkfish*
> *6 scallops (4 oz; 115 g)*
> *³/₄ cup (6 oz) milk*
> *2 cloves garlic, peeled and chopped*
> *¹/₂ lb (225 g) raw shrimp, shelled*
> *2 Tb butter*
> *3 Tb flour*
> *¹/₄ cup (2 oz) light or single cream*
> *1 cup (4 oz; 115 g) grated Emmenthal or*
> *   Gruyère cheese*
> *2 Tb chopped fresh parsley*
> *Salt and black pepper*
> *1¹/₂ Tb sunflower or vegetable oil for frying*

First make the pancake batter. Mix the flour and salt in a mixing bowl. Make a well in the center and pour in the egg, oil, and half of the milk. Catch the edges of the flour with a whisk and

SEAFOOD PANCAKES, CONTINUED

beat until it is thoroughly mixed in. Beat to a smooth batter and stir in the remaining milk.

Alternatively, mix the flour and salt in a food processor. Then add the egg, oil, and milk through the funnel. Pour the batter into a jug and let it stand for 30 minutes while you make the filling. (You can make the batter the day before and refrigerate, if you wish.)

Remove any skin from the monkfish, rinse it under the cold tap, and cut it off the bone and into bite-size pieces. Pat dry. Rinse the scallops in cold water, pat them dry, and cut them in half. If you have king scallops (scallops with an orange roe), cut out the roe with a sharp knife and set aside. Pour the milk into a saucepan, add the garlic, and bring to a simmer. Add all the fish except for the shrimp and any scallop roe. Simmer for 5–6 minutes, then add the roe and shrimp. When the shrimp turn pink, remove all the fish to a bowl and set aside. Strain the fish milk and reserve for the sauce.

Place the butter in a saucepan and melt over moderately low heat. Add the flour and stir continuously for 2 minutes, then pour in the reserved milk and the cream. Continue to stir, and simmer for a few minutes until you have a smooth sauce. Turn the heat to low, mix in the cheese and parsley, and season to taste with salt and black pepper. Thoroughly mix with the fish and set aside.

Preheat the oven to 350°F (180°C; gas 4).

Place a small frying pan or an omelet pan over high heat. Lightly grease it with a little oil. Beat the pancake batter, then pour 3 tablespoons of it into the pan. Turn the pan so that the bottom is covered evenly with the batter and cook for about 40–60 seconds, or until the underside is lightly browned. Then turn the pancake, and cook 30–40 seconds more, or until it is lightly browned. Transfer to a large plate. Continue to cook all the pancakes in this way. There should be enough batter for 10 pancakes. Place an equal amount of filling (about 3 tablespoons) in the center of each pancake. Fold the sides over the filling and arrange in an ovenproof dish just large enough to hold the pancakes. Place in the oven for 20 minutes, or until the pancakes are hot through. Serve immediately.

Celery Hearts with Mozzarella and Tomato Sauce

An imaginative dish for this creative, watery sign of the zodiac. Very easy to make, it is also a beneficial food for this sign, since cheese is rich in the Cancerian's cell salt, fluoride of lime, and helps to strengthen tooth enamel and keep the skin elastic. *Serves 4*

Tomato sauce

    2 Tb olive oil

    1 medium onion, peeled and finely chopped

    2 cloves garlic, peeled and pushed through a press

    1 lb tomatoes, peeled and finely chopped

    1/2 tsp superfine or castor sugar

    1/4 tsp dried basil, or 1/2 tsp chopped fresh

    Salt and black pepper

    Olive oil

    One 18 1/2-oz (524-g) can of 4 celery hearts, drained, or 4 celery hearts, cooked and drained

    1/2 lb (225 g) mozzarella cheese

Preheat the oven to 375°F (190°C; gas 5).

Rub a little olive oil over the bottom of an ovenproof dish, just large enough to hold 4 wrapped celery hearts. Then prepare the tomato sauce.

Heat the 2 tablespoons of oil in a frying pan over moderate heat, add the onion and garlic, and sauté for 6–8 minutes, turning and stirring occasionally. Mix in the tomatoes, sugar, and basil, and simmer for 2–3 minutes. Increase the heat to moderately high and sauté for about 10 minutes to reduce some of the liquid from the tomatoes. Season to taste with salt and black pepper, and remove from the heat.

Slice the mozzarella into eight 1/8-inch-thick slices approximately 2 1/2 inches by 4 inches (depending on the size of your celery hearts). Lay 4 pieces along the bottom of the ovenproof dish. Cover each slice with a celery heart and then with a slice of cheese. Pour the tomato sauce over. Place in the oven and cook for 20 minutes, or until the hearts are hot through and the cheese is bubbling. Serve hot.

Spaghetti with Mussels and Garlic

Pasta is perfect for the sign of the zodiac that likes to feel a full stomach by the end of a meal (Cancer rules the stomach). Mixed with creamy mussels, a food that observes the motions of the Moon, Spaghetti with Mussels and Garlic makes a scrumptious meal and is particularly delicious served with a green salad, a hot crusty loaf, and a cold white Italian wine. *Serves 4*

2 lb (900 g) mussels

1/2 cup (4 oz) dry white wine

3 Tb (1 1/2 oz) olive oil

2 medium onions, peeled and finely chopped

8 cloves garlic, peeled and finely sliced

2 Tb tomato paste

1 medium carrot, peeled and grated

1/2 lb (225 g) mushrooms, wiped clean and finely sliced

1/4 tsp dried basil, or 1/2 tsp chopped fresh

3/4 cup (6 oz) light or single cream

1 Tb chopped fresh parsley

Black pepper

1 lb spaghetti

2 Tb butter

Scrub the mussels clean in several changes of cold water. If any mussels are open when you have finished, throw them out. Place the mussels and wine in a pan over moderately low heat, cover, and cook for 5 minutes, or until the mussels have steamed open. Then remove the mussels from the pan and set aside in a bowl to cool; strain the mussel liquor through cheesecloth or muslin and set aside.

Heat the oil in a frying pan over moderately low heat. Add the onions, and, stirring occasionally, sauté for 15 minutes, or until tender. Stir in the garlic, tomato paste, carrot, mushrooms, basil, and mussel liquor. Increase the heat to moderately high and let the mixture bubble for about 10–15 minutes, stirring occasionally, or until most of the liquid has cooked off. While the sauce is cooking, remove the mussels from their shells and discard the shells. Lower the heat, and return the mussels to the pan. Stir in the cream and parsley, heat through, and season to taste with black pepper.

Meanwhile, cook the spaghetti in a pot of boiling salted water until *al dente,* drain, and turn into a warmed serving dish. Stir the butter into the pasta, then spoon the hot sauce into the center. Serve immediately.

Roast Crab with Ginger and Scallions

The image of the crab symbolizes this sign of the zodiac, representing the Cancerians' tenacity and providing a shell where they can hide in times of need for solitude. The strong taste and crooked irregular forms of the crab should also appeal to this sign. Serve this spectacular dish with Quick-Fried Turnips with Soy Sauce and Yogurt (see page 94), and a bowl of noodles or rice, lots of cold beer or wine, and finger bowls, because it is messy to eat. *Serves 2*

> Two 1¼–1½-lb crabs, cooked, with the poison sacs and gills removed
>
> 10 scallions or spring onions
>
> 2½-inch piece of gingerroot, peeled and finely chopped
>
> 6 Tb (3 oz) corn oil
>
> 3 Tb (1½ oz) lemon juice
>
> 3 Tb (1½ oz) soy sauce
>
> 4½ Tb medium sweet sherry
>
> 1 large clove garlic, peeled and pushed through a press
>
> ½ tsp cayenne
>
> Black pepper to taste

Preheat the oven to 350°F (180°C; gas 4).

Wipe the crab shells clean. Break the legs off the crabs and crack them with nutcrackers or a hammer. Chop the scallions finely. Place the crabs and crab legs in a roasting pan just large enough to hold them and sprinkle the scallions and gingerroot over. In a small bowl or jar, mix together the oil, lemon juice, soy sauce, sherry, and garlic. Pour over the crab. Season with cayenne and black pepper. Cook in the oven for 20 minutes, basting every 5 minutes. Serve hot.

Pork Pot with Hot Pepperoni

This peasant dish is appropriate for this sign of the zodiac because the Moon (Cancer's ruling planet) represents the common people and the physical senses, and because of the liquid the dish absorbs in the cooking process. Containing an entire meal in one pot, it is an ideal dish for a lunch or dinner party, and delicious served with a French loaf and plenty of young French red wine. *Serves 8*

> 1½ cups (¾ lb) navy or haricot beans, soaked overnight in 2–3 inches of water to cover
>
> ¾ lb (340 g) white cabbage, any rough outer leaves discarded
>
> 2 lb (900 g) pork belly
>
> 6 ribs of celery, ends and strings removed, chopped
>
> ¾ lb (340 g) carrots, peeled and cubed
>
> 8 small white onions, peeled
>
> 4 cloves garlic, peeled and chopped
>
> ¾ lb (340 g) turnips, peeled and cubed
>
> 1 lb (450 g) potatoes (preferably new), peeled and cubed
>
> 2½ cups (1 Imperial pint) chicken stock
>
> ½ tsp dried thyme, or 1 tsp chopped fresh
>
> ½ tsp dried marjoram, or 1 tsp chopped fresh
>
> 2 bay leaves
>
> Salt and black pepper
>
> ½ lb (225 g) hot pepperoni or other thin spicy sausage, cooked, sliced, and skinned

Drain the beans, place them in a saucepan, and cover with a few inches of cold water. Bring to a boil, cover, and simmer for about an hour, unsalted, or until the beans are tender, then drain them.

Preheat the oven to 350°F (180°C; gas 4).

Shred the cabbage and discard the center core. Place the pork in a very large casserole, and surround with the beans and all the vegetables. Pour the stock over. Add the herbs and season with salt and black pepper. Cover and cook in the oven for 1 hour. Remove the casserole, add the pepperoni, cover again, and return it to the oven for 20–30 minutes. Remove the meat to a board, slice it, and transfer it to a large warmed serving dish. Surround it with all the vegetables and serve.

Beef and Apple Stew

Apples lightly flavor this stew, making it both unusual and delicious. Cancer's symbol of two semicircles suggests the horns of a cow, an animal sacred to the Moon in mythology. It is best served hot from the oven with creamed potatoes and buttered parsleyed baby carrots, creating an ideal dish for a cold winter night. *Serves 6*

6 Tb flour

Salt and black pepper

2 lb chuck steak, cut into 1-inch cubes

Vegetable oil

3 large onions, peeled and sliced

1 cup (8 oz) cider

1 cup (8 oz) beef stock or water

2 bay leaves

3 medium cooking apples

1 lb baby pork chipolatas

Preheat the oven to 350°F (180°C; gas 4).

Mix the flour with 1 teaspoon of salt and 1/4 teaspoon of black pepper. Roll the beef cubes in the flour and shake off any excess. Heat 4 tablespoons of oil in a large frying pan over high heat, then very quickly brown the meat on all sides to seal in the juices. Do this in two or three batches so you don't crowd the pan. Transfer the meat to a casserole. Lower the heat slightly and add 3 tablespoons of oil. Mix in some of the onions (cook these in two or three batches so you don't crowd the pan, adding more oil if necessary), and sauté, turning occasionally, for 3–5 minutes. Then transfer the onions to the casserole. Pour the cider and stock over, add the bay leaves, stir, cover, and place in the oven for 1 1/4–1 1/2 hours, or until the meat is tender. When the beef and onions are nearly ready, peel and core the apples, cut them into medium-size slices, and add them to the casserole. Remove the bay leaves, and cook 20 minutes longer. While the apples are cooking, grease a frying pan with a little oil and place it over moderate heat. Prick the sausages with the end of a sharp knife, put them in the frying pan, and sauté them for 5 minutes, turning so they brown lightly and evenly all over. Add the sausages to the casserole and cook the stew 10 minutes longer. Remove from the oven. Adjust seasoning to taste with salt and black pepper, and serve hot.

Eggplant and Zucchini au Gratin

Unusual flavorings combine to make a simple but tempting supper dish or a dish for an informal dinner party. Served cold it can be made easily in advance and makes a perfect dish for a hot summer evening, served with a green salad and boiled new potatoes. *Serves 4*

> *One 12-oz (340-g) eggplant or aubergine*
> *Salt*
> *1 lb zucchini or courgette*
> *3–4 Tb olive oil*
> *1 medium onion, peeled and finely chopped*
> *2 cloves garlic, peeled and pushed through a press*
> *1/4 tsp dried rosemary, or 1/2 tsp chopped fresh*
> *1/4 tsp dried thyme, or 1/2 tsp chopped fresh*
> *1/2 tsp curry powder*
> *Black pepper*
> *3 medium eggs*
> *1 1/4 cups (10 oz) light or single cream*
> *Pinch of nutmeg*
> *3/4 cup (3 oz; 85 g) grated Gruyère cheese*

Preheat the oven to 375°F, (190°C; gas 5).

Peel the eggplant, and cut it into 1-inch cubes. Place it on a plate and sprinkle with salt. Leave to sweat for 20 minutes. Wash and dry the zucchini, slice it into 1/4–1/2-inch diagonal slices. Sprinkle with salt and leave to sweat for 20 minutes. Then pat the eggplant and zucchini dry. Heat the oil in a large saucepan over moderate heat (it is best to use as little oil as possible because you don't want the baked dish to be greasy), add the onion, eggplant, and garlic, turn in the oil, and cover. Cook, turning occasionally, for 20 minutes. Then add the zucchini, rosemary, thyme, and curry powder. Cover, and cook 10–15 minutes longer, or until the zucchini is tender. Season to taste with salt and black pepper. Remove from the heat and turn into a 2–2 1/2-inch-deep, 5-cup ovenproof dish. In a mixing bowl lightly beat the eggs and beat in the cream. Pour over the vegetable mixture. Sprinkle with nutmeg and grated cheese. Bake for 15–20 minutes, or until set. Serve hot or cold.

Roast Duck with Chili-Cherry Sauce

Roast duck served with a deliciously spicy sauce should prove an irresistible combination for the sign of the zodiac that combines a watery nature with the fieriness of a cardinal sign. Serve it with Sweet-and-Sour Red Cabbage (see page 93), boiled new potatoes, and a chilled white Sancerre wine. For just two or three people, halve the sauce ingredients and cook one duck. *Serves 4 to 6*

> Two 4-lb ducks, cleaned
> 1 clove garlic, peeled
> Salt and black pepper

Chili-cherry sauce
> 1 lb fresh or canned cherries
> 2 Tb Kirsch
> 2 Tb brown sugar
> 1 Tb cornstarch
> 1 Tb malt vinegar
> 1 small clove garlic, peeled and pushed
>   through a press
> 1 tsp chili powder

Thoroughly dry the ducks inside and outside, with a paper towel or clean dishcloth. Then prick the skin all over with a fork or needle and leave them in a dry, airy place for a few hours.

Preheat the oven to 350°F (180°C; gas 4).

Pat the ducks dry again. Rub the skin with the garlic and then with salt. Season generously with black pepper. Arrange the ducks on a rack in a roasting pan. Place them in the oven and cook them for 60 minutes without opening the door. Drain the fat off the pan and return the ducks to the oven and cook 30–60 minutes longer, for medium-rare or medium. While the ducks are cooking, make the sauce.

If using fresh cherries rinse them in cold water, pat dry, and remove the pits. Canned cherries should be drained completely. Place in a saucepan with 1 tablespoon Kirsch and the sugar and bring to a simmer over low heat. Cover, and cook for 10 minutes, or until the cherries are tender. Then turn them into a food processor or blender and purée. Mix the cornstarch with the remaining Kirsch. Return the cherry purée to the saucepan and whisk in the cornstarch and Kirsch, vinegar, a pinch of salt, garlic, and chili powder. Place over moderately low heat and bring to a simmer. Stir continuously until the mixture thickens to a smooth sauce, and simmer for a few minutes. Then transfer the sauce to a bowl, cover, and leave to cool until you wish to serve the duck.

When the ducks are cooked, remove them from the oven. Transfer to a platter and let them sit for 10 minutes before carving, and serve accompanied by the sauce.

Chicken, Zucchini, and Shrimp Tart

Here is a dish with a subtle combination of tastes—an unusual and delicious quiche—that provides an excellent way for using leftover chicken. Serve it with Spinach, Cress, and Water Chestnut Salad (see page 291) and a chilled bottle of white wine. *Serves 4*

> *Shortcrust pastry to fit 10-inch pie pan*
>   *(see page 12)*
> *1 lb zucchini or courgette, washed and dried*
> *Salt*
> *1 Tb butter*
> *4 cloves garlic, peeled and pushed through a press*
> *1½ cups (200 g) flaked cooked chicken*
> *¼ lb (115 g) cooked and peeled shrimp*
> *1 cup (2 oz; 60 g) grated Cheddar cheese*
> *5 medium eggs, lightly beaten*
> *½ cup (4 oz) light or single cream*
> *1 Tb lemon juice*
> *1 tsp English mustard*
> *1 Tb chopped fresh parsley*
> *Black pepper*

Prepare the pastry as described on page 12. While the pastry is chilling, prepare the zucchini.

Remove the ends from the zucchini and slice them thinly crosswise. Place them on a large plate or board and sprinkle them with ½ teaspoon salt. Leave to sweat.

Preheat the oven to 425°F (220°C; gas 7).

Roll the pastry out on a floured board, ease it into the pie pan, and prick the bottom and sides with a fork. Bake for 10 minutes. Remove from the oven and set aside. Lower the oven heat to 350°F (180°C; gas 4) and prepare the filling.

Pat the zucchini dry. In a frying pan, melt the butter over moderately low heat. Add the zucchini and garlic, and sauté for 15 minutes, stirring occasionally. Remove from the heat and allow to cool slightly. In a large mixing bowl, thoroughly mix zucchini with all the remaining ingredients. Season to taste with salt and black pepper, turn into the pie shell, and bake 40–45 minutes, or until the pie has set. Serve hot or at room temperature.

Sweet-and-Sour Red Cabbage

Rich in calcium and potassium, red cabbage is a valuable food for this sign of the zodiac, since it aids digestion and the assimilation of food and helps relieve gastric upsets, all possible Cancerian complaints. Sweet-and-Sour Red Cabbage also goes particularly well with pork, roast pheasant, or Roast Duck with Chili-Cherry Sauce (see page 91). *Serves 4 to 6*

2 Tb butter
2 medium onions, peeled and finely chopped
3 cloves garlic, peeled and pushed through a press
3 medium ribs of celery, chopped
2 medium cooking apples
1 lb red cabbage
1 tsp cinnamon
Salt and black pepper
1 Tb brown sugar
4 Tb red wine vinegar

Heat the butter in a very large frying pan over moderate heat, add the onions, garlic, and celery, and sauté, stirring occasionally, for 5 minutes. Core and chop the apples. Stir them into the onion-and-celery mixture, and cook 5 minutes longer. Meanwhile, finely shred the cabbage, discarding the core and any tough outer leaves. Add the shredded cabbage to the onion-and-apple mixture. Increase the heat slightly and, stirring continuously, sauté for 5 minutes.

Preheat the oven to 350°F (180°C; gas 4).

Mix the cinnamon into the cabbage and season to taste with salt and black pepper. Lower the heat and cook 10–15 minutes longer, stirring occasionally, until the cabbage is tender. Stir in the sugar and vinegar. Turn into an ovenproof casserole, cover, and cook in the oven for 15 minutes. Serve hot.

Quick-Fried Turnips with Soy Sauce and Yogurt

An unusual side dish with a taste of the Orient that is delightful served with Roast Crab with Ginger and Scallions (see page 87). *Serves 2 to 3*

> *³/4 lb (340 g) turnips*
> *¹/2 small green pepper*
> *2 scallions or spring onions*

Sauce
> *1 Tb soy sauce*
> *2 Tb brown sugar*
> *¹/4 cup plain yogurt*
> *2 Tb medium-sweet sherry or Shaosing wine*
> *1 Tb cornstarch*
> *2 Tb corn or vegetable oil*
> *Salt and black pepper*

Peel the turnips and rinse them in cold water. Slice them very thinly and place in a pan of boiling salted water. Cover, boil for 5 minutes, and drain. While the turnips are cooking, remove the stalk, seeds, and whitish membrane from the sides of the green pepper, and chop it very fine. Chop the scallions finely. Place the soy sauce, brown sugar, yogurt, and sherry in a bowl and whisk in the cornstarch. Heat the oil in a frying pan over high heat, lower the heat slightly, and add the turnips, green pepper, and scallions. Stir-fry for 3 minutes. Lower the heat to moderate and stir in the yogurt mixture. Cook, turning and stirring continuously, for 5 minutes. Season to taste with salt and black pepper. Remove from the heat and serve.

Chocolate Mousse

Chocolate mousse is a classic French dessert that is delectably light and very easy to do. Its color and shape suggest the dark face of the Moon, in her form as Persephone in the underworld. *Serves 6*

> *1 Tb butter*
> *4 oz (115 g) semisweet chocolate, broken into squares*
> *3 medium egg yolks*
> *1 Tb Cointreau or Grand Marnier*
> *4 medium egg whites*

Place the butter and chocolate in the top of a double boiler over simmering water. Stir occasionally until the chocolate has completely melted. Remove from the heat and beat in the egg yolks. Then turn into a bowl and mix in the Cointreau. In a separate bowl beat the egg whites until stiff. Fold them into the chocolate mixture, gently but thoroughly. Turn into 6 ramekin dishes or a glass bowl, and chill overnight before serving.

Pumpkin Pie

Pumpkin Pie is the amber of Cancer; it is the full harvest moon that shines over the golden cornfields promising fulfillment, making a perfect dish for Thanksgiving. *Serves 8*

Pastry

1½ cups (8 oz; 225 g) flour

¼ tsp salt

2 Tb (1 oz; 30 g) superfine or castor sugar

Grated rind of 1 orange

9 Tb (4½ oz; 125 g) butter

2–3 Tb fresh orange juice

Filling

1½ lb (675 g) of pumpkin, seeds removed, or 2 cups canned pumpkin purée

5 medium eggs

¾ cup (4 oz; 120 g) light brown sugar

1 cup (8 oz) light or single cream

¼ tsp ground ginger

¼ tsp ground cloves

Pinch of salt

¼ tsp nutmeg

Peel the pumpkin and cut it into about 1½-inch pieces. Then place it in the top of a steamer over boiling water. Cover, and steam for 30–40 minutes, or until the pumpkin is tender. While the pumpkin is cooking, prepare the pastry.

Place the flour, salt, superfine sugar, and orange rind in a large bowl and cut in the butter. Mix lightly with your fingertips, and work the flour and butter together until the mixture has the consistency of bread crumbs. Make a well in the center and fill it with the orange juice. Then catch the edges of the flour mixture with a fork, until the orange juice is mixed in. Or alternatively, you can make this pastry in a food processor. First mix the flour, salt, sugar, orange rind, and butter together until the mixture is the consistency of coarse bread crumbs. Then add the orange juice through the funnel. Mix to a dough and shape into a round piece. Wrap it in plastic wrap and chill for 20–30 minutes.

Preheat the oven to 375°F (190°C; gas 5).

When the pumpkin is cooked, turn it into a food processor or blender and purée (there should be 2 cups). In a mixing bowl, beat the eggs with the brown sugar, pumpkin purée, cream, ginger, cloves, and salt.

Roll the pastry out on a floured board to line a 9- or 10-inch pie pan. Ease the pastry into the pie pan and trim and crimp the edges. Turn the pumpkin mixture into the pie shell and sprinkle the nutmeg over. Bake for 35–40 minutes, or until the pie has set. Leave to cool slightly before serving.

Baked Custard with Apricot Jam and Cream

This is a delicious way of serving custard, making it impressive enough for a dinner party as well as a favorite with the family. Dairy products are also good for and enjoyed by this home-loving and family-minded sign of the zodiac—this is indicated by the Moon's rulership of the breasts and the fluoride of lime content (Cancer's cell salt), which helps to strengthen teeth and eyesight. *Serves 4 to 6*

> 5 medium eggs
> 1/2 cup (4 oz; 115 g) superfine or castor sugar
> Pinch of salt
> Few drops of vanilla
> 3 cups (24 oz) milk
> 1/4 tsp nutmeg
> 4 Tb apricot jam
> 1 cup (8 oz) heavy or double cream
> 1/4 cup (1 oz) grated milk chocolate

Preheat the oven to 300°F (150°C; gas 2).

Grease a 5-cup ovenproof dish that's about 2 1/2 inches deep. In a mixing bowl lightly beat the eggs, then mix in the sugar, salt, vanilla, and milk. Turn into the greased ovenproof dish and sprinkle the nutmeg evenly over. Set the dish in a pan of cold water and bake for 75–80 minutes, or until a knife plunged into the center of the custard comes out clean. (While the custard is cooking make sure that the water surrounding it does not reach the boiling point, or the custard will separate.) Remove the custard from the oven and leave to cool. Place the jam in a small saucepan over low heat. Gently melt it, but do not allow it to boil, then spread it evenly over the top of the custard. Turn the cream into a bowl and beat until it is stiff. Spread it over the top of the jam. Cover with grated chocolate. Chill before serving.

Lemon Snow with Custard

The pure white of snow with the fresh tang of lemon, this dessert makes an ideal dish for the white Moon goddess and indicates the light and promise that the pale crescent of the Moon brings.
Serves 6

   3 Tb (1½ oz) cold water
   1 Tb plus ½ tsp gelatin
   1 cup (8 oz) boiling water
   ¾ cup (6 oz) fresh lemon juice
   2 Tb Cointreau
   2 Tb gin
   ½ cup (4 oz) or 5 medium egg whites
   6 Tb (3 oz; 85 g) superfine or castor sugar

Custard
   3 medium egg yolks
   3 Tb brown sugar
   1 cup (8 oz) milk
   1 Tb Cointreau

Pour the cold water into a bowl and sprinkle the gelatin over. Let it soak for a few minutes, then add the boiling water and stir continuously until the gelatin is completely dissolved. Thoroughly mix in the lemon juice, Cointreau, and gin, and leave to chill for 1½–2 hours, or until the mixture is just beginning to set. Now beat it until it is well mixed. In a separate bowl, with clean beaters, whip the egg whites until stiff, then fold the egg whites and superfine sugar into the lemon mixture. When it is thoroughly mixed turn into a 5-cup glass serving dish and chill for several hours or overnight, until set.

Just before you wish to serve the Lemon Snow, make the custard. In the top of a double boiler mix the egg yolks with the brown sugar. Place over barely simmering water and stir in the milk. Stir continuously until the mixture thickens to a custard. Remove from the heat, and stir in the Cointreau. Serve with the Lemon Snow.

Layered Fruit Sponge Cake

In Greek and Roman mythology the Moon was divided into three phases, of maiden, woman, and old woman, representing its stages of new, full, and old. Its colors were white, red, and black, indicating the changing temperaments and forms of which the Moon was capable. The layered fruit in this dessert relates to that concept —the white litchis have the delicate perfume of a young girl, the red cherries the voluptuousness of a woman, and the black currants a dark intensity that comes with maturity. The Victoria Sponge Cake is good for using as a pudding base. *Serves 6 to 8*

Victoria sponge cake (makes two 8-inch cakes)

    8 Tb (4 oz; 115 g) soft butter

    1 cup (7 oz; 200 g) superfine or castor sugar

    2 large eggs

    1/4 tsp vanilla

    1 cup (5 oz; 140 g) flour

    1 tsp baking powder

    1 1/2 cups (12 oz) heavy or double cream

    3 Tb superfine or castor sugar

    1/2 cup cherry brandy

    1/4 lb (115 g) black currants, or blackberries, hulled and cooked

    1/2 lb (225 g) cherries, pitted

    1/2 lb peeled and pitted litchis, or one 15-oz (425-g) can, drained

Preheat the oven to 325°F (165°C; gas 3).

Butter and dust with flour two 8-inch cake pans.

In a mixing bowl, beat the butter and sugar until pale and fluffy. In a small bowl lightly beat the eggs and very gradually beat into the butter and sugar, along with the vanilla. Mix the flour with the baking powder, and fold them into the egg mixture. Turn into the cake pans and bake for 20–25 minutes, or until a knife inserted into the center of the cakes comes out clean. Turn out onto a rack and allow to cool.

While the cakes are cooling, beat the cream in a mixing bowl until it is stiff. Fold in the superfine sugar. Slice each layer in half to create two layers. Place one layer on the bottom of a 2-quart glass bowl just large enough in diameter to hold the cake. Sprinkle a third of the brandy over, then evenly cover the sponge with the black currants. Spread a third of the cream over. Place a second layer of cake on top of the cream. Sprinkle half the remaining brandy evenly over, then spread the cherries over and cover with half the remaining cream. Discard (or use for another purpose) one of the remaining layers of sponge and lay the other layer over the cherries and cream. Sprinkle with the remaining brandy. Spread the remaining cream over the sponge in an even layer, then cover the top with litchis. Serve immediately, or chill before serving.

Rhubarb Pudding with Strawberries

Summer fruits, rose-pink and scarlet (the color that promises resurrection after death), combine to make a fresh and piquant pudding similar to a cheesecake. Make it easily in advance of a lunch or dinner party, only add the strawberries at the last minute. *Serves 6 to 8*

1¹/₂ lb (675 g) rhubarb, washed and dried

³/₄ cup (5 oz; 150 g) granulated sugar

5 Tb (2¹/₂ oz) fresh orange juice

Crumb crust

10 graham crackers or digestive biscuits (5 oz)

2 Tb superfine or castor sugar

5 Tb (2¹/₂ oz; 75 g) melted butter

1 Tb plus 2 tsp gelatin

1 cup (8 oz) light or single cream

1 pint (¹/₂ lb; 225 g) strawberries

Remove the leaves and the ends from the rhubarb and cut the stalks into 2-inch pieces. Put into a medium-size saucepan with the granulated sugar and 2 tablespoons of orange juice. Place over low heat, cover, and simmer for 15–20 minutes, or until the rhubarb is tender.

While the rhubarb is cooking, prepare the crumb crust. In a food processor or with a rolling pin, crush the graham crackers. (If you are not using a food processor turn the crushed crackers into a bowl.) Then thoroughly mix in the superfine sugar and butter. Press the mixture into the bottom of a 9¹/₂- to 10-inch pie pan and leave to chill.

When the rhubarb is nearly cooked, place the remaining orange juice in a bowl and sprin-kle the gelatin over. Let it soak for a few minutes. Turn the rhubarb into a food processor or blender and purée. Return it to the saucepan, and bring to a simmer. Now pour it over the softened gelatin and stir continuously until the gelatin has completely dissolved. Let the rhubarb cool slightly and then mix it with the cream and turn into the crumb crust. Chill for several hours or overnight until it has set. Before serving, hull and halve the strawberries lengthwise and arrange them over the top of the rhubarb.

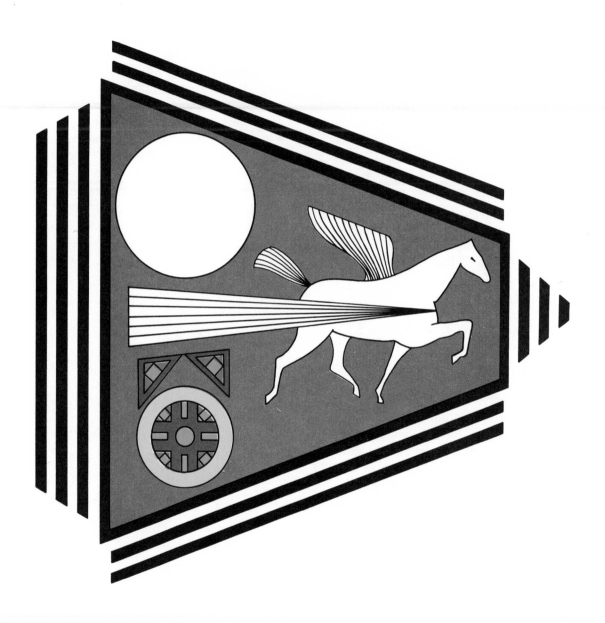

LEO

JULY 24–AUGUST 23

Rules the fifth house, the house of pleasure and the arts

RULING PLANET
The Sun
♌

ELEMENT
Fire
♌

QUALITIES
Fixed, active
♌

CHARACTERISTICS
Assertive, courageous, domineering, generous,
magnanimous, strong
♌

OPPOSITE SIGN
Aquarius
♌

BODY AREA
Heart, back
♌

GEMSTONE
Topaz, yellow diamond
♌

COLOR
Yellow
♌

FLAVOR
Sweet and pungent
♌

METAL
Gold
♌

FAUNA
Caviar, cockerel, eggs, lamb
♌

FLORA
Apples, dandelions, honey, nuts, oranges, palm trees, sunflowers, tomatoes, vine leaves
♌

HERBS AND SPICES
Angelica, balm, bay leaves, cinnamon,
ginger, lovage, rosemary, saffron
♌

CELL SALT
Phosphate of magnesia (Mag. Phos.),
found in barley, cucumber, eggs, figs,
rye, walnuts
♌

LEO THE COOK

Leos love to show off their beautiful homes and their ability as cooks. This is a generous and loving sign of the zodiac, who really enjoys being surrounded by friends and family. They excel when they have an audience, and really love entertaining; dinner parties are likely to take place frequently in their households.

So if a Leo asks you to dinner you can go prepared for a grand and luxurious evening. He or she will want to impress you. Leos also like things to be done properly—the table will be beautifully set, flowers will be arranged, and, being very conventional at heart, foods will be served in the correct order. They love to sit down together with their families at mealtime, not so much for the food but because it's right and proper that they should, and it gives the family an opportunity to get together. Leos like food for the function it fulfills, and are fond of the ritual of eating; they will take to the barbecue with flourish on a hot evening, or turn the meal into a gala picnic.

Leo rules a time of year when the sun is fixed high overhead, ripening the fruits and shining golden over wheatfields swaying in the breeze. It is a time of year when the pleasures of the earth are ready to be enjoyed, giving a feeling of eternity. In the same way, Leo is a fixed and stable sign of the zodiac, which suggests a nature that is determined and often inflexible. If a Leo decides to hold a large dinner party he or she will excel in the organization of the whole event. Leos are particularly good at directing other people, and their kitchens will probably be full of helpers charmed into assisting.

Leos make creative cooks (Leo rules the fifth house of the zodiac, which is concerned with creativity), but their creativity tends to be well thought out and controlled. They are more concerned with the end product than the process (as their seasonal association indicates), and the menu for the evening will have been planned in advance and will be balanced (because Leo is the harmony of fire). Leos mostly enjoy cooking for other people. If there is someone to appreciate their labors in the kitchen they will quite happily spend time perfecting a magnificently showy dish, but alone, without an adoring audience for their masterpiece, they see very little point in bothering.

A dinner party is likely to capture their imaginations, and foods they will most enjoy preparing will be impressive and extravagant, with sweetly pungent flavors. A lobster dish is a possibility since it is the king of shellfish, or a crown roast of lamb, which suggests the crown this regal sign feels is rightfully theirs. Flambéed dishes are also popular with this fiery sign, or they might prepare a showy meringue dish, which is not too difficult to do but looks wonderful. (Because the Sun rules the sight, it rules the right eye in a man and the left in a woman.) The Leo doesn't really want to spend longer than necessary in the kitchen when there are so many other pleasures waiting to be enjoyed.

If a Leo invites you to dinner, you can put the evening aside to total pleasure. No expense will be spared, and you will be treated to an evening of great elegance.

RECIPES FOR LEO

MENU SUGGESTIONS FOR LEO

First Courses

Bombay Monkfish
Caviar Pie
Stuffed Vine Leaves
Red, White, and Black Salad
Parma Ham with Melon
Salmon Tartare
Vichyssoise with Pecans

Main Courses

Crown of Lamb
Kaori's Oven-Baked Spareribs
Cod with Tomatoes and Olives
Lobster Thermidor
Gingered Chicken with Apricots
Pipérade
Polynesian Pork

Side Dishes

Beets in Orange Sauce
Palm Heart and Smoked Oyster Salad

Desserts

Walnut Tart
Caramelized Oranges
Crêpes Suzette
Choux Pastry Ring with Chocolate Sauce
Raspberry-Meringue Pyramid
Crème Brûlée

Caviar Pie
Lobster Thermidor
Crêpes Suzette
Ω

Stuffed Vine Leaves
Pipérade
Caramelized Oranges
Ω

Bombay Monkfish
Gingered Chicken with Apricots
Choux Pastry Ring with Chocolate Sauce
Ω

Red, White, and Black Salad
Polynesian Pork
Raspberry-Meringue Pyramid
Ω

Vichyssoise with Pecans
Kaori's Oven-Baked Spareribs
Raspberry-Meringue Pyramid
Ω

Parma Ham with Melon
Cod with Tomatoes and Olives
Walnut Tart
Ω

Salmon Tartare
Crown of Lamb
Crème Brûlée

LEO THE GUEST

Leos thoroughly enjoy being invited out to dine; luxuriating in being fed good food, in the same way as they enjoy all the pleasurable things in life. Leo's warm and sunny nature is bound to brighten your table, so dinner should be a delightful occasion.

This is a fire sign, and Leos possess a personality full of the force and heat characteristic of their element. But theirs is the balanced, harmonious part of fire—the air of fire, which is contained and controlled and dignified. Leos will be generous and enthusiastic (they will probably sweep in magnanimously bearing gifts), and although they will desire attention, they will demand it gracefully. They will love being catered to, being greeted with champagne, and no matter what other guests you may have invited, Leos will be quite sure that the evening was engineered especially for their pleasure. After all, this is the most regal sign of the zodiac and like the lion (the king of beasts) that symbolizes them, Leos expect to be treated with the respect and extravagance that is reserved for kings.

Because this sign of the zodiac is ruled by the Sun, Leos embody all the strength and force of this hot, aggressive planet, reflecting its importance in their own strong awareness of their place in the world. The Sun also endows a warm and joyous nature that knows life is here to be enjoyed and not to be spent toiling over a hot stove; so they will be sure to appreciate all your labors.

Leos will flatter your other guests, because flattery is something they love to receive and because they possess an ability to have fun. Leo rules the fifth house of the zodiac, the house concerned with pleasure, love affairs, and the arts, making this sign romantic, fond of beauty and the best in food and drink. Leos will arrive at your dinner party quite prepared to have a good time. However, it is worth noting that they are most compatible with other fire signs or air signs, but you could invite a Capricorn, who will also enjoy a festive occasion.

You won't need to fuss over the details of the food too much with this sign of the zodiac, so long as the overall effect is spectacular. The grand gesture is what interests Leos, so perhaps feed them some roasted meats rubbed golden with saffron, a color traditionally associated with kings. Or a flaming Crêpes Suzette, to match the fire that burns within this sign. And feed them well-formed, rounded foods such as tomatoes, oranges, or apricots to match the golden orb of their ruling planet, the Sun, foods that have proportion and symmetry with clear dignified lines, or you can give them a steak tartare to appeal to the beast in them.

Really, the only drink for this noble creature is champagne, but failing that, try your Leo guest on a rich red or a golden wine the color of the Sun. And make sure that it's the best you can afford. Don't sit them in a dark corner—the head of the table is the place for the Sun, the god of light.

Bombay Monkfish

Individual dishes of monkfish and shrimp are baked in egg and cream and flavored with curry to make an appetizing and stylish way to begin a meal. For a light lunch dish for two, cook this in one ovenproof dish and serve it with a green salad and boiled new potatoes. *Serves 4*

1 lb monkfish, skinned
Milk to cover
1/4 lb (115 g) shrimp, shelled
2 medium eggs
3 Tb tomato paste
1/2 tsp curry powder
2 tsp lemon juice
Pinch of dried rosemary, or 1/4 tsp chopped fresh
Pinch of saffron or turmeric
3/4 cup (6 oz) light or single cream
Salt and black pepper to taste

Garnishes
1 lemon, quartered
Whole wheat Italian bread, warmed in the oven

Preheat the oven to 350°F (180°C; gas 4).

Put the monkfish in a pan just large enough to hold it. Pour the milk over and place the pan over moderate heat. Bring to a simmer, cover, and cook for 8 minutes. Turn the fish and cook 7 minutes longer, or until the monkfish is cooked through. When the monkfish is nearly done, add the shrimp and cook 2–3 minutes, or until they turn pink. Drain the fish and shrimp, discarding the milk, and transfer to a wooden board. Cut the monkfish into bite-size pieces. In a mixing bowl, beat the eggs with the tomato paste, curry powder, lemon juice, rosemary, saffron, and 1/2 cup (4 oz) cream. Mix in the fish and season to taste with salt and black pepper. Turn into 4 individual ramekin dishes and pour an equal amount of the remaining cream over the top of each dish. Bake for 20 minutes, or until set, and serve hot with a squeeze of lemon and a crusty loaf.

Caviar Pie

A sheet of dense caviar covers the golden of eggs chopped with onion and iced with sour cream, making a magnificent and unusual dish that should be served very cold. Cut it like a pie and serve accompanied by wedges of lemon and thin slices of whole wheat bread and butter. Delicious with champagne, Caviar Pie makes an impressive starter, regal enough for the king of beasts, and no trouble to prepare. *Serves 8*

9 medium eggs, hard-boiled and finely chopped

6 Tb (3 oz; 85 g) melted unsalted butter

1 medium onion, peeled and finely chopped

Freshly ground black pepper

3/4 cup (6 oz) sour cream

1 1/4 cups (9 oz; 250 g) caviar or Danish lumpfish caviar

Garnishes

2 lemons, each cut into 4 wedges

8 thin slices of whole wheat bread, buttered and cut in half

In a mixing bowl, thoroughly combine the eggs and butter with the onion. Season generously with black pepper. Press the mixture into the base of a 9-inch pie plate. Spread the sour cream evenly over the top of the egg-and-onion mixture. Chill for several hours or overnight, or in the freezer until very cold, but not frozen. Then spread the caviar evenly over the sour cream, so that the top is completely covered with caviar and no white shows through. Serve chilled with lemon wedges and whole wheat bread.

Stuffed Vine Leaves

The Sun-warmed vines are sacred to Apollo as the immortal part of Dionysus, reflecting his joy and sensuous enjoyment of pleasure. Apollo is god of sunlight and also a shepherd god who played the lyre as he watched over his flocks. Vine leaves filled with a delicious combination of lamb and rice, with the fresh taste of mint, make a superb dish for the Sun-ruled Leo, and a wonderfully tempting way to begin a meal. *Serves 4 to 5*

3 oz (85 g) or 26 vine leaves

2 Tb olive oil

1 medium onion, peeled and finely chopped

2 cloves garlic, peeled and pushed through a press

1 Tb tomato paste

2 medium tomatoes (about 6 oz; 180 g), peeled and finely chopped

1/2 lb (225 g) minced lamb

2 Tb port or red wine

1/2 tsp dried oregano, or 1 tsp fresh

Generous pinch of cinnamon

1/4 cup (2 oz; 60 g) long-grain rice

1/2 tsp dried mint, or 1 tsp chopped fresh

Salt and black pepper

Preheat the oven to 350°F (180°C; gas 4).

Place the vine leaves in a large bowl. Cover with boiling water and let them soak for 15 minutes. Drain and rinse in cold water, then pat the leaves dry.

In a large frying pan, heat the oil over moderate heat. Add the onion and sauté for about 8 minutes, or until soft. Mix in the garlic, tomato paste, tomatoes, lamb, port, oregano, and cinnamon, stirring and turning to break up any lumps

a moderate oven for 20 minutes. Then turn the leaves over, check that they are smeared with oil, and return them to the oven for 15 minutes more. Transfer the leaves to a warmed serving dish and serve hot.

of meat. Simmer gently for 15–20 minutes, or until the meat has browned and any liquid has reduced.

Meanwhile, cook the rice in 3 cups (1¼ Imperial pints) boiling salted water. Simmer without stirring for 15–20 minutes, or until tender. Drain and thoroughly mix into the browned meat with the mint. Season to taste with salt and black pepper, and remove from the heat. Then place 1 tablespoon of the filling in the center of each vine leaf (on its veiny side). Wrap the right and left sides of each leaf over the filling, then roll up so you have a small package. Coat the bottom of an ovenproof dish with some olive oil. Arrange the vine leaves seam-side down in it. Brush the tops of the leaves generously with olive oil, cover the dish with foil, and cook in

Red, White, and Black Salad

Round tomatoes, a sweet scarlet fruit of the Sun, are beautifully complemented by the white savory mozzarella, salty black olives, and basil dressing, creating a decorative and delicious starter. Prepare this easy-to-make dish just before you wish to eat it—the tomatoes can become watery—and serve it with rolls or crunchy bread. *Serves 4*

Basil dressing

> 2 Tb olive oil
>
> 1 Tb lemon juice
>
> 1/2 tsp honey
>
> 1/2 tsp Dijon mustard
>
> 1/4 tsp dried basil, or 1/2 tsp chopped fresh
>
> Salt and black pepper to taste

> 2 scallions or spring onions
>
> 1 lb (450 g) tomatoes, or 2 large ripe tomatoes, peeled
>
> 7 oz (200 g) mozzarella cheese

Garnish

> 1/3 cup (1 oz; 30 g) black olives

In a small bowl or jar mix together the dressing ingredients. Chop the scallions finely crosswise. Slice the tomatoes thinly crosswise. Slice the mozzarella into about 1/8-inch thickness and into pieces of about 2 by 2 inches. Arrange the tomatoes and mozzarella alternately in a shallow dish just large enough to hold them. Sprinkle the scallions and olives over. Pour the dressing over and serve.

Parma Ham with Melon

The full round curves of this Sun-kissed fruit—yellow with a hint of green, the color of the finest gold—relate directly to Leo, the sign of the zodiac ruled by the golden sphere of the Sun. Flattered by the savory Parma ham, this dish is joyously easy to prepare and makes a gloriously summery way to begin a meal. *Serves 4*

> 8 thin slices (about 8 oz; 225 g) Parma ham
>
> 1 ripe honeydew melon (about 1 1/4 lb; 560 g), chilled
>
> Black pepper

Garnish

> 1 lemon, quartered

Remove the rind and any surrounding fat from the Parma ham. Place two slices of ham on each plate, to one side of the plate. Cut the melon in half lengthwise. Scoop out and discard the pips. Cut the melon in half again lengthwise. Cut the skin off the melon. Then cut each piece of melon into 3 slices lengthwise. Arrange 3 slices of melon beside the ham. Season to taste with black pepper, and serve with wedges of lemon.

Salmon Tartare

Salmon Tartare is a mixture of chopped raw fish subtly blended with spices to make a luxurious and most unusual starter, topped with caviar and a raw quail egg. Serve it with thin slices of brown toast and a very cold bottle of white Burgundy wine. *Serves 6*

1/2 lb (225 g) salmon, skinned and filleted

6 oz (180 g) halibut or turbot, skinned and filleted

1 small onion, peeled and finely chopped (2 1/2 Tb)

3 Tb capers, finely chopped

3/4 tsp Tabasco

1 tsp Worcestershire sauce

2 Tb finely chopped fresh parsley

Salt and freshly ground black pepper

1 Tb caviar or Danish lumpfish caviar

6 quail eggs

Garnishes

6 slices of thinly sliced bread, toasted, buttered, and halved

Tabasco

Chopped onion

Capers

Black pepper

Chop the fish finely with a sharp knife. Place it in a mixing bowl with the onion, capers, Tabasco, Worcestershire sauce, and parsley, and season to taste with salt and black pepper. Shape the mixture into 6 equal rounds. Place each one on the center of a plate and press the mixture flat, so it looks like a burger. Place 1/2 teaspoon of caviar in the center of each patty. Crack a quail egg

over the top of the caviar. Serve accompanied by the garnishes, so that each person may vary the spiciness of his or her fish.

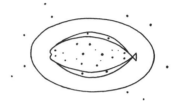

Vichyssoise with Pecans

A delicious cool, creamy soup, with the rough texture of sweet pecans and full of the goodness of root vegetables; Vichyssoise with Pecans is an ideal dish for a hot summer evening. *Serves 8*

> *1½ lb leeks*
> *2 ribs of celery, chopped*
> *4 Tb (2 oz) butter*
> *1 lb potatoes*
> *2½ cups (1 Imperial pint) chicken stock*
> *2 cups milk*
> *Salt and black pepper*
> *2 cups (8 oz; 225 g) pecans, whole or pieces*
> *1¼ cups (½ Imperial pint) heavy or double cream*

Garnishes

> *2 tsp chopped fresh chives*
> *2 Tb chopped fresh parsley*
> *8 thin slices of whole wheat bread, buttered and halved*

Remove the roots, ragged ends, and rough outer leaves from the leeks, slice them crosswise, and thoroughly wash. Wash and dry the celery, remove the ends and strings, and chop. Melt 4 tablespoons of butter in a large saucepan over moderately low heat, mix in the celery and leeks, cover, and cook, stirring occasionally, for 15 minutes, or until they are tender. While the leeks and celery are cooking, peel and chop the potatoes. Stir the potatoes, stock, and milk into the vegetables, and season to taste with salt and black pepper. Bring to a boil, cover, and simmer for about 20 minutes, or until the potatoes are tender. Turn into a food processor or blender, and purée in batches with the nuts and cream, check the seasoning, turn into a soup tureen, and chill for 2–3 hours. Sprinkle with the chives and parsley, and serve with thin slices of buttered whole wheat bread on the side.

MAIN COURSES

Crown of Lamb

Crown of lamb is perfect for such a regal and dignified sign of the zodiac as Leo, symbolized by a lion, the king of the animal kingdom. This spectacular dish must be the king of meat dishes and makes a surprisingly easy meal for a dinner party. For a colorful finish, serve it with the center filled with petit pois and accompanied by baby carrots, boiled new potatoes, and a delicious bottle of red wine. *Serves 6 to 8*

> One prepared 16-rib crown of lamb
> (about 3¼ lb; 1615 g)
> 1 clove garlic, peeled
> 1 tsp dried rosemary, or 2 tsp fresh
> Salt and freshly ground black pepper

Garnishes
> Paper frills
> Petits pois

Preheat the oven to 325°F (165°C; gas 3).

Remove any trimmings from the joint that the butcher may have left in the center. Rub the meat with garlic, rosemary, and salt and season lightly with black pepper. Cover the ends of the ribs with foil. Fill the center of the crown with foil so it will hold its shape. Place the crown in a roasting pan. Roast for 1 hour (15–18 minutes for each pound), depending on how well done you like it. Then remove the lamb from the oven, discard all the foil, and let rest 10–15 minutes before carving. For a decorative finish, cover the ends of the ribs with paper frills. Fill the center with petits pois and serve.

Kaori's Oven-Baked Spareribs

This dish for the hungry lion is easy to make and fun to eat. If it is hot enough to barbecue outdoors, bake the ribs until tender, then cook them on the barbecue, to match the heat and vitality embodied in this fiery sign of the zodiac. Serve with the sauce and a bowl of noodles and stir-fried vegetables or a green salad. *Serves 4*

> 3 lb pork spareribs
> 2-inch piece of gingerroot, peeled and cut into
>   4 pieces

Sauce
> 6 Tb (3 oz) dark soy sauce
> ¾ cup (6 oz) tomato ketchup
> ¼ cup (2 oz) oyster sauce
> 2 cloves garlic, peeled and pushed through a press
> ½ tsp ground ginger
>
> Vegetable or sunflower oil

Preheat the oven to 350°F (180°C; gas 4).

Arrange the ribs in a large ovenproof dish or roasting pan with the ginger. Cover with water and then foil. Bake for 1½ hours, or until the ribs are tender. While the ribs are cooking, prepare the sauce. In a mixing bowl, beat or thoroughly mix together the sauce ingredients. When the ribs are tender, drain them, set aside, and discard the ginger. Wipe the dish or roasting pan clean, rub the bottom with a little oil, and return the ribs to the dish. Pour the sauce over the ribs and cover with foil. Return to the oven for 25 minutes, then remove the foil. Turn the ribs in the sauce and cook 15 minutes longer. Serve hot.

Cod with Tomatoes and Olives

A simple but unusual and delicious fish dish with the full, rich flavor of tomatoes and olives mixed with the spicy aroma of bay leaves. Nicholas Culpeper, the famous seventeenth-century astrologer and physician, attributed the bay to the Sun in Leo and claimed that it was by nature healing and able to resist witchcraft. Serve this dish for a family supper or a dinner party, with rice or mashed potatoes, a green vegetable or salad, and a very cold white wine. *Serves 4*

> 3 Tb (1½ oz) olive oil
>
> 4 medium onions, peeled and thinly sliced
>
> 2 cloves garlic, peeled and pushed through a press
>
> 1 lb tomatoes, peeled and chopped
>
> 2 bay leaves
>
> ¼ tsp dried basil, or ½ tsp chopped fresh
>
> ⅔ cup (2 oz; 60 g) green olives, pitted and sliced crosswise
>
> 1 Tb capers
>
> 2 lb (or 4 pieces) cod or haddock, skinned, from the thick end of fillet
>
> Salt and black pepper

Heat the oil in a large frying pan over moderately low heat. Add the onions and garlic, and sauté, turning occasionally, for 20 minutes, or until the onions are soft. Then add the tomatoes, bay leaves, basil, olives, and capers. Increase the heat slightly, and simmer the tomatoes for 5 minutes, stirring frequently. Add the fish and season to taste with salt and black pepper. Cook the fish for 5 minutes on each side. Discard the bay leaves; check the seasoning and correct if necessary. Transfer to a warmed serving dish.

Lobster Thermidor

Lobster Thermidor is a luxuriously extravagant meal, a dish to heighten the enjoyment of life. And it is just right for this warm and generous sign of the zodiac, who loves to impress and be impressed. Serve it with some rice, a green salad, and champagne or a very chilled white wine. *Serves 2*

> One 1½–1¾-lb lobster, cooked and cut in half lengthwise, the gray brain and black intestines discarded
>
> 4 Tb (2 oz) butter
>
> ¼ lb (115 g) mushrooms, wiped clean and thinly sliced
>
> 2 Tb flour
>
> ½ cup plus 1 Tb (4½ oz) milk
>
> ½ cup (4 oz) heavy or double cream
>
> 1 Tb dry sherry
>
> 1 tsp Dijon mustard
>
> Salt and black pepper
>
> 2 Tb freshly grated Parmesan
>
> Cayenne

Preheat the oven to 425°F (220°C; gas 7).

Remove the claws of the lobster from the body. Crack them with nutcrackers or a hammer. Remove all the flesh from the claws and shell of the lobster, discard the claws, and set the shells aside. Cut the flesh into ½–¾-inch cubes and set aside.

In a small saucepan, melt 1 tablespoon of the butter over moderate heat, mix in the mushrooms, and sauté, stirring occasionally, for 5 minutes. Remove from the heat and set aside.

Melt 2 tablespoons butter in a saucepan over

moderately low heat. Stir in the flour, and continue to stir for 2 minutes. Gradually add the milk and cream, and stir continuously until you have a smooth sauce. Simmer for a few minutes. Mix in the mushrooms, sherry, mustard, and lobster pieces. Heat through and season to taste with salt and black pepper. Then fill the shells with the mixture and place them in a baking dish. Sprinkle the cheese and cayenne evenly over. Dot with the remaining tablespoon of butter and bake for 10 minutes, or until the cheese is golden. Transfer to a warmed serving dish.

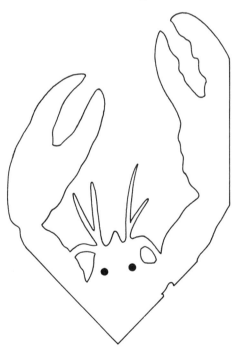

Gingered Chicken with Apricots

A golden bird the color of Leo, which relates to the warmth and energy of the incandescent Sun. Serve this glorious dish with boiled new potatoes and a green salad, and with the apricot juices that surround the chicken in place of gravy. *Serves 4*

> 8 oz (225 g) dried apricots
> 1½ cups (12 oz) apricot juice

Stuffing

> 3 scallions or spring onions, finely chopped
> 2 cups (4 oz; 115 g) soft whole wheat
>   bread crumbs
> 4 dried apricots (from the 8 oz soaked), chopped
> ½ cup (2 oz) chopped mixed nuts
> 1 Tb soft butter
> 1 large egg
> 1 Tb chopped stem ginger in syrup or candied
>   ginger, wiped clean

> Salt and black pepper to taste
> Two 2-lb chickens, or one 4-lb chicken, cleaned
> 2 tsp ground ginger
> ⅓ cup (2½ oz) sherry
> 1 Tb honey

Place the apricots in a bowl and pour the apricot juice over. Let them soak for about 4 hours or overnight. Drain the apricots, reserving the apricot juice. Then prepare the stuffing.

Preheat the oven to 325°F (165°C; gas 3).

In a mixing bowl thoroughly mix all the stuffing ingredients. Season to taste with salt and black pepper. Wash and dry the chickens. Rub the skin with ground ginger and season with

GINGERED CHICKEN, CONTINUED

salt and black pepper. Divide the stuffing into 2 equal portions and stuff the birds. Fasten the body cavities with a skewer to hold in the stuffing, and truss to keep the birds intact. Place them breast-side up in a roasting pan just slightly larger than the chickens. Pour the sherry over and place in the oven. (Figure 25 minutes per pound for cooking time.) After 15 minutes pour the apricot juice over and baste with the surrounding juices. Roast 15 minutes longer, then smear the birds' skin with the honey and surround them with the apricots. (If you are cooking a larger bird, add the apricots about 20 minutes before the chicken is cooked.) Baste with the apricot juice and surrounding juices. For the smaller chickens, baste one more time; for the larger one, continue to baste every 15 minutes. When the chickens are cooked, remove them to a platter and let them sit for 10 minutes before carving. Pour the juices into a jug, and serve them with the chicken.

Pipérade

Pipérade is a famous Basque peasant dish in which a purée of tomatoes, peppers, and onions is mixed with eggs. In Egyptian mythology the Sun was an egg laid every day by a heavenly goose. Since eggs are representative of creation, their yolk and white being the symbol for the Sun—a dot surrounded by a circle, life surrounded by eternity—Pipérade makes an ideal lunch or supper dish for this Sun-ruled sign. Serve hot, with plenty of whole wheat bread and a young Rioja. *Serves 4*

> *1 medium red pepper (about 6 oz; 180 g)*
> *1 medium yellow pepper (about 6 oz; 180 g)*
> *¼ cup (2 oz) olive oil*
> *2 Spanish onions, peeled and thinly sliced*
> *3 cloves garlic, peeled and pushed through a press*
> *2 large ripe tomatoes (about 1 lb; 450 g), peeled and chopped*
> *1 tsp dried oregano, or 2 tsp chopped fresh*
> *½ tsp dried basil, or 1 tsp chopped fresh*
> *12 medium eggs*
> *⅛ tsp paprika*
> *Salt and black pepper*
> *4 Tb (2 oz) butter*

Quarter the peppers lengthwise, and from both peppers remove the seeds, stalk, and whitish membrane. Slice them thinly across. Heat the oil in a large frying pan over moderately low heat, add the onions, peppers, and garlic, and turn them in the oil. Sauté gently for 30 minutes, or until soft, turning them occasionally. Then add the tomatoes, oregano, and basil. Increase the heat to moderate and leave uncovered. Let

Polynesian Pork

the mixture bubble for 25–35 minutes, stirring occasionally, or until the liquid has reduced and the vegetables are very well cooked.

When the vegetables are nearly ready, beat 6 eggs in a mixing bowl with a pinch of paprika and salt and black pepper to taste. Then place a 9–10-inch omelet pan, or nonstick frying pan, over high heat with 2 tablespoons of butter. When it foams, pour in the eggs, tilting the pan so that the eggs spread and cook evenly, lifting the edges of the omelet so the uncooked egg runs underneath. When the eggs have cooked on the outside, but are still soft in the center, spread half of the vegetable mixture on one side of the omelet. Roll the other half of the omelet over the filling and turn out onto a warmed serving dish. Keep the omelet warm while you cook the remaining eggs in the same way, filling them with the remaining filling. Then transfer the second omelet to the serving dish and serve each omelet cut into slices crosswise.

Polynesian Pork is a deliciously different combination of pork and spicy sausage, cooked in fresh orange juice with almonds and peas. It makes an ideal dish for a dinner party, since it is a complete meal in one pot and only needs to be accompanied by a bowl of hot rice and a fruity red wine. *Serves 4*

3–4 Tb flour
1/2 tsp salt
1/4 tsp black pepper
1 lb shoulder of pork, cut into small cubes and trimmed of any fat
2 Tb sunflower oil
Peeled rind of 1 orange, without pith
1 cup (8 oz) fresh orange juice
1 1/2 cups (12 oz) chicken stock
3/4 lb (340 g) spicy garlic pork sausages
1/2 lb (225 g) shelled peas
1/2 cup (1 1/2 oz; 45 g) slivered almonds
1/4 cup (2 oz) heavy or double cream

Preheat the oven to 350°F (180°C; gas 4).

Mix the flour with the salt and pepper. Roll the pork cubes in the flour and shake off any excess. Heat the oil in a frying pan over high heat, then very quickly brown the meat on each side, to seal the juices. Do this in two or three batches so you don't crowd the pan. Transfer the meat to a casserole. Add the orange rind. Pour the orange juice and stock over. Cover, place in the oven, and cook for 1 1/4–1 1/2 hours, or until the meat is tender. When the meat is nearly tender, rub a frying pan with oil and place it over moderate heat. When the pan is hot, add

POLYNESIAN PORK, CONTINUED

Beets in Orange Sauce

the sausages and sauté, turning, for 10–15 minutes, or until lightly browned. Remove the sausages to a wooden board and cut them into ³/4–1-inch pieces. Remove the casserole from the oven, add the sausages, and return it to the oven for 10 minutes. Then add the peas and cook 5 minutes longer. Mix in the almonds and cream and return the casserole to the oven for 5 minutes, or until the almonds and cream are hot through and the peas are cooked. Serve hot.

Red beets suggest the red heartbeat, the pulse of life that symbolizes creativity and the part of the body ruled by Leo, the sign of the zodiac that lives more from the heart than the head. *Serves 4*

1¹/4 lb small beets
2 Tb butter
2 Tb flour
1¹/4 cups (¹/2 Imperial pint) fresh orange juice
1¹/2 Tb brown sugar
Salt and black pepper

Cut the leaves off the beets and trim the stalks, leaving 1 inch and the roots intact. Wash in plenty of cold water without scrubbing or the beets will bleed. Place them in a saucepan with 1–2 inches of water to cover. Boil gently for 45–60 minutes, or until the beets are tender. When the beets are nearly ready prepare the sauce.

Place the butter in a saucepan over moderately low heat. When it has melted mix in the flour and cook, stirring constantly, for 2 minutes. Then gradually stir in the orange juice until you have a smooth sauce. Mix in the sugar and simmer for a few minutes. Season to taste with salt and black pepper. Remove from the heat, cover, and keep warm.

When the beets are cooked, drain them and cool slightly by rinsing in cold water. Peel off the skins and remove the tapering root and tops. Arrange in a warmed serving dish. Pour the sauce over and serve hot.

Palm Heart and Smoked Oyster Salad

The palm tree is poetically connected with birth, because it grows by the sea, which represents the universal mother, and Apollo was born beneath a palm, which was sacred to him. Palm Heart and Smoked Oyster Salad is an exotic dish that can be served for a light lunch with some bread and cheese, as an accompaniment to a main meal, or as a starter. *Serves 4*

Vinaigrette

    4 Tb (2 oz) olive oil
    1 Tb lemon juice
    Salt and black pepper to taste

    1/2 head crisp green lettuce, washed and dried
    2 oz (60 g) or a small head of radicchio, washed and dried
    One 14-oz (425-g) can palm tree hearts, drained
    One 3 1/2-oz (105-g) can smoked oysters, drained
    3 scallions or spring onions
    1 Tb finely chopped fresh parsley

In a small mixing bowl or jar mix together the vinaigrette ingredients. Shred the lettuce into small pieces and arrange it over the bottom of a salad bowl. Arrange the radicchio leaves around the edge of the bowl. Chop the palm tree hearts into about 1-inch slices crosswise and arrange them and the oysters over the bed of lettuce. Chop the scallions finely crosswise. Scatter them and the parsley over. Just before serving, pour the vinaigrette over and toss.

Walnut Tart

Nuts relate to the radiant Sun as a creative source of energy because they are the seeds of life. Walnuts are particularly good for this sign of the zodiac because they contain Leo's cell salt, magnesium phosphate, which helps combat cramps, shooting pains, and spasmodic palpitations of the heart—often a vulnerable organ with this sign of the zodiac. The crust for Walnut Tart is especially good if you substitute orange juice for the milk in the pastry recipe. *Serves 6 to 8*

Sweet shortcrust pastry
(to line a 9-inch tart pan)

    1 1/4 cups (6 1/4 oz; 175 g) flour
    1/4 tsp salt
    2 Tb superfine or castor sugar
    7 Tb (3 1/2 oz; 100 g) butter
    1 medium egg yolk
    2–3 Tb milk (or orange juice)

Filling

    6 Tb (3 oz; 85 g) butter
    2/3 cup (5 oz) corn syrup or golden syrup
    3 medium eggs
    Few drops of vanilla
    Grated rind of 1 orange
    Grated rind of 1 lemon
    3 Tb (1 1/2 oz) fresh lemon juice
    1 1/4 cups (5 oz; 140 g) finely chopped walnuts

WALNUT TART, CONTINUED

To prepare the pastry: Place the flour, salt, and sugar in a large bowl. Cut in the butter and with your fingertips work the flour and butter together until the mixture has the consistency of coarse bread crumbs. Make a well in the center and fill it with the egg yolk and milk. Stir the flour mixture into the egg and milk with a fork, until the egg and milk are all absorbed. Alternatively, you can make this pastry in a food processor. First mix the flour, salt, sugar, and butter until the mixture resembles coarse bread crumbs, then add the egg yolk and milk through the feed tube. Process until a dough forms. Shape into a ball, wrap it in plastic wrap, and refrigerate for 20–30 minutes.

Preheat the oven to 425°F (220°C; gas 7).

Roll the pastry out on a floured board. Transfer it to a 9-inch tart pan, press the dough in all around, and trim the edges. Prick the bottom and sides with a fork and bake for 10 minutes.

Lower the oven heat to 375°F (190C°; gas 5).

While the pastry is cooling, make the filling. Heat the butter and syrup in a small saucepan over low heat, stirring occasionally, until the butter has melted. Remove from the heat and leave to cool. In a mixing bowl or food processor beat or mix the eggs, vanilla, orange and lemon rinds, and lemon juice. Mix in the butter-and-syrup mixture and the nuts. Turn into the tart pan and bake for 20–25 minutes, or until firm to the touch. Serve cold with whipped cream and a sweet white dessert wine or a glass of port.

Caramelized Oranges

These Sun-filled oranges shine from under a sweet golden glaze, suggesting the glorious and intense energy of the Sun. They make a delightfully simple and refreshing end to a meal. *Serves 4*

> 4 large oranges
> 1/2 cup (4 oz) superfine or castor sugar
> 3 Tb fresh orange juice, or the juice reserved from the sliced oranges

Slice the top and base off the oranges. Stand 1 upright on a wooden board. Using a sharp knife, cut off the peel and pith from the sides of the orange. Then repeat this process with the remaining 3 oranges. (Reserve any juice they shed.) Slice the oranges thinly crosswise. Remove any pips and arrange slices, overlapping, decoratively on a serving dish.

Place the sugar and orange juice in a saucepan over low heat. Simmer and bubble the sugar until its color changes to caramel — this will take about 5 minutes. Pour the caramel evenly over the sliced oranges and serve.

Crêpes Suzette

Delicious crêpes flamed in brandy and Cointreau make a suitably fiery and showy dish, to capture the imagination of this flamboyant and commanding sign of the zodiac. *Serves 4*

> 1 1/4 cups (1/2 Imperial pint) milk
> Pinch of salt
> 3 Tb (1 1/2 oz; 45 g) superfine or castor sugar
> 1 cup (5 oz; 140 g) flour
> 2 medium eggs
> 2 Tb melted butter
> 6 Tb Cointreau
> Grated rind of 1 orange
> 7 Tb brandy

Pour two-thirds of the milk into a mixing bowl. Add the salt, 2 tablespoons of the sugar, and the flour and eggs, and beat thoroughly. Beat in the remaining milk, melted butter, and 3 tablespoons of Cointreau. (Make the batter either the night before or a few hours before you wish to use it.) Place a 7-inch omelet pan or small nonstick frying pan over high heat. When hot, lightly grease it with butter, then add 2 tablespoons of batter. Turn the pan so that the bottom has an even coating of batter. Cook about a minute, or until golden, then flip the crêpe, and cook 30 seconds more, or until the underside is golden. Fold in half and half again. Place on a metal dish. Continue to cook the crêpes in this way until all the batter is used up. Sprinkle with the remaining sugar and the orange rind. Place over moderate heat. Drizzle the brandy and remaining Cointreau over and when the liquor begins to bubble, flame it. Remove from the heat, spoon the pan juices over the crêpes, and serve immediately.

Choux Pastry Ring with Chocolate Sauce

This beautifully elegant ring of choux pastry is filled with whipped cream and coated with chocolate and slivered almonds. Its soft round form echoes the shape of the Sun, the chocolate coating makes it a food worthy of kings, and it is an excellent dish for this Sun-ruled sign of the zodiac.
Serves 6

1/2 cup (4 oz) water
Pinch of salt
4 Tb (2 oz; 60 g) butter
3/4 cup plus 2 Tb (4 oz; 123 g) flour
2 medium eggs
Few drops of vanilla
1 1/4 cups (1/2 Imperial pint) heavy or double cream
2 Tb superfine or castor sugar

Sauce
1 Tb butter
2 Tb cocoa
2 Tb milk
1 medium egg yolk
Few drops of vanilla
1/2 cup (2 oz; 60 g) confectioners or icing sugar

1/4 cup (1 oz; 30 g) toasted slivered almonds

Preheat the oven to 375°F (190°C; gas 5).

Place the water and salt in a saucepan over moderate heat. Add the butter, and when the butter has melted, mix all the flour in together. Stir continuously until the dough forms a ball. Remove from the heat and turn into a bowl or food processor. Thoroughly beat or mix in the eggs and the vanilla. Leave to cool slightly. Shape the dough into a ring 6 1/2 inches in diameter, 1 1/4 inches thick, and place on a buttered baking sheet. Bake for 40–45 minutes. Remove from the oven and leave to cool. Then, using a sharp knife, slice off the top of the pastry ring.

While the ring is cooling, turn the cream into a mixing bowl and beat it with the superfine sugar until just stiff. Spoon the cream into the two pastry halves. Put the two halves together and leave to chill while you prepare the sauce.

Place the butter in a saucepan over moderate heat, whisk in the cocoa and milk until thoroughly mixed. Remove from the heat, and cool for 1 minute. Then mix in the egg yolk and vanilla. Beat in the confectioners sugar until the sauce is smooth. Spread the sauce over the ring, sprinkle evenly with the almonds, and serve.

Raspberry-Meringue Pyramid

A spectacular and delectable dish of fresh raspberries, meringues, and cream built into a pyramid. Raspberries are a fruit that ripens with the Sun's joyous entry into the constellation of Leo, the sign of the zodiac that rules a time of year synonymous with the enjoyment of the fruits of the harvest. Apollo, god of solar light, ripens and protects the fruits of the earth. You can prepare the ingredients for this dish in advance, but it's best to assemble the pyramid just before you wish to eat it, or it goes soft. *Serves 4*

Meringues

  2 medium egg whites, at room temperature
  1/2 cup (4 oz; 115 g) superfine or castor sugar
  Few drops of vanilla

  1 1/4 cups (1/2 Imperial pint) heavy or double cream
  2 Tb superfine or castor sugar
  Few drops of vanilla
  1 medium egg white
  1 1/4–1 1/2 pints (3/4–1 lb) fresh raspberries, hulled
  3 Tb (1/2 oz; 15 g) toasted slivered almonds

Preheat the oven to 250°F (120°C; gas 1/2).

In a mixing bowl beat the egg whites stiff, then gradually beat in the sugar and vanilla. Place 12 small spoonfuls of meringue on wax or greaseproof paper. Place in the oven and bake for 1 1/2–2 hours. Remove the meringues from the oven and set aside while you prepare the filling. In a mixing bowl, beat the cream until it is stiff. Mix in the sugar and vanilla. Then beat the egg white until it is stiff. Fold it into the cream mixture until all are well mixed. Place

4 meringues on a serving dish. Cover with some of the cream mixture and raspberries, then 3 more meringues. Continue to build the meringues into a pyramid (the next two layers will have 2 meringues), fixing each layer with cream and raspberries. End with 1 meringue and cream and raspberries for the top of the pyramid. Sprinkle the slivered almonds over and serve.

Crème Brûlée

Although the Greeks saw Apollo as a solar god, the Sun was personified by a separate divinity called Helios, who rose from an eastern swamp each morning and traveled through the sky in a golden chariot drawn by winged horses. He would then rest in the west before he traveled back through the night to re-emerge in the east ready for the next morning. Crème Brûlée shines round like Helios; it is reminiscent of the golden midday Sun as it reaches the highest point in its journey west and reigns sovereign over other desserts. Make the custard in advance if you wish, but caramelize it shortly before you eat it, or it will go soft. *Serves 6*

> 8 medium egg yolks
> 1/2 cup (3 oz; 85 g) light brown sugar
> 2 tsp cornstarch
> 2 cups (16 oz) heavy or double cream
> 1/2 cup (3 oz; 85 g) demerara or turbinado sugar

In the top of a double boiler, whisk the egg yolks with the light brown sugar and cornstarch. Place over barely simmering water, stir in the cream gradually, and continue to stir until the mixture thickens to a custard. Cook 1 minute longer to cook the cornstarch. Turn into a 3-cup (1¼–Imperial pint), 2-inch-deep ovenproof dish and chill until very cold.

Preheat the broiler.

Sprinkle the top of the custard with an even layer of demerara sugar so the whole surface is completely covered. (The amount of sugar you need to use will depend on the size of the dish.) Place the top of the custard 1 inch from the broiler, and cook for 1–3 minutes, or until the sugar has melted. If necessary, turn the dish so that the sugar melts evenly. Chill for 15 minutes so that the top can harden, and serve.

VIRGO

AUGUST 24–SEPTEMBER 23

Rules the sixth house, the house of service and health

RULING PLANET
Mercury
♍

ELEMENT
Earth
♍

QUALITIES
Mutable, passive
♍

CHARACTERISTICS
Analytical, discriminating, industrious,
intellectual, meticulous
♍

OPPOSITE SIGN
Pisces
♍

BODY AREA
Abdomen, intestines
♍

GEMSTONE
Jade, jasper, peridot
♍

COLOR
Yellow-green
♍

FLAVOR
Sharp, clean
♍

METAL
Platinum
♍

FAUNA
Beef, birds, fish
♍

FLORA
Carrots, cereals, citrus fruits, cucumber,
fennel, mulberries, mushrooms, parsnips
♍

HERBS
Aniseed, caraway, dill, lavender, parsley
♍

CELL SALT
Potassium sulphate (Kali. Sulph.), found
in bread, raw and dried fruit, carrots, chicory,
cucumber, endive, nuts, oatmeal, globe artichokes, semolina
♍

VIRGO THE COOK

Virgos love an opportunity to plan and cook for a dinner party, and will be quite undeterred by the work involved since they shine with perpetual action and love to be constantly busy burning up their abundance of nervous energy.

So if a Virgo invites you to dinner, it should be an evening to look forward to. Virgos are sticklers for punctuality and it's wise to arrive on time—but not too hungry; they don't apply the punctuality rule to themselves and may well keep you waiting while they spend hours putting the finishing touches on their meal. They set very high standards and they will want their food and their homes to be perfect—and they won't relax until they have realized this aim. The wait will be worth it, though: flowers will garnish a meticulously clean house, the table will be set with precision and charm, and because Virgos combine a natural gift for cooking with a cool reasoning nature, the dinner will always turn out well. Moreover, this receptive and understanding sign of the zodiac will cater to your every need and, cherishing comfort themselves, will make sure you are comfortable.

Virgo is symbolized by the Earth goddess Demeter, who represents the fertile soil. It is a reflective and passive sign of the zodiac, mellow like the harvest, and as a cook your Virgo friend will be practical in a down-to-earth way, able to prepare most foods at his or her disposal, often in very inventive ways. This sign of the zodiac is not particularly extravagant, because their essence of Earth makes them materialistic. Also Virgos don't feel the need to impress with expense—

they would rather demonstrate their expertise as cooks and keep their money safely in the bank.

The Virgoan kitchen is likely to be very well organized. Pots and pans will probably sparkle with cleanliness, reflecting the purity that is embedded within this sign, which is signified by their symbol of the Virgin. It also suggests a solitariness, and this sign of the zodiac is quite self-contained. As cooks, Virgos like to work alone quietly and speedily in an orderly kitchen (they often clean up as they go along). But don't be afraid to interrupt their quiet, because Virgos are sociable and do like company. The contradiction of an earthy practicality combined with an airy intellectual nature (Mercury is the planet of communication and exchange of ideas) gives this mutable sign its duality.

True to Virgo's symbol of purity, it is healthy dishes, not junk foods, that will be favorites in their households, and you may be fed a wholesome and earthy Steak and Kidney Pie or macaroni and cheese, or a fresh and clean fruit salad, full of the goodness of the sun-warmed earth. Seasonal vegetables will have been carefully chosen and then steamed lightly, to retain their full flavor and crisp texture. And although the food and drink will not be obviously extravagant, they will certainly be of good quality.

An evening with a Virgo will run smoothly and should leave you feeling that you have dined well.

RECIPES FOR VIRGO

MENU SUGGESTIONS FOR VIRGO

First Courses

Semolina Gnocchi
Quail Eggs in Pastry
Artichoke Bottoms with Parma Ham
Corn Soup
Bute Street Salad
Mushroom Pâté
Crab Salad

Main Courses

Salade Niçoise
Lemon Sole with Cucumber and Dill
Stir-Fried Vegetables with Monkfish
Parsnip Soufflé
Ham Véronique
Roast Grouse
Steak and Kidney Pie

Side Dishes

Coleslaw with Caraway
Cucumber Salad with Yogurt and Mint

Desserts

Pistachio Ice Cream
Floating Islands
Carrot Torte
Mixed Melon and Mango with
    Apricot Sauce
Rice Caramel
Lady Scott's Lemon Pudding

Semolina Gnocchi
Roast Grouse
Mixed Melon and Mango with Apricot Sauce
♍

Quail Eggs in Pastry
Stir-Fried Vegetables with Monkfish
Carrot Torte
♍

Artichoke Bottoms with Parma Ham
Steak and Kidney Pie
Rice Caramel
♍

Corn Soup
Salade Niçoise
Lady Scott's Lemon Pudding
♍

Mushroom Pâté
Lemon Sole with Cucumber and Dill
Pistachio Ice Cream
♍

Bute Street Salad
Ham Véronique
Floating Islands
♍

Crab Salad
Parsnip Soufflé
Mixed Melon and Mango with Apricot Sauce

VIRGO THE GUEST

Persuade your Virgo friend to stop whatever he or she is doing—this sign of the zodiac is bound to be doing something—and invite him to dinner. He will probably accept eagerly because he will love an opportunity to be social, and won't want to miss out.

It's a good idea not to let Virgos into your kitchen; this sign of the zodiac is very particular about what they eat and you are bound to be putting something into the pot that won't agree with them. They are often very fussy about food and can excel in finding fault or telling you how to do something better.

But kept in the sitting room with the other guests, Virgos make charming company. Versatile and changeable, this is a mutable sign, representing the water and motion of earth, so Virgos will get along with all kinds of people. Moreover, since they are ruled by Mercury, the god of eloquence and communication, they are good at making conversation and getting people to mix. If you have invited more than one Virgo to dinner, you are in for a lively evening. Seat them as far away from each other as possible, or they will talk to each other almost without catching a breath all night. For a bit of peace and quiet, try feeding them foods that have a certain individuality, such as Roast Grouse or Parsnip Soufflé, which combines their dual currents of lightness and earthiness. And feed them some clean healthy foods such as salads and stir-fried vegetables, since Virgo rules the sixth house of the zodiac, which is concerned with health.

Although Virgos have a cautious nature, they are open to new ideas and are extremely fond of good food (Virgo rules the intestines). It would be safer to stick to delicately spiced foods than to get carried away with a wildly colorful curry. So if you want the evening to flow, try feeding your Virgoan friend a well-presented and unusual fish dish (which reflects the nature of their ruling planet, Mercury). And make sure your food looks good; Virgos will always appreciate your painstaking labors in the kitchen and will take note of that last garnish that transformed the pie into a masterpiece.

Virgos tend to burn up a lot of nervous energy (Mercury rules the nervous system), so they are likely to arrive hungry. Foods rich in protein, or containing their cell salt, potassium sulphate, will be enjoyed.

Fed well in good company, Virgos will probably endear themselves to you by staying behind and helping you clean up because they have had such a good time.

Semolina Gnocchi

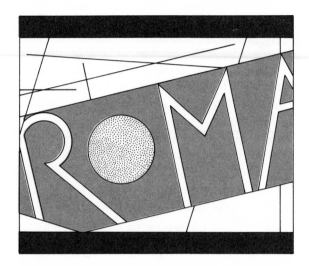

Semolina is milled from wheat, a cereal that belongs to the Earth Mother and Roman goddess Ceres, who represents Virgo, the sign of the zodiac that is concerned with the work necessary to produce the fruits of the earth. Semolina Gnocchi is a classic Italian starter that should be served Roman-style with a very chilled bottle of Italian wine. *Serves 4*

2¹/2 cups (1 Imperial pint) milk
³/4 cup (4 oz; 115 g) fine-grain semolina
¹/2 cup (2 oz; 60 g) grated Cheddar cheese
¹/2 tsp dry mustard
3 Tb (1¹/2 oz; 45 g) butter
Salt and black pepper
¹/4 cup (1 oz; 30 g) grated Parmesan

Place the milk in the top of a double boiler over simmering water. When it is very hot, gradually mix in the semolina, stirring constantly to prevent any lumps from forming, until the mixture thickens. Remove from the heat and thoroughly mix in the Cheddar cheese, mustard, and 1¹/2 tablespoons butter. Stir until the cheese and butter have melted. Season to taste with salt and black pepper, turn onto a flat or shallow buttered dish, spread the mixture so it is ¹/4 inch deep, and leave until cold. Preheat the broiler. Now cut out rounds about 1¹/2 inches in diameter. Arrange them overlapping in a buttered oven-proof dish. Dot generously with the remaining butter, sprinkle the Parmesan over, and dust lightly with black pepper. Place under the broiler, 2 inches from the broiler element, and cook for 5–6 minutes, or until the top is golden brown and bubbling. Serve immediately.

Quail Eggs in Pastry

Individual tarts of quail eggs resting over anchovy-flavored mayonnaise make a charming start to a meal. Virgos are often good pastry cooks because their ruling planet, Mercury, endows a light touch and skilled hands (Mercury rules the hands and arms in the sign of Gemini). *Serves 4*

Shortcrust pastry

    1 cup (5 oz; 140 g) flour

    1/4 tsp salt

    5 Tb (2 1/2 oz; 75 g) butter

    2–3 Tb cold water

    One 2 oz (55-g) can anchovy fillets, drained and chopped

    1/4 cup (2 oz) milk

    1/2 cup (4 oz) mayonnaise (see page 59)

    1/2 cup finely shredded lettuce, washed and dried

    2 Tb chopped fresh parsley

    Black pepper

    12 quail eggs, hard-boiled and peeled

Preheat the oven to 425°F (220°C; gas 7).

First make the pastry. Place the flour and salt in a large bowl and cut in the butter, mixing lightly. Then, with your fingertips, work the flour and butter together until the mixture has the consistency of bread crumbs. Pour the water in, mixing with a fork, until it is all absorbed. Or alternatively, you can make this pastry in a food processor. First spin the flour, salt, and butter together until the mixture resembles large bread crumbs, then with the machine going, add the water through the funnel, mixing until a dough forms. Remove and shape into one round piece. Wrap it in plastic wrap and leave to chill for 20–30 minutes. Divide the pastry into four equal pieces and roll them out on a floured board, then ease them into four 3–3 1/2-inch tart pans. Prick the bottoms and bake for 15–20 minutes, or until the pastry is golden.

While the pastry is baking, place the anchovy fillets in a small bowl, cover them with the milk, and leave them to soak while you prepare your own mayonnaise. Place 1/2 cup of the mayonnaise in a mixing bowl. Drain the anchovies and mix them thoroughly with the mayonnaise, lettuce, and parsley. Season to taste with black pepper. Remove the tart shells from the oven and let them cool. Then spread 2 tablespoons of the mayonnaise mixture over the bottom of each tart. Place 3 quail eggs on top of each so they are evenly arranged, and serve.

Artichoke Bottoms with Parma Ham

A simple but delicious combination of tastes that makes a perfect dish for a hot summer evening. Serve it with a chilled Italian wine such as a Frascati and thin slices of whole wheat bread and butter. *Serves 5*

> 5 artichokes
>
> ½ lemon
>
> 1 clove garlic
>
> 10 thin slices (about 10 oz; 285 g)
>   Parma ham
>
> 2½–3 Tb mayonnaise (see page 59)
>
> Black pepper to taste

Garnishes

> 5 wedges of lemon
>
> Mayonnaise (see page 59)
>
> 5 thin slices of whole wheat bread,
>   buttered and halved

If you are using fresh artichokes, cut two-thirds of the leaves off the top of the artichokes and the stem and discard. Remove the remaining leaves until you reach the lighter inner leaves. Pull off the inside leaves and spoon out the hairy choke. Trim the bottom of the artichokes so they stand upright and rub them all over with a little lemon juice to prevent them from discoloring. Then place the artichoke bottoms in the top of a steamer over boiling water, with a clove of garlic in the water. Cover and steam for 15–20 minutes, or until they are tender when pierced with a knife. Drain upside down.

Remove the rind and any surrounding fat from the Parma ham. Lay the slices of ham in equal portions on five plates. Fill the center of each artichoke bottom with about ½ tablespoon of mayonnaise and set one on the center of each plate. Season with black pepper and serve with wedges of lemon, a small bowl of mayonnaise, and a plate of buttered whole wheat bread.

Corn Soup

Virgo is represented by the goddess of the golden harvest, Isis in Egyptian mythology, Demeter in Greek, and Ceres in Roman, who is often depicted wearing a crown of wheat and holding sheaves of wheat in her hand. This sweet-tasting golden corn soup makes a beautifully simple way to start a meal and should be served with lots of fresh crusty bread. *Serves 4*

2 thick slices (2 oz; 60 g) streaky bacon, rind
   removed, cut into small pieces
2 Tb butter
2 small onions, peeled and finely chopped
1 Tb flour
1¼ cups (½ Imperial pint) chicken or
   vegetable stock
1¼ cups (½ Imperial pint) milk
2½ cups (1 lb) fresh or frozen corn kernels
1 Tb light brown sugar
¼ cup (2 oz) light or single cream
Salt and black pepper

Place a large saucepan over moderate heat. Mix in the bacon and sauté, stirring frequently, for about 8 minutes, or until the bacon is cooked but not crisp. Drain and set aside. Pour most of the fat from the pan. Reduce the heat to moderately low, mix in the butter, and when it has melted add the onions. Sauté for 15 minutes, stirring occasionally, or until the onions are soft. Stir in the flour and cook, stirring continuously, for 2 minutes. Gradually pour in the stock and milk, stirring until the mixture is smooth. Add the corn, bacon, and sugar. Cover and simmer for 15 minutes, stirring occasionally. Mix in the cream and season to taste with salt and black pepper.

Transfer the soup to a food processor or blender, and purée for a few seconds, so that the soup retains a rough texture. Return to the saucepan. Heat through, turn into a warmed soup tureen, and serve hot.

Bute Street Salad

The flavor of this salad improves if it is made ahead, but it should not be served straight from the fridge. Combining sweet and savory tastes with a variety of textures, it makes a perfect dish for this dual sign of the zodiac—as a first course or a light lunch dish, if accompanied by bread and a selection of cheeses and a chilled German wine. *Serves 6*

> 1 lb new potatoes
> 5 scallions or spring onions
> 4 pickled herring fillets (7 oz; 200 g)
> 2 Granny Smith apples
> 6 Tb sour cream
> 1 Tb lemon juice
> Salt and black pepper to taste

Garnishes

> 6 lettuce leaves, washed and dried
> 2 tsp chopped fresh chives
> 6 thin slices of whole wheat bread,
>   buttered and halved

Scrub the potatoes clean, place them in a pan, and cover with salted water. Cover, and boil for 15–20 minutes, or until the potatoes are tender. Drain and leave to cool. Chop the scallions thinly. Cut the herring into bite-size pieces and the potatoes into about 3/4-inch cubes. Peel, core, and cube the apples. In a mixing bowl, beat together the sour cream and lemon juice, then fold in the potatoes, herring, apples, and scallions, and season. Place the lettuce leaves on the centers of 6 plates or 1 large plate. Divide the salad evenly among the plates. Scatter the chives over and serve with slices of buttered bread.

Mushroom Pâté

Most wild mushrooms grow in the quiet solitary late summer fields of Virgo. Precious jewels dotted with glistening dew, they suggest the purity and privacy embodied in this sign. *Serves 4 to 6*

> 8 Tb (4 oz; 115 g) butter
> 1 clove garlic, peeled and pushed through a press
> 1 small onion, peeled and finely chopped
> 1/2 lb (225 g) fresh cèpes (Boletes) or
>   cultivated mushrooms
> 1/4 tsp dried marjoram, or 1/2 tsp chopped fresh
> Salt and black pepper
> 3/4 cup (1 oz; 30 g) soft whole wheat bread crumbs
> 2 tsp lemon juice
> 1/2 cup (4 oz) tofu (bean curd)
> 1 Tb chopped fresh parsley

Garnishes

> 6–8 thin slices of bread, toasted
> Butter

Heat the butter in a frying pan over moderately low heat. Mix in the garlic, onion, mushrooms, and marjoram; cover, and sauté for 15 minutes, or until soft, stirring occasionally. Season to taste with salt and black pepper. Turn into a food processor or blender, and purée with the bread crumbs, lemon juice, tofu, and parsley until the mixture is well blended but still has a slightly rough texture. Check the seasoning. Turn into 2 small serving dishes, and chill for 1–2 hours, or until cold. Serve with slices of hot toast and butter.

Crab Salad

The beauty of this dish lies in its presentation, and Virgos, with their wonderful eye for intricate detail and precision, will find pleasure in composing the salad. The simplicity of the treatment of the ingredients also allows the taste and texture of the crabmeat to be sensitively enhanced, rather than dominated. *Serves 6*

One 2½–3-lb cooked crab, with the poison sacs
   and gills removed, or ¾ lb (340 g)
   fresh crabmeat
3 medium eggs, hard-boiled, peeled,
   and finely chopped
8 scallions or spring onions
½ small head of lettuce, washed and dried
1 large avocado
1 tsp lemon juice

Vinaigrette
6 Tb (3 oz) olive oil
3 Tb (1½ oz) lemon juice
1 tsp Dijon mustard
1 tsp superfine or castor sugar
¾ tsp Tabasco
Salt and black pepper

Garnish
6 thin slices of buttered whole wheat bread,
   crusts removed

Break the legs off the crab and crack them with nutcrackers or a hammer. Remove the flesh from the shells and chop it finely. Arrange it in a flat round in the center of a large serving plate. Surround the crabmeat with crescents of chopped egg. Chop the scallions finely, and scatter them over the crab and egg. Arrange the lettuce in leaves (or partly shredded leaves if they are large) around the crab. Peel the avocado, slice it in half lengthwise, and pit it. Place it flat-side down on a wooden board and slice it thinly lengthwise. Arrange it over the lettuce and sprinkle with lemon juice. Then, in a small bowl or jar, thoroughly mix together the vinaigrette ingredients and season to taste with salt and black pepper. Sprinkle the dressing over the whole salad and serve with slices of buttered whole wheat bread.

MAIN COURSES

Salade Niçoise

Salade Niçoise is a colorful French salad, full of the good things of summer, that should be served with a crusty loaf and a young French red wine. Prepare and dress it just before you wish to eat or it will get soft. *Serves 4*

> *½ lb (225 g) green beans*
>
> *1 clove garlic*
>
> *One 2-oz (55-g) can anchovy fillets, drained*
>
> *¼ cup (2 oz) milk*
>
> *1 medium-size head of crisp lettuce*
>
> *One 6½-oz (185-g) can tuna fish, drained and flaked*
>
> *6 medium eggs, hard-boiled and peeled*
>
> *One 4½-oz (120-g) can sardines, drained*
>
> *½ cup (2 oz; 60 g) washed, dried, and trimmed radishes*
>
> *2 medium tomatoes (about ½ lb)*
>
> *16–20 black olives*
>
> *6 scallions or spring onions*
>
> *2 Tb chopped fresh parsley*

Vinaigrette

> *5 Tb (2½ oz) olive oil*
>
> *2 Tb red wine vinegar*
>
> *1 tsp Dijon mustard*
>
> *1 tsp superfine or castor sugar*
>
> *1 small clove garlic, peeled and pushed through a press*
>
> *Salt and black pepper*

Top and tail the beans and wash them in cold water. Place them in the top of a steamer over boiling water, with a clove of garlic in the water. Cover and steam for 10 minutes, or until the beans are tender. When the beans are cooked, refresh them in cold water, then pat them dry with a paper towel and set aside. While the beans are cooking, put the anchovies in a small bowl and pour the milk over. Leave them to soak while you prepare the rest of the vegetables.

Remove any rough outer leaves from the lettuce. Break up the remaining leaves, and wash and dry them. Shred the lettuce, and put it at the bottom of a salad bowl. Arrange the tuna fish over the lettuce, then cut the eggs in half lengthwise and arrange them sunnyside up around the edge of the dish, interspersed with the sardines. Thinly slice the radishes and sprinkle them over the tuna fish. Quarter the tomatoes and scatter them over, along with the beans and olives. Drain the anchovies, pat them dry, arrange them in crosses over the top of the dish, and sprinkle the scallions and parsley over. In a small bowl or jar mix together thoroughly all the vinaigrette ingredients and season to taste with salt and black pepper. Pour the vinaigrette over the salad, toss, and serve.

Lemon Sole with Cucumber and Dill

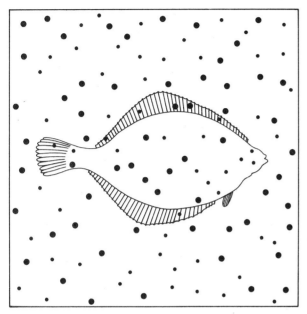

Rinse the fish in cold water and pat it dry with a paper towel. Mix ¼ teaspoon of salt and ⅛ teaspoon of black pepper with the flour. Roll the fish in the flour so that it is evenly coated and shake off any excess. Heat 3 tablespoons of butter in a frying pan over moderately high heat. Add the fish, and sauté for 3–4 minutes on each side. Then remove the fish to a hot serving plate and keep it warm while you prepare the cucumber.

Add the remaining butter to the pan. When it is hot, mix in the cucumber, lemon juice, and dill. Simmer, stirring and turning, for 5 minutes. Season to taste with salt and black pepper. Spoon over the fish and serve.

The swiftness of fish and the changeable color typical of their scales relates to the nature of the god Mercury, Virgo's ruling planet. Lemon sole is served with a cucumber sauce that combines the fresh tang of lemon with the aroma of dill, also an herb of Mercury. Serve this delicious dish with rice, a green vegetable, or Coleslaw with Caraway (see page 141) and a very cold dry white wine. *Serves 2*

> *12 oz lemon sole or flounder, filleted and skinned*
> *Salt and black pepper*
> *2–3 Tb flour*
> *4 Tb butter*
> *1 cup (5 oz; 140 g) peeled, seeded, and cubed cucumber*
> *2 Tb fresh lemon juice*
> *1 Tb chopped fresh dill weed, or 1½ tsp dried*

Stir-Fried Vegetables with Monkfish

This Oriental stir-fry is extremely healthy as well as quite delicious, and should appeal to the health-conscious Virgo, who also likes good food (Virgo rules the sixth house of the zodiac, the house concerned with health). Serve it Chinese-style with noodles and either beer or a very cold dry white wine. *Serves 4*

> 1 lb small to medium-small zucchini or courgette, washed and dried
>
> Salt
>
> 1/2 lb green beans, washed and dried
>
> 2 lb monkfish, skinned and boned
>
> 3 Tb (1 1/2 oz) ground nut or sunflower oil
>
> 3 cloves garlic, peeled and pushed through a press
>
> 1-inch piece of gingerroot, peeled and finely chopped
>
> 3 Tb (1 1/2 oz) dark soy sauce
>
> 1/4 cup (1 oz; 30 g) toasted slivered almonds
>
> Black pepper

Cut the zucchini in half lengthwise, and then into 3-by-1/4-inch diagonal slices. Place them on a large dish, sprinkle with salt, and leave them to sweat for 15 minutes. Cut the beans into 3-by-1/4-inch diagonal slices. Wash the fish, pat it dry, and cut it into 1-inch slices lengthwise. Now pat the zucchini dry. Heat 2 tablespoons of the oil in a wok or large nonstick frying pan over high heat. Add the garlic, ginger, zucchini, beans, and 2 tablespoons of the soy sauce. Stir-fry for 3–4 minutes, or until the vegetables are tender but still crisp. Transfer the vegetables to a warmed serving dish and keep them warm while you prepare the fish.

Lower the heat to moderate and add the remaining oil and soy sauce to the pan. Add the fish and cook it, turning frequently, for 6–8 minutes, or until the center is cooked. Arrange the fish in the vegetable dish among the vegetables. Scatter the almonds over. Season to taste with salt and black pepper, and serve.

Parsnip Soufflé

Here earthy parsnips are transformed into a light and airy soufflé, suggesting the conflict and duality within this most airy intellectual of earth signs. Serve Parsnip Soufflé with a green salad, boiled new potatoes, and a cool white wine. *Serves 4*

1 lb parsnips
2 Tb butter
2 Tb flour
1 cup (8 oz) milk
1 tsp light brown sugar
1/4 tsp curry powder
Pinch of nutmeg
5 medium eggs, separated
Salt and black pepper

Preheat the oven to 375°F (190°C; gas 5).

Butter a 1½-quart soufflé dish. Cut off the tops and roots of the parsnips, peel, and cut them into 1-inch pieces. Place the parsnips in a pan with about 2 inches of boiling water, cover, and simmer for 10 minutes, or until they are tender. While the parsnips are cooking, place the butter in a saucepan and melt it over low heat. Mix in the flour and, stirring continuously, cook for 2 minutes. Whisk in the milk until you have a smooth sauce. Bring to a boil, and simmer for a few minutes, stirring occasionally. Remove from the heat. When the parsnips have cooked, drain them, and put in a food processor or blender with the white sauce, sugar, curry powder, nutmeg, and egg yolks. Purée and season to taste with salt and black pepper. In a bowl beat the egg whites stiff. Pour the parsnip mixture down the side of the bowl in which the egg whites were beaten and gently fold into the egg whites until they are thoroughly mixed. Turn into the buttered soufflé dish, and bake for 35 minutes, or until the soufflé has risen and cooked through. Serve immediately.

Ham Véronique

Véronique is a French term for a dish served in a sauce made from cream, white wine, and usually seedless grapes. Often used for fish, it is particularly good with ham because the saltiness of the ham perfectly complements the sweetness of the grapes. Ham Véronique also makes an imaginative way of using up any leftover ham. Serve it with mashed potatoes or rice to soak up the sauce, green beans, and a chilled white California wine. *Serves 4*

> 8 medium-thin slices (1–1¼ lb) cooked ham
> 1 cup (6 oz; 180 g) white seedless grapes
> 3 Tb (1½ oz; 45 g) butter
> 3 Tb (¾ oz; 26 g) flour
> 1 cup (8 oz) chicken stock
> ¼ cup (2 oz) heavy or double cream
> 1 tsp Dijon mustard
> Salt and black pepper
> 3–4 Tb sherry or dry white wine

Preheat the oven to 350°F (180°C; gas 4).

Remove any fat from the ham, and halve the grapes.

Melt the butter in a saucepan over moderately low heat. Mix in the flour and, stirring continuously, cook for 2 minutes. Stir in the chicken stock until you have a smooth sauce. Bring to a boil and simmer for a few minutes, then stir in the cream, mustard, and grapes. Season to taste with salt (very lightly because of the ham's saltiness) and black pepper, remove from the heat, and stir in the sherry or wine. Fold the ham slices in half and arrange them in tiers in an ovenproof dish just large enough to hold them. Pour the sauce over so the ham is evenly covered and bake in the oven for 10 minutes, or until the ham is hot through. Serve hot.

Roast Grouse

The wings of the grouse relate to the wings and flight of Mercury (Virgo's ruling planet) and its distinct taste to the particularity of this sign of the zodiac. Grouse is available from the "glorious twelfth of August" until December and should be served rare, with the meat and juices pale pink, unlike light-meat game birds, which need to be served well done. Serve the grouse on fried bread with a green vegetable and freshly fried potato chips or roast potatoes, a gravy made from the pan juices, and a good claret. *Serves 2*

Two 1-lb grouse, cleaned
Salt
5 Tb (2½ oz; 75 g) butter
Black pepper

Stuffing

2 small onions, peeled
2 Tb cranberries, washed and dried,
    or ½ Granny Smith apple, peeled,
    cored, and cut in quarters

4 slices (3 oz; 85 g) streaky bacon, rind removed
2 slices of bread, crusts removed

Garnishes

Watercress
Cranberry sauce

Preheat the oven to 425°F (220°C; gas 7).

Dry the insides of the birds and rub them inside and out with a little salt, then rub the birds all over with 1 tablespoon of butter each, and dust lightly with black pepper. Stuff each bird with an onion and an equal amount of cranberries or apple. Fasten the body cavities with a skewer to hold the stuffing in, and truss to keep the birds intact. Place the birds breast-side up in a roasting pan just large enough to hold them, and cover their breasts with the bacon. (If necessary, cut it to fit the lengths of the birds.) Roast, basting every 10 minutes, for 30 minutes, or until the birds are cooked. They are ready when the juices run pale pink; don't cook longer or they will be overdone.

While the birds are roasting, melt the remaining butter over fairly hot heat and fry the bread for 1–2 minutes on each side, or until lightly browned and crisp. Place a piece of bread on 2 warmed plates, place 1 grouse on each piece of bread (with the bacon, which complements the grouse well), garnish with watercress, and serve with cranberry sauce.

Steak and Kidney Pie

A delicious combination of beef, kidney, and mushrooms lies covered by a layer of pastry, making a substantial family dish for the earthy Virgo. The Egyptian goddess Isis, who represents Virgo, wore as her headdress a disk that lay between the horns of a cow. Steak and kidney pie is a typically English dish that should be served with mashed potatoes, a green vegetable such as brussels sprouts, and a cold beer. *Serves 4*

1 lb beef chuck steak, cut into 1-inch pieces
1/2 lb (225 g) beef kidneys
5 Tb (1 1/2 oz; 45 g) flour
Salt and black pepper
4 Tb (2 oz) sunflower or vegetable oil
3 Tb (1 1/2 oz) butter
2 medium onions, peeled and thinly sliced
1/4 lb (115 g) button mushrooms, wiped clean and cut in half
1 cup (8 oz) beef stock
1 tsp Worcestershire sauce
2 Tb dry red wine or sherry
Shortcrust pastry to line a 10-inch pie pan (see page 12)
1 Tb milk

Preheat the oven to 300°F (150°C; gas 2).

Trim any fat from the beef. Remove the central core of fat from the kidneys and cut them into 1-inch pieces. Mix 3 tablespoons of the flour with 1/2 teaspoon of salt and 1/4 teaspoon of black pepper. Roll the beef and kidney in it and shake off any excess. Heat the oil in a large frying pan over high heat and quickly brown the meat on all sides, to seal in the juices. Do this in two or three batches so you don't crowd the pan. Transfer the meat to a 5-cup (2-Imperial pint) deep pie plate and set aside. Reduce the heat to moderately low and add the butter to the frying pan. When the butter begins to bubble, mix in the onions and sauté, turning occasionally, for 10 minutes. Add the mushrooms, and cook 5 minutes longer. Sprinkle in the remaining flour and, stirring continuously, cook for 2 minutes. Add the onions and mushrooms to the pie plate. Pour the stock, Worcestershire, and wine or sherry over. Stir well, season to taste with salt and black pepper, and cover with foil. Cook in a low oven for 1 1/2 hours, or until the meat is tender. When the meat has been cooking for nearly an hour, prepare the pastry as described on page 12. Wrap it in plastic wrap and chill for 20–30 minutes. Then roll out on a floured board to cover the pie plate, with 3/4 inch to spare around the edge. When the meat is ready, remove it from the oven.

Turn the oven to 375°F (190°C; gas 5).

Place a shallow cup upside down in the center of the pie plate to support the pastry and draw in the meat juices. Lay the crust over the top of the pie so there is an equal amount of pastry extending over the edges of the pie dish. Crimp the edges of the pastry and cut two 2-inch slits in it so that steam can escape. Brush the top of the pie with the milk. Bake for 30 minutes, or until the pastry is golden brown. Remove from the oven and let it sit for 5–10 minutes before serving.

Coleslaw with Caraway

Full of the goodness of raw vegetables, caraway seeds (an appetite stimulant), and parsley (an herb of Mercury that is particularly good for this sign's frequent nervous conditions), Coleslaw with Caraway is an easy dish to prepare. It goes particularly well with cold meats and fish. *Serves 4*

> 1/2 lb (225 g) carrots
> 3/4 lb (340 g) white cabbage, rough outer
>   leaves and core removed
> 4 scallions or spring onions
> 2 Tb golden raisins or sultanas
> 2 Tb chopped fresh Italian parsley
> 2 tsp lemon juice
> 1/3 cup (2 2/3 oz) mayonnaise (see page 59)
> 1 tsp caraway seeds
> Salt and black pepper

Peel and grate the carrots and put them in a large bowl. Shred the cabbage and add it to the carrots. Thinly slice the scallions, and add them to the vegetables along with the golden raisins and parsley. Beat the lemon juice with the mayonnaise and caraway seeds, then mix thoroughly into the vegetables. Season to taste with salt and black pepper. Turn into a salad bowl or serving dish and serve.

Cucumber Salad with Yogurt and Mint

Cucumber Salad with Yogurt and Mint is a traditional Greek dish that can be served as a first course or a side dish. Cool cucumber, the palest of greens, is clothed in a sheet of virgin white, flecked with the rich green of mint, suggesting the purity and freshness that is an essential part of the sign of the zodiac that is symbolized by the Virgin. *Serves 4*

3 scallions or spring onions
1 large cucumber
1 clove garlic, peeled and pushed through a press
1 cup (8 oz) plain yogurt
3 Tb chopped fresh mint
1 tsp lemon juice
Salt and black pepper

Garnish
4 pita breads, warmed in the oven

Chop the scallions finely crosswise. Peel the cucumber and slice it thinly crosswise. In a mixing bowl mix thoroughly the garlic, yogurt, mint, and lemon juice. Mix in the cucumber and scallions and season to taste with salt and black pepper. Pour into a shallow dish and serve with the warm pita bread.

Pistachio Ice Cream

Pistachios are the yellow-green of Virgo and the color of new grass that is untouched and perfect. Pistachio Ice Cream—cool, creamy, and nutty—is not hard to make and is an ideal dish to have at hand in the freezer during the late summer month of Virgo. *Serves 6*

1/2 cup (4 oz; 115 g) superfine or castor sugar
3 medium egg yolks
1 1/2 cups (12 oz) milk
2/3 cup (3 oz; 85 g) finely chopped, toasted, salted pistachio nuts
1 1/4 cups (1/2 Imperial pint) heavy or double cream
A drop of almond extract

In the top of a double boiler, mix the sugar with the egg yolks. Place over barely simmering water and pour in the milk. Stir until the mixture has thickened, then remove from the heat and turn into a bowl. Mix in the pistachios and leave to cool for 10 minutes. Turn the heavy cream into a bowl and beat until stiff, then fold it into the custard mixture with the almond extract. Pour into an ice tray, and chill in the freezer for 2 1/2 hours, or until it is half-frozen. (If you have an ice cream maker, make the ice cream following the manufacturer's directions.) Remove the ice cream from the freezer and whisk it with a fork so that the crystallized edges are mixed into the center. Return to the freezer and leave at least 4 hours or overnight before serving. Remove the ice cream from the freezer and place in the refrigerator a few hours before you wish to serve it so it can soften.

Floating Islands

Floating Islands is a clever assembly of ingredients in which islands of snow-white meringue top a pale sea of custard. It is a reminder that Virgos can be an island unto themselves. *Serves 4*

3 medium eggs, separated
3 Tb superfine or castor sugar
Few drops of vanilla
1 Tb cornstarch
¼ cup (1¾ oz; 60 g) granulated sugar
2½ cups (1 Imperial pint) milk
2 Tb sweet sherry

Place a very wide saucepan half full of water over moderately low heat. Bring the water to a simmer. While it is heating, put the egg whites in a bowl and beat them, gradually adding the superfine sugar and vanilla, until they are stiff. Then scoop up 3 tablespoons of the meringue and scrape it off onto the simmering water. Add 1 or 2 more meringues, cover, and poach very gently for 1–2 minutes, or until the meringues are firm to the touch. Transfer the meringues to a large plate and cook the remaining meringues in the same way. (You should have about 8.) Set aside while you prepare the custard.

In the top of a double boiler, mix the cornstarch with the granulated sugar, then with the egg yolks. Place over barely simmering water and gradually stir in the milk. Stir continuously until the mixture thickens, then 1 minute longer so the cornstarch cooks. Remove from the heat, mix in the sherry, and turn into a shallow bowl with a large surface area. Drain any water from the meringues, and place them on top of the custard, chill, and serve cold.

Carrot Torte

Carrot Torte is a single-layered moist cake topped with Cointreau-flavored cream and toasted slivered almonds. It makes a light dessert, or a delectable snack for during the day, when Virgos need to replace some of their expended energy. Carrots, rich in vitamin A, also contain Virgo's cell salt, potassium sulphate, which helps to keep the skin conditioned. *Serves 6 to 8*

> 4 eggs, separated
> ³⁄₄ cup (4 oz; 120 g) light brown sugar
> 1 cup (4 oz; 120 g) ground almonds
> Grated rind of 1 orange
> 2¹⁄₂ cups (8 oz; 225 g) grated carrot
> 2 Tb Cointreau or Grand Marnier
> ¹⁄₂ cup (2¹⁄₂ oz; 70 g) flour
> 1 tsp baking powder
> Pinch of salt

Topping
> ⁵⁄₈ cup (5 oz) heavy or double cream
> 1 Tb superfine or castor sugar
> 1 Tb Cointreau or Grand Marnier
> ¹⁄₄ cup (1 oz; 30 g) toasted slivered almonds

Preheat the oven to 325°F (165°C; gas 3). Butter and dust with flour one 9-inch cake pan.

In a food processor or mixing bowl, mix or beat the egg yolks with the brown sugar, until thick and lighter in color. Then mix in the ground almonds, orange rind, grated carrot, and Cointreau. Mix the flour, baking powder, and salt together, and fold them into the carrot mixture. Then in a separate bowl beat the egg whites until stiff and fold them into the cake mixture.

Turn the mixture into the cake pan and bake for 35–40 minutes, or until a knife plunged into the center of the cake comes out clean. Leave it in the pan for 5 minutes, then turn it out onto a cake rack to cool. While it is cooling prepare the topping.

In a mixing bowl, beat the cream until it is stiff. Fold in the superfine sugar and Cointreau. Place the cake on a serving dish. Spread the cream evenly over the top of the cake, sprinkle the toasted almonds over, and serve.

Mixed Melon and Mango with Apricot Sauce

Exotic fruits of red, pale green, and amber are served with a delicate apricot sauce to make a refreshing way to end a meal—an appropriate dish for the sign of the Virgin, whose purity of spirit and capacity for reflection are sympathetic to the nature of the Moon, and these Moon-ruled fruits. *Serves 6 to 8*

¾ lb (340 g) fresh apricots
3 Tb light brown sugar
2 Tb apricot brandy
1 small (1¼ lb) honeydew melon, halved
1 mango or papaya
One 1¼-lb slice watermelon

Rinse the apricots in cold water and pat them dry with a paper towel. Then slice them in half and remove the pits. Place in a saucepan over low heat with the brown sugar and 1 tablespoon of apricot brandy. When they begin to simmer, cover, and cook for 10 minutes, or until the apricots are tender. Remove from the heat and turn into a food processor or blender and purée. Scoop out and discard the pips from the honeydew melon and scoop out the flesh in balls with a spoon or scoop. Place in a colander to drain off any excess liquid while you prepare the remaining fruits. Peel the mango or papaya, slice in half, and remove the pit (and seeds, if using papaya). Cut the flesh into 1-inch cubes. Add it to the colander while you slice the watermelon off its skin and cut into 1-inch cubes. Gently mix the fruits together and turn them into a glass bowl or individual glass dishes. Sprinkle the remaining tablespoon of apricot brandy over and chill the fruits and the puréed apricot sauce separately for about an hour, or until cold. Serve with the sauce dribbled over the fruits.

Rice Caramel

Rice Caramel has a soft, creamy base of rice hidden beneath a crunchy caramelized top. It transforms that old favorite, rice pudding, into something very special, for either the family or a dinner party. You can make the pudding the night before you wish to eat it, but caramelize it just before you serve it or the caramel may go soft. *Serves 4 to 6*

3/8 cup (3 oz; 85 g) short-grain rice, washed
1 1/4 cups (10 oz) milk
1 1/4 cups (10 oz) light or single cream
1/3 cup (2 1/4 oz; 75 g) granulated sugar
1/3 cup (1 1/2 oz; 45 g) washed currants
Pinch of nutmeg
1 vanilla bean
1/2 cup (4 oz) heavy or double cream
1/2 cup (3 oz; 85 g) raw, turbinado,
*   or demerara sugar*

Put the rice, milk, light cream, granulated sugar, currants, nutmeg, and vanilla bean in the top of a double boiler. Place over simmering water, mix thoroughly, cover, and cook for 30 minutes. Then remove the vanilla bean and cook 1 hour longer, or until the rice is cooked, and has absorbed the liquid. Stir occasionally to prevent any lumps from forming and every 20–30 minutes check to see if the water in the double boiler needs refilling. When the rice is cooked you should have a thick, creamy mixture. Remove from the heat and let it cool. Then turn the heavy cream into a bowl and beat it until it is nearly stiff. Fold it into the rice mixture, and turn into a 2-inch-deep ovenproof dish. Chill for 1–2 hours, or until cold. Preheat the broiler and sprinkle the top of the pudding with an even layer of raw sugar, so the whole surface is completely covered. (The amount of sugar you need will depend on the size of the dish.) Place the top of the pudding 1 inch from the broiler and cook for 2 minutes, or until the sugar has melted. Chill slightly and serve.

Lady Scott's Lemon Pudding

Lady Scott's Lemon Pudding shines golden yellow, the color of Mercury (Virgo's ruling planet), the planet of the mind and intellectual expression. It is a delectably light, buttery dessert, full of the rich taste of lemons and oranges, and makes an ideal dish for a dinner party. *Serves 4 to 6*

16 ladyfingers
4 Tb (2 oz) Grand Marnier or Cointreau
8 Tb (4 oz; 115 g) butter
1/4 cup (2 oz; 60 g) superfine or castor sugar
1 cup (8 oz; 225 g) lemon curd (recipe follows)
1 Tb lemon juice
Grated rind of 1 lemon
Grated rind of 1 orange
3 medium eggs, separated, the yolks lightly beaten
1 1/4 cups (1/2 Imperial pint) heavy or double cream

Place the ladyfingers in one layer in a shallow dish and sprinkle them with Grand Marnier or Cointreau. (The amount of ladyfingers and liqueur you need will depend on the size of the dish you use for the dessert.) In a mixing bowl or food processor, beat the butter and sugar together until pale. Then beat in the lemon curd, lemon juice, and lemon and orange rinds. Very gradually beat in the egg yolks, drop by drop to begin with, and then in a thin, steady stream. If the lemon mixture is not in a bowl, pour it into one, and in a separate bowl, with clean beaters, beat the egg whites until stiff. Fold them into the lemon mixture. Line a 5-cup (2–Imperial pint) deep dish with 8 ladyfingers, breaking a few up if necessary to fit them into the bottom of the dish.

Cover them with half of the lemon mixture. Lay the remaining ladyfingers over and then cover them with the remaining lemon mixture. Chill in the refrigerator for 1–2 hours, or until cold. Beat the heavy cream in a bowl until it is just stiff. Spread it evenly over the top of the pudding and serve.

Lemon Curd

1 large egg
6 Tb (3 oz; 85 g) superfine or castor sugar
Juice of 1 lemon
3 Tb soft butter

Lightly beat the egg in the top of a double boiler and mix in the sugar, lemon juice, and butter. Place over barely simmering water and stir until the mixture thickens. Turn into a clean jar and cover. Refrigerate until you wish to use.

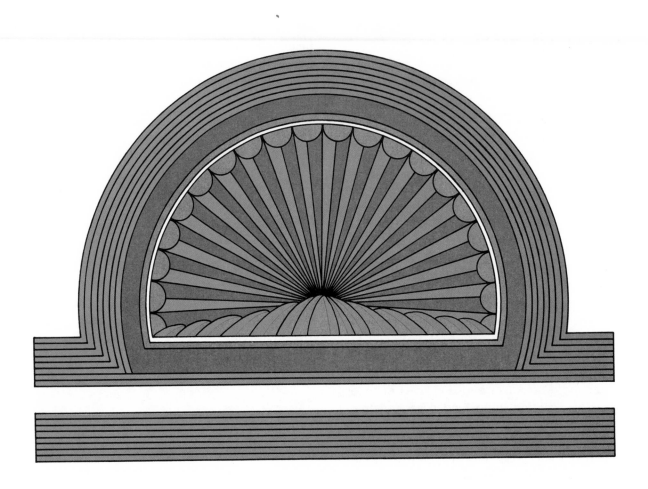

LIBRA

SEPTEMBER 24–OCTOBER 23

Rules the seventh house, the house of marriage and partnership

RULING PLANET	ELEMENT	QUALITIES
Venus	Air	Cardinal, active
♎	♎	♎

CHARACTERISTICS

Artistic, changeable, charming, diplomatic,
harmonious, indecisive, romantic

♎

OPPOSITE SIGN	BODY AREA	GEMSTONE
Aries	Kidneys	Sapphire
♎	♎	♎

COLOR

Green

♎

FLAVOR	METAL	FAUNA
Sweet, fragrant	Bronze	Birds, fish, lamb, shellfish
♎	♎	♎

FLORA

Almonds, apples, avocados, bananas, beans, berries, cherries,
chocolate, figs, grapes, legumes, peaches, pears, plums, roses, sugar

♎

HERBS AND SPICES

Cinnamon, coriander, marshmallow,
mints, sorrel, violets

♎

CELL SALT

Sodium phosphate (Nat. Phos.), found in
almonds, apples, asparagus, beets, carrots,
celery, corn, dried fruit, peaches, peas,
watercress, wheat

♎

LIBRA THE COOK

Don't be surprised, if you are invited to dinner, to find your Libran hostess lying gracefully on her chaise longue, contemplating the beauty of life and not at all concerned about the state of dinner. This doesn't mean that things are not in order; she probably had a spurt of frenzied activity earlier in the afternoon and is now replenishing her strength.

So relax. The menu was undoubtedly planned well in advance—which is just as well, because Librans, who are imaginative and like to please their guests, find it very difficult to make decisions and can strive for hours trying to strike a perfect balance.

This sign of the zodiac is symbolized by the scales, and Librans' emotions are constantly dipping from one extreme to another in their attempt to balance and harmonize. Also, their ruling planet, Venus (the Roman version of the Greek goddess Aphrodite), in addition to being goddess of love, was born from the ocean and was also a sea goddess. From her comes a burning desire for harmony, but she also embodies the fluctuating moods of the sea.

As goddess of love, the pure charm and graciousness within Venus shines through Librans and is obvious in their choices of foods. Chicken is a probability in this household since birds relate to the goddess whose love encourages man to rise above the earth, as well as foods of love such as oysters, scallops, and tuna. Soft, curved mousses and sensual fruits that reflect the gentle curves of Venus are also likely to be on the menu, as well as tender meats and sweet pastries.

The Libran kitchen will probably be remarkably well organized, well fitted out with gadgets to aid them in their role as chef (Saturn, the planet of discipline, is exalted in this sign), and Librans tend to think through what they are going to create before they begin. They will welcome your help and conversation as they cook; surroundings and people are very important to this sign of the zodiac, and their homes will reflect this, providing a relaxed and welcome atmosphere.

Wine is quite likely to flow in this household, and it could be either white or red, depending on the present mood. Since Librans often experience periods of extremes of hard work, which are followed by complete relaxation, as well as bursts of spending and not spending, it's a good idea to check that your invitation is going to fall during a period of exertion and extravagance, or dinner could be a scant affair. On a good day, dining with a Libran should be a memorable occasion, full of the delights of Venus and well worth making the effort for.

RECIPES FOR LIBRA

MENU SUGGESTIONS FOR LIBRA

First Courses

Oysters with Hot Tomato Sauce
Guacamole
Tropical Smoked Salmon
Cheese-Salami Croissants
Chicory Salad with Apple and Bacon
Pea and Mint Soup
Coquilles St. Jacques

Main Courses

Salmon Wrapped in Pastry
Breaded Lamb Chops
Flamed Chicken with Cherries
Sweet Corn Soufflé
Crab Ring with Mussels
Kidney Stew
Spaghetti with Red and Black Caviar

Side Dishes

Lentil Salad with Yogurt and Parsley
French Beans with Toasted Almonds

Desserts

Raspberry-Marshmallow Pudding
Pears in Port
Apfel Strudel
Figs with Rum in Chocolate Sauce
Rose Petal Ice Cream
Peach and Grape Cream Salad

Guacamole
Breaded Lamb Chops
Figs with Rum in Chocolate Sauce

♎

Oysters with Hot Tomato Sauce
Flamed Chicken with Cherries
Rose Petal Ice Cream

♎

Tropical Smoked Salmon
Spaghetti with Red and Black Caviar
Pears in Port

♎

Cheese-Salami Croissants
Kidney Stew
Peach and Grape Cream Salad

♎

Pea and Mint Soup
Crab Ring with Mussels
Apfel Strudel

♎

Chicory Salad with Apple and Bacon
Salmon Wrapped in Pastry
Raspberry-Marshmallow Pudding

♎

Coquilles St. Jacques
Sweet Corn Soufflé
Rose Petal Ice Cream

LIBRA THE GUEST

Librans make very rewarding guests—that is if they will ever say yes to your invitation definitively. This sign of the zodiac likes to keep its options open, allowing it the chance to go whichever way the wind blows.

If it blows your way, then you should have a pleasant evening in store, because Librans are relaxed people who have the ability to enjoy themselves. This is an air sign; it is the falling leaves of autumn that turn first one way and then another, fluttering, changeable, and enchanting as they tumble. Catch them if you can, because Librans are full of sociability and will gracefully appreciate all your hard labors in the kitchen. Libra rules the seventh house of the zodiac, which is concerned with close relationships and partnerships, and true to this, Librans are very caring, appreciative, and interested in people they meet.

This is a much more fiery and outgoing air sign than either Gemini or Aquarius. It is a cardinal sign of the zodiac, ruling a time of year when the fall is rapidly bursting forth—the beginning of the season when the gold-fringed fields are burning scarlet and the leaves on the trees are changing from green to vibrant reds and yellows. Libra is full of the flamboyance of the turning year, and, like the changing leaves, Librans' emotions change color, often leaving you unsure of where you are. So if you want the evening to run as smoothly as possible, note that Librans are most compatible with other air and fire signs. Because this sign of the zodiac can be quite argumentative, they like to stimulate conversation and debate, and they are quite capable of changing from one side of an argu-

ment to another, happily seeing everyone's point of view.

An evening with a Libran should be fun—full of laughter and wit and variety—especially when he or she is well fed. Librans like good food; in fact they enjoy all the luxurious and sweet things that life provides. Try a flambéed dish on them, or perhaps a flamed chicken to attract their flamboyant personality and capture their imagination. Or a delicate fish or soufflé to appeal to their element of air, following with foods of love such as figs, grapes, and cherries in honor of their ruling planet, Venus. Harmonious surroundings are also important to Librans, and a well-set table with flowers and candlelight will enchant them and appeal to their fundamentally romantic and gullible nature.

Feed your Libran friend beautifully proportioned and well-arranged dishes, because harmony and balance is the key to this sign. Offer Librans delicious wines and sweet pastries, and the evening should be a delightfully cultured and aesthetic affair.

Oysters with Hot Tomato Sauce

Oysters are traditionally a food of love. Tightly wrapped in a mother-of-pearl shell, their flesh has a soft and delicate tenderness, which is rich in copper (the metal of Venus) and said to have aphrodisiac qualities. Oysters should be opened just before serving and are complemented best by a chilled Chablis. *Serves 4*

Hot tomato sauce

   2 Tb olive oil

   1 small onion, peeled and thinly sliced

   1 clove garlic, peeled and thinly sliced

   1/2 red chili, stalk removed and thinly sliced

   1/2 lb (225 g) tomatoes, peeled and sliced

   Salt and black pepper

   32–48 oysters

   2 tsp lemon juice

   1 Tb heavy or double cream

Garnishes

   Seaweed

   4–8 thin slices of whole wheat bread, buttered

Heat the oil in a frying pan over moderately low heat. Mix in the onion, garlic, and chili and cook, stirring frequently, for 8 minutes. Add the tomatoes and cook about 8 minutes longer, stirring occasionally, until any liquid has cooked off and you have a purée of vegetables. Season to taste with salt and black pepper and turn into a food processor or blender, and purée. Pour into a bowl and leave to chill while you open the oysters.

   To open the oysters, wrap one in a cloth (the shells are sharp and can cut quite badly if not covered) with the hinge exposed. Hold it flat-side up in your hand and prize the joint open with an oyster or wide-bladed knife. Lay the deeper shell on a bed of ice with the oyster and its juices in it. Continue to open all the oysters in this way and add them to the bed of ice. (They should be eaten within 3–4 hours of being opened.) Then mix the lemon juice and cream into the tomato sauce, turn it into a small glass bowl, and place it in the center of the oysters. Garnish the ice with seaweed and serve accompanied by slices of buttered whole wheat bread.

Guacamole

Guacamole, the lightly spiced salad of mashed avocado from Mexico, can be prepared in minutes and makes a very nourishing starter for a meal or dip for a party. *Serves 4 to 6*

> 1/4 lb (about 3 small) tomatoes, skinned, chopped, and seeded
> 1 small onion, peeled and grated
> 1 small clove garlic, peeled and pushed through a press
> 2 tsp lime or lemon juice
> 1/4 tsp chili powder
> 1/2 tsp ground coriander
> 1/2 tsp Tabasco
> 1 tsp salt
> Black pepper to taste
> 3 ripe avocados

Garnish
> Tortilla chips

Place all the ingredients except the avocados in a food processor or blender and mix thoroughly. Halve the avocados, remove the pits, and spoon the flesh into the food processor. Mix lightly so that the avocado retains a slightly rough texture. Check the seasoning and turn into a serving bowl. Serve with tortilla chips soon after preparing— or the delicate green of the avocado will darken.

Tropical Smoked Salmon

Tropical Smoked Salmon is an exotic starter in which rose-pink slices of salmon are covered with soft, sensual green fruits, creating a dish that reflects the loveliness and colors of Venus (Libra's ruling planet). It is easy to do and best prepared just before you wish to eat it or the avocado will discolor. *Serves 4*

> 8 oz (225 g) wafer-thin slices of smoked salmon
> 4 kiwi fruit
> 1 medium avocado

Dressing
> 2 Tb olive oil
> 3 Tb (1 1/2 oz) lime juice
> Black pepper

Garnish
> 4 thin slices of whole wheat bread, buttered and halved

Arrange the smoked salmon on a serving plate, or divide equally among 4 plates. Peel the kiwi fruit, and slice thinly lengthwise. Halve the avocado lengthwise, remove the pit, and lay flesh-side down on a plate or wooden board. Using a sharp knife, pierce the skin down the center from top to bottom and peel it off. Slice thinly lengthwise and arrange over the smoked salmon with the kiwi fruit. Mix together the dressing ingredients, season to taste with black pepper, and sprinkle over the fruits and salmon. Serve with a plate of buttered whole wheat bread.

Cheese-Salami Croissants

This is a simple but very delicious combination of tastes, ideal for days when the sociable Libran has little time to spend in the kitchen. Serve it as a starter or a light lunch dish, with a green salad and red Italian wine. *Serves 4*

4 croissants

1¹/2 Tb soft butter

2 oz (60 g; 8 slices) thinly sliced Genoa (Italian) salami

4 oz (115 g) thinly sliced Gruyère cheese

Salt and black pepper

Preheat the oven to 350°F (180°C; gas 4).

Slice each croissant open, starting from the front and leaving the back unbroken. Then spread the butter over the bottom half of each. Divide the salami into 4 equal portions and arrange over the bottom of each croissant. Cover with the cheese and season to taste with salt and black pepper. Place in the oven for 10 minutes, or until the croissants are hot through and the cheese has melted. Cut the croissants in half and serve hot.

Chicory Salad with Apple and Bacon

Hot, crisp bacon tossed over the colorful combination of chicory, radicchio, and apple provides a salad with a delightful texture and an interesting combination of sweet and savory tastes—a reflection of the oscillating emotions of sweet and sour that this sign of the zodiac tends to experience. *Serves 4*

2 medium heads chicory

1 small head radicchio

3 scallions or spring onions

1¹/4 cups (5 oz; 140 g) grated Gruyère cheese

¹/2 lb (or 2) crisp eating apples

3 Tb (1¹/2 oz) lemon juice

8 slices (¹/2 lb; 225 g) streaky bacon

1 Tb olive oil

Salt and black pepper

Break the chicory and radicchio into leaves and wash and dry them. Shred the radicchio and cut 1 head of chicory into ¹/2-inch slices crosswise. Arrange the remaining leaves of chicory around the edge of a salad bowl, with the chopped chicory and radicchio mixed in the center. Chop the scallions, and scatter them and the cheese over. Then peel, core, and chop the apple, scatter the pieces over, and sprinkle with lemon juice. Cut the rind off the bacon, if necessary, and cut it into small pieces. Heat the oil in a frying pan over moderately high heat; when it is hot add the bacon, and sauté, stirring constantly, for 5–6 minutes, or until crisp. Toss the bacon and some of the fat over the salad, season to taste with salt and black pepper, and serve immediately.

Pea and Mint Soup

Pea soup is the velvet green of a secluded forest glade, smooth with a delicate hint of mint, which is both refreshing and reviving. It also contains Libra's cell salt, sodium phosphate, which helps control the acids in the body and the digestion of fatty foods, as well as being beneficial for conditions of rheumatism, heartburn, and headaches. Make this soup the night before a dinner party if you wish and serve it either hot or cold with rolls warm from the oven. *Serves 6*

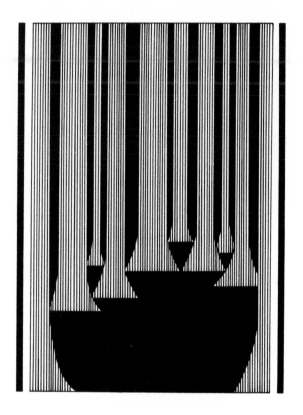

> 2 Tb (1 oz; 30 g) butter
> 1 small onion, peeled and finely chopped
> 1 clove garlic, peeled and pushed through a press
> 2 lb shelled fresh or frozen peas
> 1½ cups (12 oz) milk
> 2 cups (16 oz) chicken stock
> ½ cup plus 2 Tb (5 oz) light or single cream
> ¼ cup (4 Tb) chopped fresh mint
> Salt and black pepper

Garnish
> 6 warmed rolls

Melt the butter in a large saucepan over moderately low heat. Mix in the onion and garlic, cover, and sauté for 15 minutes, stirring occasionally. Add the peas, milk, and chicken stock, bring to a boil, cover, and simmer gently for 10 minutes, or until the peas are tender. Pour into a food processor or blender, and purée with the cream and mint. Return to the saucepan, season to taste with salt and black pepper, heat through, and serve. Or alternatively, chill the soup for several hours or overnight, and serve with rolls.

Coquilles St. Jacques

Aphrodite, the Greek goddess of love, was born from the white foam of the sea and carried across it on a scallop shell. So scallops were sacred to her and the floor of her palace sanctuary at Knossos was carpeted with shells. Coquilles St. Jacques, the classic French dish of scallops and mushrooms, served in a scallop shell and often edged with mashed potato, is a delicious food of love and beauty, which is ideal for the romantic Libran who is ruled by this goddess. *Serves 6*

1½ lb (about 18) scallops

7 Tb (3½ oz; 100 g) butter

6 oz (180 g) mushrooms, wiped clean and sliced

1 clove garlic, peeled and pushed through a press

¾ cup (6 oz) dry white wine

1½ lb potatoes

Salt

6 Tb (3 oz) milk

Black pepper

3 Tb (1½ oz; 40 g) flour

¼ cup (2 oz) heavy or double cream

2 Tb chopped fresh parsley

Butter 6 clean scallop shells. Rinse the scallops in cold water, pat them dry, and then cut them in half. If you have king scallops (scallops with an orange roe), separate the roe with a sharp knife and set it aside. Melt 2 tablespoons of butter in a frying pan over low heat. Mix in the mushrooms and garlic, and cook for 3 minutes, then add the wine and scallops, cover, and simmer for 3–4 minutes longer, or until the scallops are just tender. (If you have any roe, add this to the pan after the scallops have been cooking for 2 minutes.) Remove from the heat, drain, and set aside, reserving the liquor.

Peel the potatoes, cut into large chunks, put in a pan with ½ teaspoon of salt, and cover with cold water. Bring to a boil, and simmer for 15–20 minutes, or until tender. Drain, return to the pan, and place over very low heat. Stir in the milk and 3 tablespoons of butter, and mash the potatoes until smooth. Season to taste with salt and black pepper.

Preheat the oven to 350°F (180°C; gas 4).

While the potatoes are cooking, make the sauce. Melt the remaining 2 tablespoons of butter in a pan over low heat, add the flour, and stir continuously for 2 minutes. Add the reserved liquor and cream, stirring continuously until you have a smooth sauce. Simmer for a few minutes and season to taste with salt and black pepper. Mix the scallops, mushrooms, and parsley into the sauce, and check the seasoning. Spoon equal amounts of mixture into the centers of the scallop shells and, using a pastry bag with a rosette nozzle, pipe the mashed potato around the edges of the shells. Place in the oven for about 5 minutes, or until hot through, and serve.

Salmon Wrapped in Pastry

Two salmon fillets sandwiched together with currants and butter and wrapped in pastry suggest the closeness of love, making a perfectly romantic dish for the sign of the zodiac that is concerned with partnership and love. Serve this dish for a special occasion with French Beans with Toasted Almonds (see page 165), boiled new potatoes, and a cold white Burgundy wine. *Serves 2*

Quick flaky pastry

> *1¹/3 cups (6 oz; 180 g) flour*
> *³/4 tsp baking powder*
> *Pinch of salt*
> *8 Tb (4 oz; 115 g) butter*
> *3¹/2–4 Tb cold water*

> *Two 6-oz (180-g) boned and skinned salmon fillets*
> *3 Tb (1¹/2 oz; 45 g) soft butter*
> *2 Tb washed currants*
> *Salt and black pepper*
> *1 Tb milk*

Preheat the oven to 425°F (220°C; gas 7).

Place the flour, baking powder, and salt in a large bowl and cut in the butter. Mix lightly, then, with your fingertips, work the flour and butter together until the mixture resembles bread crumbs. Pour in the water, mixing with a fork until the liquid is all absorbed. Or alternatively, you can make this pastry in a food processor. First mix the flour, baking powder, salt, and butter together, and then add the water through the funnel, continuing to process until the dough forms a ball. Remove and place on a floured wooden board. Roll out to ¹/8-inch thickness and cut out a rectangle about 8 by 12 inches. Then place 1 fish fillet on a separate board or plate. Mix the butter with the currants and season to taste with salt and black pepper. Spread the mixture evenly over the top of the fillet. Cover with the remaining fillet and then place the fish in the center of the pastry so that it lies lengthwise across the 8-inch width. Fold the pastry over the top of the salmon, and trim the edges so the pastry only overlaps about ¹/4 inch. Brush the ends of the pastry with milk and press them together, crimp so that you have a small parcel, and place it seam-side down on a greased baking sheet. Cut four ¹/4-inch slits along the long edges of the pastry, so that the steam can escape, brush with milk, and bake for 25 minutes.

Breaded Lamb Chops

In this easy, delicious dish, breaded lamb chops, filled with a slice of pâté, are dipped in egg and fried—very appropriate for the peace-loving Libran, since the tenderness of the lamb relates directly to the tenderness and gentleness of their ruling planet, Venus. Serve with boiled new potatoes, Lentil Salad with Yogurt and Parsley (see page 165), and a red Burgundy wine. *Serves 4*

> *4 loin lamb chops, a generous 1 inch thick*
> *4 Tb (3 oz; 85 g) meat or vegetable pâté*
>   *(see pages 141 and 132)*
> *Salt*
> *2 small eggs*
> *2 cloves garlic, peeled and pushed through a press*
> *Black pepper*
> *6 Tb (1½ oz; 45 g) very fine dry bread crumbs*
> *Vegetable or sunflower oil*

Garnish
> *A bunch of trimmed watercress*

Trim any excess fat from the outside of the chops. Lay 1 chop flat-side down on a wooden board and cut a 2-inch slit halfway down the fatty edge and through to the bone. Stuff it with 1 tablespoon of pâté and press the edges back together. Repeat this process with the remaining chops. Sprinkle the chops with a little salt on both sides. In a bowl beat the eggs with the garlic and season to taste with salt and black pepper. Cover a large plate or wooden board with the bread crumbs and coat the chops with them so they have an even covering on each side. Press them in firmly, then shake off any excess. Pour enough oil into a frying pan to fill ¼ inch, place over high heat, and when the oil is hot, lower the heat to moderately high. Place the bowl of eggs by the side of the frying pan and dip the lamb chops in the egg just before you add them to the pan. Sauté for 5 minutes on each side, then transfer them briefly to a plate covered with a paper towel to drain some of the fat. Arrange the chops on a warmed serving dish, garnish with watercress, and serve hot.

Flamed Chicken with Cherries

Chicken, cooked with cherries and flavored with rosemary, is then flamed with Armagnac to make an exceptionally delicious combination of flavors and a pretty dish, which should be a favorite with this most fiery and flamboyant air sign. Serve it with French Beans with Toasted Almonds (see page 165), roast potatoes, and a red wine. *Serves 4*

Two 2-lb or one 4-lb chicken(s)

Stock

Chicken giblets

1 bay leaf

1 medium onion, peeled and halved

2 cups water

Salt and black pepper to taste

Stuffing

3 cups (6 oz; 180 g) soft whole wheat
  bread crumbs

1/4 cup (1 1/2 oz; 45 g) chopped almonds

1 medium egg

2 Tb melted butter

1/3 cup (2 oz; 60 g) pitted cherries

1 Tb dried rosemary, or 2 Tb chopped fresh

1 small onion, peeled and finely chopped

Salt and black pepper to taste

1 1/2 Tb dried rosemary, or 3 Tb fresh

4 Tb (2 oz; 60 g) butter

2/3 cup (6 oz; 170 g) pitted fresh or
  canned cherries, or canned
  Bing cherries, drained

1 1/2 Tb flour

4 Tb (2 oz) red wine

1/3 cup (2 1/2 oz) Armagnac or Cognac

Preheat the oven to 325°F (165°C; gas 3).

Remove giblets from cavities of chickens and place them with bay leaf, onion, water, and salt and black pepper in a saucepan, bring to a boil, cover, and simmer gently for 1 1/2 hours while you prepare the chickens.

In a food processor or large bowl, thoroughly mix all the stuffing ingredients. Divide the mixture in half (if you are using two birds) and stuff the birds with it. Mix the rosemary with the butter and rub over the chickens. Season with salt and black pepper. Skewer the opening to hold the stuffing in and truss to keep the birds intact. Arrange the birds breast-side up in a roasting pan just large enough to hold them, and place in the oven. Roast for 30 minutes, basting twice, surround the chicken with the cherries, and cook 20 minutes longer, or until the birds are done. (If you are cooking a larger bird, roast it for 25 minutes per pound and add the cherries about 20 minutes before the chicken is done.) When the chickens are done, transfer them and the cherries to a serving platter and keep warm. Skim the fat from the pan juices, and reserve 2 tablespoons for gravy. Pour the juices into a jug and set aside. Place the pan over moderately low heat. Heat the reserved fat, sprinkle in the flour, and stir continuously for 2 minutes. Then mix in the pan juices, stock, and wine, stirring continuously until you have a smooth sauce, then simmer for a few minutes. Season to taste with salt and black pepper and pour into a gravy boat. Return the chickens to the roasting pan, pour over the Armagnac, and place over low heat. When the Armagnac begins to bubble, ignite it, remove pan from the heat, and spoon

Sweet Corn Soufflé

the flaming liquor over the chickens. When the flames have died, return the chickens to the platter, with the cherries around them, and serve.

Golden yellow corn, which grows in abundance in the autumnal fields of Libra, gives a sweetness to this delectably light soufflé and makes a perfect dish for such a light and airy sign of the zodiac. Serve it with a green vegetable or salad, a crusty Italian loaf, and a light white wine such as an Alsace. *Serves 4*

> *2 Tb butter*
> *2 Tb flour*
> *3/4 cup (6 oz) milk*
> *1/4 cup (2 oz) light or single cream*
> *2 cups (3/4 lb; 340 g) fresh sweet corn,*
>   *cut off the cob*
> *1 Tb light brown sugar*
> *5 medium eggs, separated*
> *Salt and black pepper*

Preheat the oven to 375°F (190°C; gas 5). Butter a 1½-quart soufflé dish.

Place the butter in a saucepan and melt it over low heat. Mix in the flour and, stirring continuously, cook for 2 minutes. Stir in the milk and cream until you have a smooth sauce. Bring to a boil and simmer for a few minutes, stirring occasionally. Remove from the heat, turn into a food processor or blender with the sweet corn, sugar, and egg yolks, and purée. Season to taste with salt and black pepper. In a bowl beat the egg whites until stiff. Pour the corn mixture down the side of the bowl in which the egg whites were beaten and gently fold the egg whites in until they are thoroughly mixed. Turn into the buttered soufflé dish and bake for 45 minutes, or until the soufflé has risen and is cooked through. Serve immediately.

Crab Ring with Mussels

Aphrodite, the Greek goddess of love, was also associated with the sea. Embodied in Libra (the sign of the zodiac that Aphrodite governs) is an inclination to swing to extremes of emotion like the ever-changing moods of the sea. Serve this luxuriously soft seafood dish with a green salad, an Italian loaf, and a delicious bottle of very cold white wine. *Serves 4*

> One 2½–3-lb crab, cooked, poison sacs and gills
>   removed, or ¾ lb (340 g) fresh crabmeat
> 4 medium eggs
> 1¼ cups (½ Imperial pint) light or single cream
> ¼ tsp Tabasco
> Salt and black pepper

Mussel filling
> 1 lb (450 g) mussels
> 3 Tb (1½ oz) sherry
> 2 Tb olive oil
> 1 medium onion, peeled and finely chopped
> 6 cloves garlic, peeled and finely chopped
> 1 Tb tomato paste
> 1 tsp curry powder
> ½ tsp ground coriander
> ¼ lb mushrooms, wiped clean and sliced
> 2 Tb chopped fresh parsley
> Black pepper

Preheat the oven to 300°F (150°C; gas 2). Butter a 4-cup (1⅗-Imperial pint) ring mold.

Crack the claws of the crab with crackers or a hammer, remove all the flesh, and flake it. In a bowl, beat the eggs with the cream and Tabasco. Mix in the crabmeat and season to taste with salt and black pepper. Turn into a ring mold and place it in a baking pan half full of cold water. Place in the oven and cook for 50 minutes, or until the crab mixture has set through to the center. While the crab is cooking, prepare the filling.

Scrub the mussels thoroughly in several changes of cold water. Discard any that are open when you have finished cleaning them. Place the mussels and sherry in a large frying pan over moderately low heat. Cover, and cook for 5 minutes, or until the mussels have steamed open. Remove them from the pan and set aside to cool; strain the mussel liquor through muslin or cheesecloth and set aside. Heat the oil in the same pan, add the onion and garlic, and cook together for 8–10 minutes, stirring occasionally. Mix in the tomato paste, curry powder, coriander,

Kidney Stew

mushrooms, and mussel liquor, and cook 5 minutes longer, stirring occasionally, until the mushrooms are tender.

Meanwhile, remove the mussels from the shells. When the crab ring is nearly done, add the mussels and parsley to the pan with the sauce, heat through, and season to taste with black pepper. Unmold the cooked crab ring onto a warmed serving dish, fill the center and surround the edge of the ring with the mussel mixture, and serve.

Kidneys are the part of the body ruled by Libra, and in this dish their taste is sweet and mild and very lightly flavored with wine and thyme. Serve this stew as a family supper dish with plenty of boiled rice and a red wine. *Serves 4*

1 lb (or 2) Spanish onions, peeled and cut into eighths
1/2 cup (4 oz) red wine
1 1/4 cups (1/2 Imperial pint) water
1/4 tsp dried thyme, or 1/2 tsp chopped fresh
Salt and black pepper to taste
10 lamb kidneys (about 1 1/2 lb; 675 g)
4 Tb flour

Place the onions, wine, and 3/4 cup (6 oz) of water in a saucepan. Season with thyme, salt, and black pepper and bring to a boil. Lower the heat, cover, and simmer for 20 minutes, or until the onions are tender. While the onions are cooking, remove any surrounding fat and the translucent membrane from the outside of the kidneys, and cut them into about 1-inch cubes. Stir the kidneys into the onion mixture, cover, and simmer for 5 minutes, or until the kidneys are nearly tender. Then blend the flour with the remaining water until it is smooth and mix it into the kidneys, stirring continuously until the mixture thickens. Simmer for a few minutes, then check the seasoning. Turn into a warmed serving dish.

Spaghetti with Red and Black Caviar

The spaghetti is scattered with jet and coral, like a broken string of beads, making a charming picture. Easy to prepare, this dish is excellent served with a tomato salad (see Red, White, and Black Salad, page 108) and a chilled Italian white wine such as Frascati. *Serves 4 to 6*

2 Tb olive oil

1 lb spaghetti

One 2-oz (50-g) jar of red caviar or lumpfish caviar

One 2-oz (50-g) jar of black caviar or Danish lumpfish caviar

Grated rind of 1 lemon

3 Tb lemon juice

1 Tb chopped fresh chives

Salt and black pepper

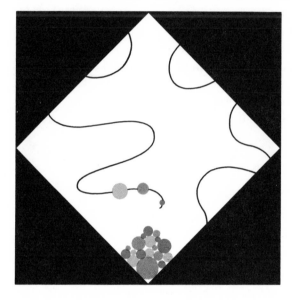

Bring a large pan of salted water with a few drops of oil to a boil, stir in the spaghetti, and cook, uncovered, until it is done *al dente*. While the spaghetti is cooking, very gently mix all the remaining ingredients together in a bowl, except for the salt and pepper. When the spaghetti is done, drain it and turn it into a warmed serving dish. Toss it in the caviar mixture until it is thoroughly mixed. Season to taste with a little salt and plenty of black pepper, and serve.

SIDE DISHES

Lentil Salad with Yogurt and Parsley

The protein-rich lentil suggests the green vibration of Venus and the color and nature of Libra; rich in nutritional value, it is an economical food that has a delicious savory taste and is especially good served as a cold salad dish, mixed with yogurt, parsley, and garlic. Serve it with Breaded Lamb Chops (see page 159) or perhaps a tomato and mixed green salad. *Serves 4*

> 1 cup (7 oz; 235 g) green lentils, washed
>
> 1 bay leaf
>
> One 1/2-inch piece gingerroot, peeled
>
> 1 tsp ground coriander
>
> Salt
>
> 2 1/2 cups (1 Imperial pint) water
>
> 3 scallions or spring onions
>
> 1 cup (8 oz) plain yogurt
>
> 1 small clove garlic, peeled and pushed through a press
>
> 1/4 cup (4 Tb) chopped fresh parsley
>
> 1 Tb lemon juice
>
> Black pepper

Place the lentils, bay leaf, gingerroot, coriander, 1/4 teaspoon of salt, and water in a saucepan. Bring to a boil, and simmer for 35 minutes, or until the lentils are tender and the water has cooked off. Turn into a bowl, discarding the bay leaf and ginger, and set aside to cool. While the lentils are cooling, chop the scallions finely crosswise. In a bowl mix thoroughly the yogurt with the garlic, parsley, lemon juice, and scallions. Mix in the lentils, season to taste with salt and black pepper, and turn into a serving dish. Serve immediately, or chill until you wish to serve.

French Beans with Toasted Almonds

The sweet taste of toasted almonds perfectly complements these elegant thin green beans as well as being particularly beneficial for this sign of the zodiac, since they contain Libra's cell salt, sodium phosphate. For an excellent meal, serve them with Flamed Chicken with Cherries (see page 160). *Serves 4*

> 1 lb young green beans or French beans
>
> 1 clove garlic, peeled
>
> 2 Tb (1 oz; 30 g) butter
>
> Salt and black pepper
>
> 1/4 cup (1 oz; 30 g) toasted slivered almonds

Trim the beans, rinse them in cold water, and pat them dry. Place them in the top of a steamer over boiling water, with a clove of garlic in the water. Cover, and steam for 8 minutes, or until tender. Turn into a warmed serving dish, toss with butter, and season to taste with salt and black pepper. Scatter the almonds over and serve.

Raspberry-Marshmallow Pudding

Raspberries are a most delicately flavored fruit whose scarlet juices suggest the fire that lies within this sign of the zodiac. Set in a bed of soft marshmallow and cream over a crumb crust, they make a delicious, sensuous dessert—one to delight the Libran's sweet tooth and enjoyment of pleasure. *Serves 8*

> *3 cups (9 oz; 256 g) marshmallows*
> *1 cup (8 oz) milk*

Crumb crust
> *7 oz (or about 13) graham crackers or digestive biscuits*
> *2 Tb superfine or castor sugar*
> *7 Tb (3½ oz; 100 g) melted butter*
> *1 cup (8 oz) heavy or double cream*
> *2 Imperial pints (1¼ lb) raspberries*

Cut the marshmallows into pieces, and place them in a saucepan with the milk. Place over low heat and gently heat without boiling (or the marshmallows will not set). Stir occasionally until the marshmallows have melted. Pour into a bowl and chill for 2–3 hours, or until the mixture has thickened. While the marshmallows are chilling, prepare the crumb crust.

In a food processor or with a rolling pin, crush the graham crackers. If you are not using a food processor turn the crushed crackers into a bowl, then mix in the sugar and butter thoroughly. Press the mixture into the bottom of a 10-inch pie pan and leave to chill.

When the marshmallow mixture has thickened, beat it until it is well mixed. In a separate bowl beat the cream until it is stiff, then fold it into the marshmallow mixture. Fold in the raspberries, and turn into the pie pan. Chill for 1–2 hours, or until set, and serve.

Pears in Port

Golden pears glow beneath a wine-red glaze like the changing red and yellow leaves of fall, the time of the year ruled by Libra. *Serves 4*

> 4 ripe Comice pears
> 1/2 cup (4 oz; 115 g) superfine or
>   castor sugar
> 1 cup (8 oz) port
> Grated rind of 1 lemon
> 1/8 tsp cinnamon

<u>Garnish</u>

> A bowl of whipped heavy or double cream

Peel the pears, leaving the stalk intact. Then trim their bottoms so they can be served upright, and lay them on their sides in a medium-size saucepan with the sugar, port, lemon rind, and cinnamon. Bring to a boil, cover, and simmer gently for 5 minutes. Turn the pears and cook 5 minutes longer, or until the pears are tender. Arrange the pears upright on a serving dish. Turn the heat to moderately high and boil the remaining juices for about 10 minutes, or until they have reduced to a thin syrup. Pour the syrup over the pears and serve at room temperature, or chilled, accompanied by a bowl of whipped cream.

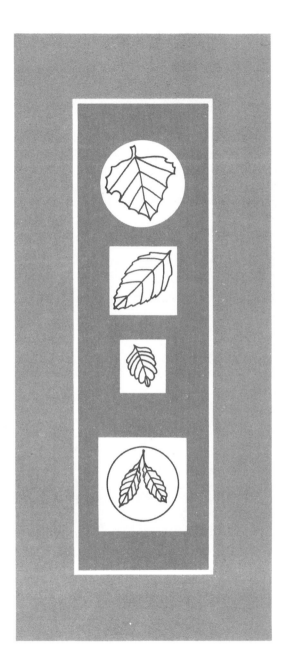

Apfel Strudel

Apples are a fruit sacred to Venus. Round and pale with a blushing hue of red, they suggest the sweet voluptuousness of this goddess. Apfel Strudel is the famous Austrian dessert in which a mixture of apple, dried fruit, and nuts is wrapped in the lightest of pastries; it makes a festive and appropriate dish for this airy sign that loves pastries and characteristically all the sweet things in life. *Serves 6*

1¼ lb McIntosh or Bramley cooking apples
½ cup (3 oz; 85 g) golden raisins or sultanas
6 Tb (1 oz; 30 g) slivered or flaked almonds
Finely grated rind of 1 lemon
¾ tsp cinnamon
¾ cup (4 oz; 115 g) light brown sugar
6 sheets filo pastry
5 Tb (2½ oz; 75 g) melted butter
1 Tb confectioners or icing sugar

Garnish

Heavy cream

Preheat the oven to 400°F (200°C; gas 6).

Peel, core, and quarter the apples and slice them very thinly. In a bowl mix thoroughly the raisins, almonds, lemon rind, cinnamon, and brown sugar, and set aside. Place a floured linen or cotton kitchen towel slightly larger than the pastry sheets over a large wooden board. Lay one sheet of the pastry on top and, using a pastry brush, brush it with melted butter. Cover with a second sheet of pastry and brush with butter, and repeat with 1 more sheet. Evenly cover the surface of the pastry with half of the apple slices, leaving ¼ inch of the pastry edges clear, then sprinkle half of the raisin mixture over so the apple is evenly covered. Cover with a sheet of pastry, brush with butter, and repeat with the remaining pastry. Cover with the remaining apple slices and raisin mixture. Fold one of the short sides of the pastry over about 1 inch of filling and then, pulling the towel toward you, roll the pastry up like a jelly roll. Lift the strudel onto a greased baking tray seam-side down and brush the top of the pastry with melted butter. Bake for 30 minutes, or until the pastry is golden. Remove the strudel to a serving platter. Put the confectioners sugar in a sieve and shake it evenly over the strudel. Serve hot or cold, accompanied by a bowl of heavy cream.

Figs with Rum in Chocolate Sauce

Figs, the sweet and succulent fruit of midsummer, are coated in a dark chocolate sauce and sprinkled with toasted almonds to make a delectable summer dessert that is delicious served with a bowl of whipped cream. *Serves 4*

> 1¾ lb (or 10) fresh figs
> ¼ cup (4 oz) dark rum
> 2 Tb brown sugar

Sauce
> 2 Tb cocoa
> 4 Tb brown sugar
> Pinch of salt
> ½ cup reserved fig juice and water
> 1 Tb butter
> 1 Tb dark rum

Garnishes
> ¼ cup (1 oz; 30 g) toasted slivered almonds
> Whipped cream

Rinse the figs in cold water and pat dry with a paper towel. Place them with the rum and 2 tablespoons of brown sugar in a saucepan over low heat, bring to a boil, cover, and simmer for 3–4 minutes, or until the figs are just tender. Thoroughly drain, reserving their juices, and arrange the figs upright in a shallow serving dish. Pour the juices in which they were cooked into a measuring cup and increase the liquid to ½ cup with a little water.

In a small saucepan mix together the cocoa, 4 tablespoons of brown sugar, and salt, gradually stir in the reserved fig juice and water, and place the pan over moderate heat. Bring to a boil, stir in the butter, and cook for about 8 minutes, or until the mixture has thickened. Remove the pan from the heat, stir in the rum, pour the sauce over the figs, and sprinkle the almonds over. Serve with a bowl of whipped cream.

Rose Petal Ice Cream

The rose is a special flower of lovers, dedicated to Venus, and white roses are said to have been stained red by the sacred blood of Aphrodite, when on her way to see her wounded lover, Adonis, she tore her flesh on a bush of white roses. Rose Petal Ice Cream, which is the softest pink color, has an exquisitely delicate and fragrant perfume and should be served in a glass bowl garnished with a full red rose. *Serves 4 to 6*

> 1½ cups (12 oz) milk
>
> 2 cups (½ oz; 15 g) fresh rose petals,
>   loosely packed
>
> ½ cup (4 oz; 115 g) superfine or castor sugar
>
> 3 medium egg yolks
>
> 1¼ cups (½ Imperial pint) heavy or double cream

<u>Garnish</u>
> 1 full red or deep pink rose, with the stem cut

Place the milk and rose petals in a saucepan over moderate heat. Bring to a boil and immediately remove from the heat. Cover and leave for 2 hours so that the rose petals infuse the milk. Then pour the milk through a sieve into a jug or small bowl and discard the rose petals. Mix the sugar with the egg yolks in the top of a double boiler. Place over barely simmering water and pour in the milk. Stir until the mixture has thickened to a custard, then remove from the heat, pour into a bowl, and set aside to cool. When the custard has cooled, pour the heavy cream into a bowl and beat until just stiff. Fold it into the custard so it is thoroughly mixed and turn into an ice tray. Chill in the freezer for 2 hours, or until half frozen. (If you have an ice cream maker, make the ice cream following the manufacturer's directions.) Remove the ice cream from the freezer and whisk it with a fork so that the crystallized edges are mixed into the center. Return it to the freezer and leave at least 4 hours or overnight before serving. Remove the ice cream from the freezer and place in the refrigerator a few hours before you wish to serve so it can soften. Serve it in scoops in a glass bowl, garnished with a rose in the center, and accompany with ice cream wafers.

Peach and Grape Cream Salad

A delicious combination of peaches and grapes, both soft, sensual fruits, sweetened with Kirsch and covered by a topping of whipped cream and sugar to make a lovely end to a meal. *Serves 4 to 6*

3/4 lb (340 g) black grapes
1 lb (450 g; or 3) peaches
1/4 lb (115 g) green seedless grapes
2 Tb Kirsch
1/2 cup (2 oz) brown sugar
1 1/4 cups (1/2 Imperial pint) heavy or double cream

Halve the black grapes lengthwise, remove the seeds, and peel them. Place the peaches in a large bowl, pour enough boiling water over to cover them, and let them soak for 30 seconds. Peel off the skins, cut the peaches in half, and discard the pits, then cut into thin slices. Arrange all the fruits in a deep 5-cup (2–Imperial pint) serving dish and sprinkle them with the Kirsch and 2 tablespoons of brown sugar. Turn the cream into a bowl and beat until stiff. Spread the whipped cream over the fruits and sprinkle the remaining sugar evenly over the top of the cream so that the whole surface is completely covered (the amount of sugar you need will depend on the size of the dish). Chill for several hours or overnight, and serve.

SCORPIO

OCTOBER 24–NOVEMBER 22

Rules the eighth house, the house of death and rebirth

RULING PLANETS
Pluto and Mars
♏

ELEMENT
Water
♏

QUALITIES
Fixed, passive
♏

CHARACTERISTICS
Determined, emotional, intense, possessive, secretive, subtle
♏

OPPOSITE SIGN
Taurus
♏

BODY AREA
Reproductive organs
♏

GEMSTONE
Bloodstone, cornelian
♏

COLOR
Green-blue
♏

FLAVOR
Extremes, bittersweet,
pungent, hot, resinous
♏

METAL
Steel
♏

FAUNA
Fish, offal, reptiles, shellfish
♏

FLORA
Asparagus, bananas, blackberries, cacti, garlic, leeks, nettles,
peppers, pine nuts, rhubarb, root vegetables
♏

HERBS AND SPICES
Basil, cayenne, ginseng, horseradish,
mustard, pepper
♏

CELL SALT
Sulphate of lime (Calc. Sulph.), found in
asparagus, cauliflower, figs, garlic,
gooseberries, leeks, mustard, onions,
prunes, radishes, watercress
♏

SCORPIO THE COOK

If a Scorpio invites you to dinner you should be extremely flattered. This sign of the zodiac is very selective about whom he or she entertains, and will only invite you if he really means it. So don't pass up the opportunity—dinner should be delicious with a Scorpio, a born gourmet who will strive for perfection.

This is a water sign—the blue-green of a calm sea whose glassy surface hides a secret and private world that is deep, colorful, and fantastic, and full of strong and powerful desires. Scorpios appear cool, but this is only a facade to hide an inner nature that burns with passion and that embodies the great force of water.

As cooks, Scorpios work with intensity and feeling, never half-heartedly. They make intuitive cooks whose instinct tends to pay off because of their fixed intent; they never lose sight of their goals and have great powers of concentration. They also know what they like and are very fond of good food.

It's probably best to stay clear of Scorpios' kitchens, partly because they will like to surprise you with whatever delight they are creating—they love to create mysteries—and also because they tend to know best and never like to appear ignorant. They are also extremely well informed. Pluto, their (more recently discovered) ruling planet, is the god of wisdom, as well as the god of the underworld, and it is his influence that gives this sign of the zodiac its secretive and probing nature. Scorpio's more traditional ruler, Mars—the Roman god of war—makes this sign of the zodiac quite fearless and adventurous in the kitchen, as well as hard-working. If a dish is

a disaster, Scorpios will not be discouraged, but they will have to know why. They enjoy a challenge, and the more demanding the dish, the more they want to master it.

Dinner with this sign of the zodiac could encompass any part of the world. Scorpios have broad tastes and like most sorts of food, especially when they are exotic, such as lobster or asparagus or crayfish. A flambéed dish will also appeal to their secretly fiery nature, as well as quite spicy flavors and foods with distinctive and unusual tastes, such as eel or mushrooms cooked with horseradish. Scorpios like to be different. They also like to live life to the fullest and thoroughly indulge themselves, so you will probably be treated to quite a variety of plentiful tastes. After all, Pluto is the god of riches, and Scorpios like to be lavish.

It's probably best to visit a Scorpio's household feeling fit. The food will certainly be good, but it could be quite rich, spicy, and plentiful, washed down with plenty of red wine. This sign of the zodiac doesn't do things by halves; it is a sign of perfectionists who like to get things right by calculating their errors.

RECIPES FOR SCORPIO

MENU SUGGESTIONS FOR SCORPIO

First Courses

Smoked Trout Pâté
Asparagus Wrapped in Parma Ham
Stuffed Peppers
Eggs in Aspic
Leeks in Cheese Sauce
Onion Soup
Mushrooms with Horseradish and Bacon

Main Courses

Chicken Livers with Marsala
Pork with Orange and Cashew Nuts
Shrimp Creole
Poached Eel with Parsley Sauce
Lobster Salad
Arroz con Pollo
Spiced Eggplant

Side Dishes

Potatoes au Gratin
Broccoli in Garlic Sauce

Desserts

Rhubarb Fool
Summer Pudding
Baked Alaska
Flambé Bananas
Prune Whip
Chocolate Cheesecake

Smoked Trout Pâté
Arroz con Pollo
Flambé Bananas

♏

Stuffed Peppers
Chicken Livers with Marsala
Rhubarb Fool

♏

Onion Soup
Lobster Salad
Summer Pudding

♏

Asparagus Wrapped in Parma Ham
Shrimp Creole
Prune Whip

♏

Eggs in Aspic
Spiced Eggplant
Baked Alaska

♏

Mushrooms with Horseradish and Bacon
Poached Eel with Parsley Sauce
Chocolate Cheesecake

♏

Leeks in Cheese Sauce
Pork with Orange and Cashew Nuts
Rhubarb Fool

SCORPIO THE GUEST

If you can recognize a Scorpio—they do like to travel in disguise—and invite them to dine, make sure that you prepare an excellent meal, because this sign of the zodiac likes to eat well and in style and won't forgive a half-hearted attempt at dinner.

Scorpios are symbolized by the scorpion, which has a deadly sting, and true to this symbol, if they don't like the look of dinner—if the lobster isn't out of its shell and presented beautifully and if the celery is not chopped in the right way, or if you pile the plates too high—they just won't touch it. Scorpios are masters of self-control and will quite happily do without rather than eat something they dislike, even though they might be starving. They will also let you know if that experiment you have spent all day perfecting is not a marvelous success. They may plot a revenge and feed you stinging nettle soup the next time you come for dinner, but usually their sting is quicker and more vocal than that and they will just tell you exactly what they think. If they tell you it's good, then you will know you have prepared a triumph.

But don't let a fear of failure put you off; Scorpios would rather have an interesting disaster than a boring success, and although they are symbolized by the scorpion, they are also represented by the phoenix that rises triumphant from the ashes. Their criticism will be constructive and given only in the hope that something better will take its place the next time they come by. This is the sign of death and rebirth.

The cycle of death and rebirth is also echoed in the time of the year that Scorpio rules, when the leaves have fallen from the trees and the air is crisp and barren. It is the death of the year that makes new beginnings possible, when the season is fixed; and it suggests someone who is quite definite about his or her likes and dislikes. Scorpios like to move forward and try new ideas, they have varied tastes and are quite prepared to try new experiments, and they also tend to have strong constitutions. So it does take quite a bad meal really to upset them.

It's a good idea to have a healthy amount of food and drink on the table for your Scorpio guests as they tend to have very good appetites and are inclined to be excessive. Having provided all these delights you shouldn't have to worry about the harmonious atmosphere. Scorpios are quite magnetic and have strong characters and are likely to draw other people to them.

Greet your Scorpio guests with a good red wine and delightful aromas. Feed them luxury and exotica, and you will be most unlikely to ever see their stings. Or match their secretive nature with hidden treasures such as Summer Pudding or a concealed pie, or a fish covered in a delicious sauce. Foods that contain their cell salt—sulphate of lime—such as prunes and onions, are also a good idea, as well as strong and pungent foods that really leave them feeling they have eaten.

Smoked Trout Pâté

Smoked trout pâté is a delightful blend of flavors. Very pale pink, scattered with green chopped chives, the dish is attractive and an easy one to prepare—a good starter or lunch dish served with a Greek Salad (see page 266). *Serves 6*

> *2 smoked trout*
> *2 tsp horseradish*
> *1 cup (1/2 lb; 225 g) cream cheese*
> *1/4 lb tomatoes, peeled*
> *2 Tb lemon juice*
> *1/2 small onion, peeled and grated*
> *1 small clove garlic, peeled and pushed through a press*
> *1 Tb chopped fresh chives*
> *Salt and black pepper*

<u>Garnishes</u>
> *Rounds of toast*
> *Butter*

Skin, bone, and flake the fish. Place it in a blender or food processor with the horseradish, cream cheese, tomatoes, lemon juice, onion, and garlic, and purée until smooth. Turn the mixture into a bowl and fold in the chives. Season to taste with salt and black pepper. Pack the pâté into one or two bowls and chill in the refrigerator overnight or until cold. Serve with rounds of toast and butter.

Asparagus Wrapped in Parma Ham

Asparagus Wrapped in Parma Ham makes an exotic starter for the early summer months and a good dish for Scorpios, who love the luxurious things in life. Serve it with champagne or a delicious chilled white wine, or if you prefer wrap the asparagus in smoked salmon (for 1 pound of asparagus use 1/2 pound of wafer-thin slices of smoked salmon). *Serves 4*

> *1 lb (450 g) asparagus (about 12 good-size spears)*
> *12 wafer-thin slices (about 12 oz; 340 g) Parma ham*

<u>Garnishes</u>
> *A bowl of mayonnaise (see page 59)*
> *4 wedges of lemon*
> *Black pepper*
> *Thin slices of whole wheat bread, buttered*

Rinse the asparagus in cold water, peel the stalks (lightly at the top and more deeply as you reach the stems), and trim any remaining woody ends. Place in the top of a steamer, over boiling water, and cover. Steam the asparagus for 5–10 minutes, or until the stems are tender when pierced with a knife. Remove from the heat and set aside to cool. Remove the rind and any surrounding fat from the Parma ham. When the asparagus is cold, wrap each spear (or 2 spears if they are slender) in 1 slice of Parma ham, leaving the tips uncovered. Arrange them on a serving dish or individual dishes, and serve accompanied by a bowl of mayonnaise, wedges of lemon, black pepper, and a plate of buttered whole wheat bread.

Stuffed Peppers

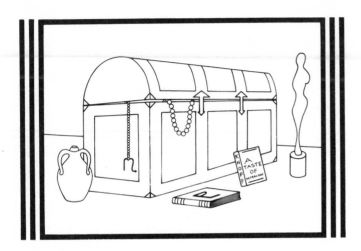

Concealed in these peppers is a host of delectable ingredients, including pine nuts and tuna and a delicate flavoring of basil, making an apt dish for the sign of the zodiac ruled by Pluto— the god of hidden treasures. Serve as a starter for six or as a lunch dish for three, with a mixed salad and chilled white wine. *Serves 6*

Six 4-oz (115-g) green peppers, or a mixture of green and red

1 medium onion, peeled and finely chopped

2 cloves garlic, peeled and pushed through a press

1/2 tsp dried basil, or 1 tsp chopped fresh

1/2 lb (225 g) tomatoes, peeled and chopped

1 cup (2 oz; 60 g) soft whole wheat bread crumbs

1/2 cup (2 1/2 oz; 75 g) pine nuts

1 medium egg, beaten

One 7-oz (200-g) can tuna fish, drained and flaked

1 cup (2 oz; 60 g) grated Cheddar cheese

Salt and black pepper to taste

Preheat the oven to 375°F (190°C; gas 5).

Cut the tops off the peppers, cut out the seeds and whitish membrane, and discard. If necessary, trim the bottoms so that they will stand upright, but be sure not to cut a hole in the bottom. Bring a large pan of water to a boil, drop in the peppers, cover, and cook for 5 minutes; thoroughly drain the peppers upside down. While the peppers are cooking, combine all the remaining ingredients in a large mixing bowl and season to taste with salt and black pepper. Divide the stuffing equally among the peppers, and arrange them standing upright in a buttered shallow ovenproof dish. Cook in the oven for 30 minutes, or until the peppers are tender. Serve hot on individual plates.

Eggs in Aspic

Lightly poached eggs lie hidden beneath a layer of consommé and caviar, suggesting the mysteries of the sea. This makes a perfect dish for the sign of the zodiac so fond of mysteries in life and can easily be made ahead of time if necessary. *Serves 4*

> One 14½-oz (411-g) can jellied beef consommé
> 1 Tb sherry
> 4 medium eggs
> 1 Tb vinegar
> Black pepper
> 6 Tb caviar or lumpfish

Thoroughly mix the consommé with the sherry and spoon 2 tablespoons of the mixture into each of 4 ramekins. Place them in the refrigerator for 15 minutes, or until set.

Meanwhile prepare the eggs. Fill a frying pan two-thirds full of water, add the vinegar, and bring to a simmer. Break an egg into a cup and then slip it into the water. Add the remaining eggs in the same way, slipping each one into a different place in the pan. Simmer for 2–3 minutes, spooning the water over the eggs, until the whites have set and the yolks are glazed. Then use a perforated spoon to transfer the eggs to a bowl of cold water, and set aside to cool for a few minutes. When the consommé has set, remove the ramekins from the refrigerator. Using a perforated spoon, lift an egg from the water and let it drain thoroughly. Pat it gently dry, and arrange it on top of the consommé; season to taste with black pepper, and pour over just enough consommé to cover the egg (about 2–3 tablespoons). Repeat this process with the remaining eggs and consommé, return the ramekins to the refrigerator, and leave to chill for about 1 hour, or until the consommé has set. Spread 1½ tablespoons of caviar on the top of the jellied consommé in each dish, glaze with the remaining consommé (about 1½ tablespoons each), and leave to set for about 1 hour, or until you wish to serve.

Leeks in Cheese Sauce

Delicately sweet leeks served in a savory cheese sauce make a very delicious way to begin a meal, or alternatively serve them as a side dish with roasted meats or a plain fish. *Serves 4*

2–2¹/₂ lb (or 8) medium leeks

Cheese sauce
3 Tb (1¹/₂ oz; 45 g) butter
3 Tb (³/₄ oz; 25 g) flour
1¹/₄ cups (¹/₂ Imperial pint) milk
3 cups (6 oz; 180 g) grated Double Gloucester
    or Cheddar cheese
Salt and black pepper

1 cup (2 oz; 60 g) soft whole wheat bread crumbs
1 Tb butter
Cayenne

Cut the roots and tough green ends off the leeks, leaving about 1¹/₂ inches of the green part. Cut a 2¹/₂-inch cross down the remaining green of the leek. Wash them thoroughly, dunking them in and out of cold water, leaf-end down. Then place them in a heavy pan with about ¹/₂ inch of water, just enough so that the leeks will not burn. Cover and simmer for 10–15 minutes, until the leeks are tender.

Preheat the broiler.

When the leeks are nearly ready, prepare the sauce. Melt the butter in a saucepan over low heat, mix in the flour, and, stirring continuously, cook for 2 minutes. Then gradually mix in the milk, stirring until the sauce has thickened and is smooth; bring to a boil and simmer for a few minutes. Thoroughly mix in the cheese until it has melted, remove pan from the heat, and season to taste with salt and black pepper.

When the leeks are tender, drain them thoroughly and arrange them in a fairly shallow ovenproof dish, pour the sauce over, and sprinkle the bread crumbs evenly on top. Dot with the butter and dust lightly with cayenne. Place under a hot broiler, 1¹/₂ inches from the heat element, and cook for 2–3 minutes, or until the top is brown and bubbling. Serve immediately.

Onion Soup

Onions grow in the dark earth—the subterranean world of Pluto—but they have the fiery quality of Mars; they appeal to both the deep emotions and hot nature of Scorpio and served as a soup they are particularly appropriate for this watery sign of the zodiac. *Serves 4*

3 Tb butter

1 lb onions, peeled and thinly sliced

1 clove garlic, peeled and pushed through a press

2 tsp brown sugar

2 cups (16 oz) beef stock

2 cups (16 oz) water

Salt and black pepper

Garnishes

4 slices of Italian or French bread,
    cut ¾ inch thick

1 Tb butter

1 cup (3 oz; 85 g) grated Gruyère or
    Emmenthal cheese

Place the butter in a large saucepan or casserole over moderately high heat. When it has melted mix in the onions, garlic, and sugar, and sauté, stirring continuously, for a few minutes, until the onions have softened slightly, then press the onions flat, turning them as they catch and turn brown, for 5–6 minutes longer, or until a caramel color. Lower the heat to moderately low and pour the beef stock and water over. Cover and simmer for 45 minutes, stirring occasionally. Season to taste with salt and black pepper.

Preheat the broiler. When the soup is nearly ready, place the slices of bread on the broiler rack, 1 inch from the broiler element, and toast one side for 1 minute or until lightly browned. Set aside.

Lower heat in oven to 400°F (200°C; gas 6). Pour soup into an ovenproof tureen or casserole. Spread the untoasted side of the bread with butter and place buttered-side up on the top of the soup. Sprinkle the cheese over the bread, pile it up quite high and let it fall over the edges of the bread if necessary. Place it in the oven for 10 minutes, or until the cheese is bubbling. Serve immediately.

Mushrooms with Horseradish and Bacon

This unusual hors d'oeuvre is a delicious combination of mushrooms and bacon flavored with cream and horseradish. Delicately hot, it also makes a good brunch or lunch dish served on toast and accompanied by a green salad. *Serves 4*

> 5 slices (5 oz) streaky bacon
> 3 Tb (1½ oz; 45 g) butter
> 1 lb (450 g) button mushrooms, wiped clean
> ¼ cup (2 oz) heavy or double cream
> 2 Tb chopped fresh chives
> 1 Tb horseradish
> Salt and black pepper
> ¼ tsp cayenne

Garnishes

> 4 slices hot toast, cut in half
> Butter

Remove the rind from the bacon and cut it into 1-inch pieces. Place a frying pan over high heat, add the bacon, and cook, stirring and turning, for 5–6 minutes, or until crisp and golden. Drain the bacon, set aside, and pour off the fat from the pan. Reduce heat to moderately high, add the butter to the pan, and when it has melted add the mushrooms. Sauté, stirring occasionally, for 5 minutes, or until the mushrooms are tender. Remove to a separate dish and set aside. Turn the heat to low and mix in the cream, chives, and horseradish, and simmer for 1 minute, then add the bacon and mushrooms to heat through. Season to taste with salt and black pepper. Turn onto a warmed serving dish, dust with cayenne, and serve either on buttered toast or accompanied by rounds of toast.

Chicken Livers with Marsala

Chicken livers flavored with Marsala have a soft, almost melting texture; they go perfectly with fried bread and a green salad, and are so uncomplicated that they can be prepared in minutes to make a delectable lunch or supper dish for the family. Offal is particularly suitable for this sign of the zodiac, since it lies buried in the body and relates to the god Pluto, who is concerned with all undersurface activities. *Serves 4*

> 1½ lb chicken livers
> 4 slices of white bread
> 4½ Tb (2¼ oz) sunflower or vegetable oil
> 4½ Tb (2¼ oz) butter
> Salt and black pepper
> ¼ cup (2 oz) Marsala, port, or sweet sherry

Rinse the livers in cold water and pat dry with a paper towel. Trim any skin, veins, and greenish spots from the livers, and set aside.

Remove the crusts from the bread and cut each slice into 4 triangles. Place 1½ tablespoons each of oil and butter in a large frying pan over high heat. When the butter and oil are bubbling, add 8 triangles of bread to the pan and sauté for 1–2 minutes on each side, or until golden. Remove to a paper towel and keep warm. Heat the same amount of oil and butter in the pan and continue to cook the remaining bread in the same way. Transfer to a paper towel and keep warm.

Reduce the heat to moderate, add the remaining butter and oil to the pan, and when they begin to bubble add the chicken livers and sauté 3–5 minutes on each side, or until browned on the outside but still pink in the middle. Season to taste with salt and black pepper. Transfer the livers to a shallow serving dish and keep warm. Increase the heat slightly and pour the Marsala into the pan, stir it around to blend it with the pan juices, and let it bubble for about 3 minutes, or until it has reduced but is not a syrup. Pour the Marsala over the chicken livers, decorate the edges of the dish with bread slices with their points sticking upward, and serve.

Pork with Orange and Cashew Nuts

Persephone was gathering flowers in a meadow when Pluto emerged from an opening in the earth in his golden chariot and stole her for his bride, at the same time taking a herd of pigs. This pork dish has a delicate aroma of oranges, which is complemented by the tender pork and nutty cashews; serve it with buttered noodles, Broccoli in Garlic Sauce (see page 190), and a good red wine. *Serves 4*

5 Tb (1½ oz; 45 g) flour
Salt and black pepper
2 lb (900 g) shoulder of pork, trimmed of any fat
*   and cut into 1-inch cubes*
4 Tb sunflower or vegetable oil
1 medium onion, peeled and thinly sliced
1 clove garlic, peeled and pushed through a press
Rind of 1 orange, without pith
6 Tb (3 oz) orange juice
2 cups chicken stock
1 Tb Worcestershire
½ cup plus 2 Tb (2½ oz; 70 g) whole raw
*   cashew nuts*

Preheat the oven to 350°F (180°C; gas 4).

Mix the flour with 1 teaspoon of salt and ¼ tsp black pepper. Roll the pork in the flour and shake off any excess. Heat 2 tablespoons of oil in a frying pan over high heat. Very quickly brown half the meat on each side, turning it to seal the juices. (Do this in batches so you don't crowd the pan.) Add the remaining oil to the pan and brown the rest of the meat in the same way. Transfer the meat to a casserole and add the sliced onion to the pan juices and, stirring continuously, sauté for 3 minutes, or until golden.

PORK WITH ORANGE AND CASHEW NUTS, CONTINUED

Add the onion to the casserole with the garlic, orange rind, orange juice, and stock, and stir so that it is well mixed. Cover and place in the oven for 1¼ hours, or until the meat is tender. Then mix in the Worcestershire and cashew nuts and cook 10 minutes longer. Transfer to a warmed serving plate that is not completely flat and serve.

Shrimp Creole

Shrimp Creole makes a tempting dinner-party dish and is delicious served with a bowl of boiled rice, a green salad, and a very cold white wine.
Serves 4

> *1 small (3–4-oz) green pepper*
> *1 Tb sunflower or vegetable oil*
> *2 Tb butter*
> *1 medium onion, peeled and thinly sliced*
> *2 cloves garlic, peeled and thinly sliced*
> *½ tsp dried thyme, or 1 tsp chopped fresh*
> *½ tsp dried oregano, or 1 tsp chopped fresh*
> *1 bay leaf*
> *2 Tb flour*
> *One 28-oz (400-g) can Italian tomatoes*
> *1 tsp superfine or castor sugar*
> *¼ cup (2 oz) white wine or dry sherry*
> *1 lb peeled raw shrimp*
> *Salt and black pepper*
> *¼ cup (2 oz) heavy or double cream*
> *2 Tb chopped fresh parsley*

Quarter the pepper lengthwise, remove the seeds, stalk, and whitish membrane, and slice it thinly. In a large pan, heat the oil and butter over moderately low heat. Mix in the onion and sauté, stirring occasionally, for 15 minutes, or until the onion is nearly soft. Then mix in the green pepper, garlic, thyme, oregano, and bay leaf and cook about 8 minutes longer, or until the pepper is soft. Add the flour and cook, stirring constantly, for 2–3 minutes to absorb the oil. Gradually stir in the tomatoes and sugar, increase the heat slightly, bring to a simmer, cover, and cook 10 minutes longer. Remove the lid and stir in the white wine or sherry, and when the mixture is simmering, stir in the shrimp. Cook for 3–5 minutes, or until the shrimp turn pink, and season to taste with salt and black pepper. While the shrimp are cooking, turn the cream into a small saucepan and heat through. Turn the Shrimp Creole into a warmed tureen. Swirl in the cream so it looks decorative and is not completely mixed in, sprinkle the parsley over, and serve.

Poached Eel with Parsley Sauce

The constellation of Scorpio was depicted in ancient times as a snake that curled around Scorpio, but that stretched from Libra to Sagittarius. Conger eel is a snakelike sea fish, with a slippery skin and a sweet and delicate flesh that is particularly delicious coated in a parsley sauce and served with mashed or boiled potatoes and carrots. *Serves 4*

Court bouillon
> *2 cups (16 oz) water*
> *1/2 cup (4 oz) white wine*
> *1 medium onion, peeled and quartered*
> *6 cloves*
> *Few sprigs of parsley*
> *10 black peppercorns*

> *One 2-lb conger eel, skinned and filleted*

Parsley sauce
> *2 Tb butter*
> *2 Tb flour*
> *1¼ cups (10 oz) milk*
> *1/4 cup (2 oz) heavy or double cream*
> *1/2 cup plus 2 Tb chopped fresh parsley*
> *Salt and black pepper*

Place all the court bouillon ingredients in a large saucepan, bring to a boil, cover, and simmer for 5 minutes. Then add the eel, cover, and simmer for 20 minutes, or until it is just cooked.

While the eel is cooking, prepare the sauce. Place the butter in a pan over moderately low heat. When it has melted, mix in the flour and stir continuously for 2 minutes. Gradually stir in the milk and cream and continue to stir until the

POACHED EEL WITH PARSLEY SAUCE, CONTINUED

mixture has thickened to a smooth sauce. Simmer for a few minutes, then remove from the heat. Mix in the parsley and season to taste with salt and black pepper. Thoroughly drain the eel and arrange it on a warmed serving dish, pour the sauce over, and serve.

Lobster Salad

Scorpio is symbolized here by a sea scorpion that wanders in the vivid waters armed with its pincers. It has a deliciously flavored and exotic meat, which is served on a bed of salad tossed in a dressing of mayonnaise, chopped spinach, and garlic. *Serves 2*

> *Two 1-lb lobsters, cooked and cut in half lengthwise, the gray brain and black intestine discarded*

Dressing
> *⅔ cup (5 oz) mayonnaise (see page 59)*
> *½ lb (225 g) spinach, cooked, thoroughly drained, and finely chopped*
> *1 clove garlic, peeled and pushed through a press*
> *1 tsp lemon juice*
> *Salt and black pepper*

Arroz con Pollo

3 scallions or spring onions
1 small head of radicchio, washed and dried
1 small head of curly endive, washed and dried
1 small head of chicory, washed and dried

<u>Garnishes</u>
1 Tb chopped fresh chives
Slices of buttered whole wheat bread

Remove the claws of the lobster, crack them with a nutcracker or hammer, and remove all the flesh from them and the lobster shells. Cut the flesh into 3/4-inch cubes and set aside.

In a mixing bowl mix thoroughly the mayonnaise with the spinach, garlic, and lemon juice, and season to taste with salt and black pepper.

Chop the scallions finely crosswise. Shred the radicchio and curly endive, and in a mixing bowl thoroughly combine the scallions, radicchio, curly endive, and chicory with the dressing. (The amount of dressing you need will vary slightly according to the size of the salad.) Arrange the salad in a bowl and place the lobster meat on top. Sprinkle the chives over and serve with slices of buttered whole wheat bread.

Arroz con Pollo is a South American chicken dish that is similar to a paella, only without the seafood. Lightly spiced and full of good things, it makes a tempting and festive meal that is delightful served with a green salad and chilled white Rioja. *Serves 4*

1 large (6-oz; 180-g) green pepper
One 2$\frac{1}{2}$-3-lb chicken, cleaned and cut
    into 8 pieces
Salt
3 Tb (1$\frac{1}{2}$ oz) olive oil
1 Spanish onion, peeled and very finely chopped
2 cloves garlic, peeled and very finely chopped
2 Tb tomato paste
1 bay leaf
1 tsp ground cumin
$\frac{1}{2}$ tsp oregano
$\frac{1}{4}$ tsp saffron, or $\frac{1}{4}$ tsp ground turmeric
3 cups (24 oz) chicken stock
$\frac{1}{2}$ cup (4 oz) dry white wine
1$\frac{3}{4}$ cups (14 oz; 400 g) long-grain rice
$\frac{1}{2}$ lb shelled peas
Black pepper

<u>Garnishes</u>
6–8 oz cooked fresh asparagus
One 7-oz (200-g) can sliced pimiento, drained
4 hard-boiled eggs, peeled and quartered

Cut the green pepper in half and remove the seeds, stalk, and whitish membrane. Then chop it very finely and set aside. Rub the chicken skin with about 1$\frac{1}{2}$ teaspoons of salt. Heat 2 tablespoons of oil in a large frying pan over high

ARROZ CON POLLO, CONTINUED

heat to moderate and mix in the chopped onion, garlic, green pepper, tomato paste, bay leaf, cumin, oregano, and saffron, and sauté for 8 minutes, or until the onion is soft. Turn the contents of the frying pan into the pan with the chicken pieces. Pour the chicken stock and wine over. Bring to a boil, cover, and simmer for 30 minutes. Add the rice, stirring it so that it is thoroughly mixed in, cover, and simmer 15 minutes longer. At this point, mix in the peas (remove the lid if you have a little too much liquid; the rice should absorb nearly all of it in the cooking process). Cook 5 minutes longer, or until the rice and peas are tender, add black pepper to taste, and check the seasoning. Turn onto a large, round warmed serving dish that is not completely flat. Remove the bay leaf and garnish the edges of the dish with asparagus, pimiento, and egg. Sprinkle the remaining oil over and serve hot.

Spiced Eggplant

Dark velvety eggplant flavored with an aromatic blending of spices makes a delicious lunch dish or vegetarian feast served with Mixed Spiced Vegetables (see page 21), rice, and a selection of chutneys. *Serves 3 to 4*

1 lb eggplant or aubergine
Salt
1 small (4-oz; 115-g) red pepper
8 Tb olive oil
1-inch piece of gingerroot, peeled and finely chopped
1 medium onion, sliced
4 cloves garlic, sliced
1/2 tsp ground cumin
1/2 tsp ground coriander
1/2 tsp ground turmeric
1/2 tsp chili powder
1/2 lb (225 g) tomatoes, peeled and chopped
1/2 lb (225 g) mushrooms, wiped clean and sliced
Black pepper

Garnish
A selection of chutneys

Wipe the eggplant clean, trim the ends, and cut it into 1-inch cubes. Place it on a large plate, sprinkle with salt, and leave to sweat for 20 minutes. Wash the red pepper, cut it in half, remove the seeds, stalk, and white membrane, and slice thinly. Meanwhile heat the oil in a fairly large saucepan over moderate heat. When it is hot, mix in the ginger, onion, garlic, and red pepper, and sauté, stirring occasionally, for 8 minutes, or until the vegetables are lightly browned.

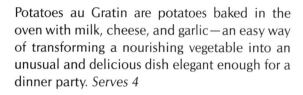

Potatoes au Gratin

Reduce the heat to moderately low, pat the eggplant dry with a paper towel, and add it to the pan with the spices and tomatoes. Stir to mix thoroughly, cover, and cook gently, stirring occasionally for 30 minutes, or until the eggplant is tender. Then add the mushrooms and cook 5 minutes longer. Season to taste with salt and black pepper, turn into a warmed serving dish, and serve with a selection of chutneys.

Potatoes au Gratin are potatoes baked in the oven with milk, cheese, and garlic—an easy way of transforming a nourishing vegetable into an unusual and delicious dish elegant enough for a dinner party. *Serves 4*

> 2 lb potatoes
> 2 cups (16 oz) milk
> 1 large egg
> 1/4 cup (2 oz) light or single cream
> 2 cloves garlic, peeled and pushed through a press
> Salt and black pepper to taste
> 1/2 cup (2 oz; 60 g) grated Gruyère cheese

Butter a 5-cup (2–Imperial pint) fairly shallow ovenproof dish. Preheat the oven to 350°F (180°C; gas 4).

Peel potatoes, rinse them in cold water, quarter them (or cut them into about 1½–2-inch cubes), and place them in a saucepan with the milk and bring to a boil. Cover, and simmer for about 10 minutes, or until the potatoes are not quite cooked. While the potatoes are cooking, in a small bowl beat the egg with the cream, garlic, and seasoning. Then turn the potatoes and the milk they were cooked in into an ovenproof dish. Pour the egg mixture over and evenly sprinkle the cheese on top. Bake for 40–45 minutes, or until the potatoes have absorbed most of the milk and the top is golden brown and bubbling. Serve hot.

Broccoli in Garlic Sauce

Prussian blue broccoli is the color of Scorpio. It suggests the dusk of the day when the green hedgerows have a blue light that moves with shadows and changing images. Dressed in a garlic sauce, with the taste of the Orient, this dish is particularly beneficial for this sign of the zodiac because garlic helps to lower blood cholesterol and fat levels and contains Scorpio's cell salt, sulphate of lime, which has a cleansing effect on the body. *Serves 4*

>   1 lb broccoli
>   1 clove garlic, peeled

Garlic sauce
>   4 Tb (2 oz) olive oil
>   2 Tb soy sauce
>   1 clove garlic, peeled and pushed through a press
>   Black pepper to taste

Thoroughly wash the broccoli in cold water, remove any tough outer leaves, trim the stalks, and slice it into florets. Place the broccoli in the top of a steamer, over boiling water with a clove of garlic in the water, and cover. Steam the broccoli for 5–8 minutes, or until the stems are tender when pierced with a knife.

While the broccoli is cooking, mix the sauce ingredients together in a small bowl or jar. Turn the broccoli into a serving dish, pour the sauce over, and toss so it is well mixed. Serve hot.

Rhubarb Fool

This is a particularly delicious and delicate way of serving rhubarb, as well as being an effortless dish to prepare. And Rhubarb Fool should act as a tonic for this often excessive sign of the zodiac. Although the leaves are poisonous, the wine-pink stems are a good blood purifier. *Serves 6*

>   1½ lb rhubarb, the leaves and ends removed
>   2 Tb orange juice
>   1 cup (8 oz; 225 g) granulated sugar
>   1¼ cups (½ Imperial pint) heavy or double cream
>   Superfine or castor sugar to taste

Garnish
>   Ladyfingers

Wash the rhubarb in cold water and cut it into 2-inch pieces. Place it in a medium-size saucepan with the orange juice and granulated sugar. Bring it to a simmer, cover, and let it cook very gently for 15–20 minutes. When the rhubarb is tender, thoroughly drain it, turn it into a food processor or blender, and purée. Set aside to cool. Put the cream in a bowl and beat so it is just stiff. Fold in the rhubarb purée and mix lightly. Taste for sweetness and add a little superfine (castor) sugar, if necessary. Turn into a glass bowl or individual glass dishes, and chill well before serving. Serve accompanied by ladyfingers.

Summer Pudding

Mixed fruits—dark reds and black—scorpionic and secretive in their encasement of bread, make a favorite for this sign of the zodiac. Summer Pudding (a traditional British pudding) can also be made with other fruits if these are not in season—such as the autumnal blackberry and apple, which are equally suitable for this sign of the zodiac—and should be served with a bowl of thick cream. *Serves 4 to 6*

> 1½ cups (8 oz; 225 g) gooseberries
>
> 1 Tb water
>
> ¾ cup plus 2 Tb (6 oz; 180 g) granulated sugar
>
> ½ cup (4 oz; 115 g) red currants
>
> ½ cup (4 oz; 115 g) black currants
>
> 1½ cups (8 oz; 225 g) raspberries
>
> About 10 medium slices of white bread

Garnish

> *Thick cream*

Lightly butter a 1-quart (32-oz) bowl or dessert basin. Top and tail the gooseberries, and rinse them in cold water. Place them in a fairly large saucepan over low heat with the water and half the sugar, and bring to a simmer. Cover, and cook very gently for about 7 minutes, or until nearly tender. While the gooseberries are cooking, top and tail the red and black currants and rinse them in cold water. Then add all the remaining fruits and sugar to the pan and let them simmer for 2–3 minutes, so that the sugar has melted but the fruits are only just tender. Remove from the heat and set aside.

Remove the crusts from the bread and line the bottom and sides of the bowl, pressing the edges of bread together so that they fit neatly and leave no gaps. Reserve ¼ cup (2 oz) of the fruit juices and turn the fruit and about ¾–1 cup of the remaining juices (enough to fill) into the bread case. Cover the top of the fruit with bread so it fits neatly together and trim any extending bread from the sides. Place on top a small plate or saucer that just fits inside the dish and rests on the top of the pudding, and cover it with a 2–3-lb weight. Chill in the refrigerator for 8 hours or overnight. Turn the pudding out onto a serving dish that is not completely flat (or the juices will overflow), pour the reserved juices over to soak any bread that is still white, and serve with a bowl of thick cream.

Baked Alaska

Baked Alaska relates to the extremes of Pluto, as it combines a light sponge base with a layer of ice cream, which is then coated with meringue, baked in the oven, and served flaming with brandy. You can make the ice cream well in advance, but the cake is best made on the day you wish to eat it. The final preparations must be done at the last minute. *Serves 6 to 8*

Vanilla ice cream

    1¹/2 cups (12 oz) milk

    1 vanilla bean

    4 medium egg yolks

    ¹/3 cup (2¹/2 oz; 75 g) superfine
        or castor sugar

    1¹/4 cups (¹/2 Imperial pint) heavy
        or double cream

    Pinch of salt

Sponge cake

    2 medium eggs

    6 Tb (3 oz; 85 g) superfine or castor sugar

    Pinch of salt

    2 Tb cold water

    ³/4 cup (3¹/2 oz; 105 g) flour

    1 tsp baking powder

    4 Tb apricot jam

Meringue

    5 medium egg whites

    6 Tb (3 oz; 85 g) superfine or castor sugar

    ¹/2 eggshell, reserved

    2 Tb brandy

Prepare the ice cream first. Place the milk and vanilla bean in a saucepan and bring to the simmering point, then remove from the heat and leave to cool for 15 minutes, so the vanilla bean can infuse. Remove the vanilla bean. In the top of a double boiler, mix the egg yolks with the sugar. Place over barely simmering water and pour in the milk. Stir until the mixture has thickened to a custard, then remove from the heat, turn into a bowl, and set aside to cool slightly. Turn the cream into a bowl and beat it until just stiff. Fold in the custard mixture and salt. Turn into an ice tray, and chill in the freezer for 2 hours or until half frozen. (If you have an ice cream maker, make the ice cream following the manufacturer's directions.) Remove the ice cream from the freezer and whisk it with a fork so that the crystallized edges are mixed into the center. Return to the freezer until it is nearly frozen or until you wish to use it.

Meanwhile prepare the sponge cake. Preheat the oven to 350°F (180°C; gas 4). Butter and dust with flour one 8-inch cake pan.

In a mixing bowl, thoroughly beat the eggs until they become a very light color. Thoroughly beat in the sugar and salt, and then the water. In a separate bowl, or on wax paper, toss the flour with the baking powder and then fold lightly into the egg mixture, until they are well mixed in. Turn the batter into the cake pan and bake for 20–25 minutes, or until a knife plunged into the center of the cake comes out clean. Remove from the oven, turn out onto a cake rack, and leave to cool.

While the cake is cooling, remove the ice

Flambé Bananas

cream from the freezer; it needs to be slightly soft so you can shape it. Slice the cake in half and spread the apricot jam over one of the layers. Cover with the remaining layer and place on a round and flat ovenproof dish about 10 inches in diameter. Take a large piece of foil about 2 feet long and lay it evenly over the sponge cake. Spread the ice cream on the foil and shape it to the size of the cake, then wrap the foil over so it is tightly sealed. Return the ice cream to the freezer for several hours, or until completely frozen.

Preheat the oven to 300°F (150°C; gas 2). When the ice cream is hard enough, turn the egg whites into a bowl and beat them until they are nearly stiff, then gradually beat in the sugar until the meringue forms soft peaks. Remove the ice cream from the freezer, peel away the foil, and place the ice cream on top of the sponge cake. Spread the meringue over the entire surface of the ice cream and cake. (The ice cream must be completely covered or it will melt.) Set the eggshell into the center of the meringue so its sides are covered with meringue but it is left open at the top, and bake for 10–15 minutes, or until the meringue is golden. Meanwhile, warm the brandy in a small pan over moderately low heat. Remove the Baked Alaska from the oven, pour the brandy into the eggshell, ignite, and serve flaming.

Golden and orange-red flamed bananas indicate a physical vitality and make a most fitting dish for the sign of the zodiac that burns inwardly with a fiery passion. *Serves 4*

> *4 ripe bananas (about 1½ lb)*
> *2 Tb butter*
> *Grated rind of 1 orange*
> *2 Tb superfine or castor sugar*
> *⅓ cup (2½ oz) Cognac*

Peel the bananas and slice them in half lengthwise. Melt the butter in a fairly large frying pan over moderate heat. When it is hot, add the orange rind and bananas, and sauté for 2 minutes on each side, or until tender. Sprinkle the sugar and the Cognac over. As the liquor begins to bubble, ignite it and remove from the heat. When the flames have died, turn the bananas onto a serving dish with the pan juices over them and serve immediately.

Prune Whip

Prune Whip is a soufflé-like combination of puréed prunes and egg whites that is cooked in the oven and served hot with a custard sauce. This fruit of the fall is appropriately very beneficial for Scorpios, since it is rich in their cell salt, sulphate of lime, which helps to maintain a good skin condition and eliminate impurities from the blood. *Serves 4 to 6*

1¼ cups (8 oz; 225 g) dried prunes
2 cups (16 oz) cold tea
1 Tb lemon juice
³⁄₈ cup (3 oz; 85 g) superfine or castor sugar
¼ cup (2 oz) light or single cream
4 medium egg whites

Custard
4 medium egg yolks
3 Tb brown sugar
1 cup (8 oz) milk
2 Tb sweet sherry

Preheat the oven to 300°F (150°C; gas 2).

Soak the prunes for 8 hours or overnight in a medium-size bowl with 1–2 inches of cold tea to cover. Then turn the prunes into a saucepan with the tea they were soaked in, bring to a boil, cover, and simmer for 20 minutes, or until tender. Drain the prunes and set aside to cool slightly, then remove the pits. Turn the pitted prunes, lemon juice, superfine sugar, and cream into a food processor or blender, and purée. In a bowl beat the egg whites stiff. Pour the prune mixture down the side of the bowl in which the egg whites were beaten and gently fold in the egg whites until they are thoroughly mixed. Turn into a 5- or 6-cup soufflé dish. Place it in a pan of cold water and cook for 65–70 minutes, or until the whip has risen and cooked.

While the prune whip is cooking, prepare the custard. In the top of a double boiler mix the egg yolks with the brown sugar. Place over barely simmering water and stir in the milk. Stir continuously until the mixture thickens to a custard. Then remove from the heat and stir in the sherry. When the whip is cooked, serve it immediately with a bowl of custard.

Chocolate Cheesecake

A cheesecake with the darkness and richness of Pluto's underground dwelling. Smooth, light, and creamy, Chocolate Cheesecake is perfectly complemented by the ginger base it rests on. *Serves 8*

Crumb crust

    8 oz (225 g; about 22) gingersnaps

    2 tsp ground ginger

    5 Tb (2½ oz; 75 g) melted butter

    3 Tb water

    1 Tb plus ½ tsp gelatin

    1 cup (7 oz; 200 g) semisweet chocolate chips or drops

    3 Tb milk

    2 medium egg yolks

    ½ cup (4 oz; 115 g) superfine or castor sugar

    2 cups (1 lb; 450 g) cream cheese

    ½ cup (4 oz) heavy or double cream

    Few drops of vanilla

    2 medium egg whites

Garnish

    ¼ cup (1 oz; 30 g) grated semisweet chocolate

In a food processor or with a rolling pin, crush the gingersnaps. (If you are not using a food processor, turn the crushed gingersnaps into a bowl.) Thoroughly mix in the ground ginger and butter. Press the mixture into the bottom of a 10-inch pie pan or springform pan, and leave to chill while you make the filling.

    Pour the water into a small saucepan, sprinkle the gelatin over, and leave to soak for 5 minutes. While the gelatin is soaking, put the chocolate drops and milk in the top of a double boiler.

Place over barely simmering water and stir occasionally until the chocolate has melted. Remove the chocolate from the heat and set aside. Place the gelatin and water over low heat and stir occasionally until the gelatin has melted (do not allow it to boil or the gelatin will not set). Set aside to cool slightly. In a large bowl or food processor thoroughly mix the egg yolks, sugar, and cream cheese; then, when the chocolate and gelatin have cooled but are still liquid enough to pour, beat or process them into the cheese mixture. In a separate bowl, beat the cream with the vanilla until just stiff and fold in the cheese mixture. In a fresh bowl, with clean beaters, beat the egg whites until they form peaks. Using a metal spoon, fold the beaten whites into the cheesecake mixture, then turn into the crumb crust. Chill for a few hours or overnight. Just before you serve it—unmolded or not as you please—dust the surface evenly with grated chocolate.

SAGITTARIUS

NOVEMBER 23–DECEMBER 21

Rules the ninth house, the house of philosophy, religion, and higher education

RULING PLANET
Jupiter
↗

ELEMENT
Fire
↗

QUALITIES
Mutable, active
↗

CHARACTERISTICS
Adaptable, adventurous, expansive, frank,
jovial, optimistic
↗

OPPOSITE SIGN
Gemini
↗

BODY AREA
Thighs
↗

GEMSTONE
Blue quartz, lapis lazuli
↗

COLOR
Blue
↗

FLAVOR
Sweet, fragrant, spicy, strong
↗

METAL
Tin
↗

FAUNA
Game birds, hare,
rabbit, venison
↗

FLORA
Apricots, asparagus, chestnuts, currants, figs, juniper berries, limes,
maple, olives, pears, strawberries, sugarcane
↗

HERBS AND SPICES
Balm, borage, cloves, marjoram,
myrrh, saffron, sage
↗

CELL SALT
Silica (Silicic. Oxide), found in fruit fiber,
vegetables, whole-meal bread, cereals
↗

SAGITTARIUS THE COOK

Sagittarians are not always the greatest cooks, but they are wonderful homemakers and entertainers, as well as being a very sociable sign of the zodiac that loves to have an audience.

Sagittarians are ruled by the planet Jupiter, and this sign of the zodiac is concerned with expansion and growth. Changing shape and form like a vast sea, Jupiter, whose Greek name was Zeus, continually alters his shape and form, becoming a bull, a shower of gold, and then a swan, as the mood and desire take him. As cooks, Sagittarians work intuitively; they like to feel free and are unlikely to be restricted by following a recipe. Unknown territories, new forms, and complete freedom of expression are what interest them, and their optimistic nature will allow them to quite happily tackle dishes other signs wouldn't touch.

Fortunately, Sagittarians' ruling planet, Jupiter, is the god of good fortune, and culinary disasters are often avoided by a stroke of luck. If they are not, Sagittarians won't be discouraged—they are much more interested in the process than the end result anyway, and they have the ability to make the best of awkward situations.

This sign of the zodiac is the play actor who loves to hold court. He or she is the joker and clown who will play the fool in order to keep everyone amused. Sagittarius is a dual sign of the zodiac, and the other face of the clown can be awkward and moody. Moderation is something that this sign seldom experiences, and he or she will have a tendency to overindulge in food and drink (especially drink), or to totally abstain, as well as experiencing great emotional extremes. This duality is symbolized by the centaur, who represents this sign of the zodiac— the mythical creature who is half man and half horse. He is the archer who shoots his arrows into the sky and gallops after them, suggesting the true vision and idealism of Sagittarius, which is hampered by earthly limitations.

Foreign smells may escape from the Sagittarian's kitchen, because this sign rules the ninth house of the zodiac, which is concerned with long-distance travel, and Sagittarians are fond of adventure and new experiences. It is also probably wise to stay clear of the kitchen while they are cooking if you want to eat well, because they can be easily distracted. They are excellent at cooking several dishes at the same time but can be quite bad at finishing any of them and attending to details.

Dinner at a Sagittarian's home should be an excursion. This sign of the zodiac will greet you with great warmth and make you feel quite at home, so you will feel at ease as he or she takes terrible risks with your dinner.

RECIPES FOR SAGITTARIUS

MENU SUGGESTIONS FOR SAGITTARIUS

First Courses

Fish Chowder
Asparagus and Chicken Salad
Scrambled Eggs with Smoked Salmon
Taramosalata
Beef Satay with Peanut Sauce
Deep-fried Mushrooms with Tartar Sauce
Monkfish and Bacon Kebabs

Main Courses

Meatballs with Mushroom Sauce
Roast Pheasant and Bread Sauce
Paella Formenterra
Pizza
Spiced Kidneys
Rabbit Stew
Shrimp and Spinach Curry

Side Dishes

Eggplant all'Uovo
Brussels Sprouts with Chestnuts

Desserts

Chestnut Soufflé
Strawberry Tart
Rummed Maple Pudding
Ginger Cream Loaf
Pears in Zabaglione
Tropical Fruit Salad

Fish Chowder
Spiced Kidneys
Pears in Zabaglione

⟳

Beef Satay with Peanut Sauce
Shrimp and Spinach Curry
Tropical Fruit Salad

⟳

Scrambled Eggs with Smoked Salmon
Roast Pheasant and Bread Sauce
Strawberry Tart

⟳

Taramosalata
Meatballs with Mushroom Sauce
Rummed Maple Pudding

⟳

Deep-fried Mushrooms with Tartar Sauce
Paella Formenterra
Tropical Fruit Salad

⟳

Asparagus and Chicken Salad
Pizza
Chestnut Soufflé

⟳

Monkfish and Bacon Kebabs
Rabbit Stew
Ginger Cream Loaf

SAGITTARIUS THE GUEST

If you invite a Sagittarian to dinner you shouldn't have to worry about how you are going to keep your guests entertained and cook the dinner at the same time, because your Sagittarian friend will quite happily do the entertaining for you—that is, if he or she arrives on time (this sign of the zodiac is often hours late).

If it was a quiet, relaxing evening that you had in mind, it would be a good idea to cross a Sagittarian off the invitation list because they like to make a lot of noise, even though they can be quite shy. This is a frank and outspoken sign of the zodiac, who often says the wrong thing without intending to offend; it's just that they speak first and think later. Yet surprisingly enough, a Sagittarian frequently is the most popular person at the party because of his or her whole-hearted enthusiasm for the present and love of being surrounded by people.

Try to keep Sagittarians out of the kitchen if possible—they tend to have the omnipresence of their ruling planet, Jupiter, and appear to be in every room at the same time—but if you can't, just keep them away from the food. Sagittarians are very accident-prone, and if you hand them the tart you spent all afternoon executing perfectly, they are quite likely to drop it. They frequently make embarrassing blunders, because of their straightforward and impulsive approach to life, but they have the miraculous art of charming themselves out of any awkward situation they may create.

Sagittarius is a fire sign, and it embodies all the warmth and feeling of its element, making people of this sign of the zodiac wonderful mixers.

They are often the life and soul of a dinner party and will probably have had conversations with all your other guests by the time they finally leave—usually last.

Sagittarius is a mutable sign of the zodiac—the changing season from autumn to winter—and in a similar way it has a changeable and dual personality. However, as host you are unlikely to see anything but the sunny and playful nature of your Sagittarian guests. But if you want to be sure to keep them happy, feed them foods that will appeal to their sense of adventure such as a paella, a Malaysian dish, or an exotic salad from the tropics, full of soft, rich fruits and pleasant smells that reflect the nature of their ruling planet, Jupiter. Or alternatively, try a hot, spicy, and colorful curry to match their fiery nature, and make sure you have plenty of wine to go with the food, because this is a very thirsty sign. Sagittarians are also outdoor people who love picnics and the ritual of eating, so if it is warm enough for you to have a barbecue, they will have a wonderful time.

Sagittarians make very rewarding guests; their big appetites for life are matched by their enjoyment of food and drink. They also like to be where they feel the action is, and you will probably have an unforgettable evening with a need for a good rest before you invite one of them again.

Fish Chowder

Fish Chowder is a replenishing soup, which relates to the mutable and watery nature of this sign of the zodiac, whose ruling planet, Jupiter, is sympathetic to and exalted in the watery sign of Cancer. *Serves 6*

1 Tb butter
1 Tb sunflower or vegetable oil
2 medium onions, peeled and finely chopped
1 lb new potatoes
1¾ cups (14 oz) water or fish stock
Salt and black pepper
1½ cups (12 oz) milk
1 lb cod or haddock fillet, skinned
One 3⅔-oz (105-g) can smoked mussels or oysters
1 Tb chopped fresh parsley

<u>Garnish</u>
A loaf of whole wheat bread, warmed in the oven

Place the butter and oil in a fairly large pan over moderately low heat, and when they begin to bubble mix in the onions. Sauté, stirring occasionally, for 8–10 minutes, or until soft. While the onions are cooking, scrub the potatoes, rinse them in cold water, and cut them into cubes of about ¾–1 inch. Add the potatoes to the pan, turning them in the onion mixture, then cover with the water or fish stock. Season to taste with salt and black pepper. Cover, and simmer for 10–15 minutes, or until the potatoes are tender. Mix in the milk, cod, and smoked mussels or oysters. Bring to a simmer, cover, and cook gently for 8 minutes longer, or until the fish is cooked. Check the seasoning and turn into a warmed soup tureen. Sprinkle the parsley over and serve accompanied by a warmed loaf of whole wheat bread.

Asparagus and Chicken Salad

Asparagus and Chicken Salad makes a nourishing hors d'oeuvre for eight or a lunch or supper dish for four. It is a good way of using up leftover chicken or potato, and the interesting Spanish-style combination of fruits and vegetables should appeal to one so fond of variety in life. A chilled white Rioja goes best with this salad. *Serves 8*

1/2–1 lb (225–450 g) fresh asparagus

1/2 cup (2 1/2 oz; 70 g) golden raisins or sultanas

1 crisp eating apple

2 Tb lemon juice

6 Tb mayonnaise (see page 59)

2 cloves garlic, peeled and pushed through a press

2 ribs of celery, ends and strings removed, chopped

15 green olives, pitted and sliced

2 cups (10 oz; 285 g) cooked and cubed new potatoes

Salt and black pepper

1 heart of lettuce, washed and dried

2 cups (10 oz; 285 g) shredded cooked chicken

Garnishes

6 small leaves radicchio, washed and dried

4 hard-boiled eggs, peeled and quartered

Mayonnaise (see page 59)

Rinse the asparagus in cold water, peel the stalks, lightly near the top and more deeply as you reach the bases, and trim off any remaining woody ends. Place in the top of a steamer, over boiling water, and cover. Steam the asparagus for 5–10 minutes, or until the stems are tender when pierced with a knife. Remove from the heat and set aside to cool. While the asparagus is cooking, place the raisins in a small bowl, cover them with water, and let them soak for about 5 minutes, to plump them. Peel, core, and cube the apple, then place the pieces in a large bowl and sprinkle on 1 tablespoon of lemon juice. Mix the mayonnaise thoroughly with the remaining lemon juice and garlic, and add it to the apple, along with the celery, olives, and potatoes. Drain the raisins, pat them dry, and mix them in. Season to taste with salt and black pepper. Arrange the lettuce on the bottom of a salad bowl and place the mayonnaise mixture on top. Cover with the shredded chicken and then the asparagus. Garnish the edges of the bowl with a few radicchio leaves and egg quarters, and serve with a bowl of mayonnaise.

Scrambled Eggs with Smoked Salmon

Scrambled eggs are one of the finest ways of preparing eggs; cooked in a way similar to Escoffier's recipe, the famous French chef who was known as "the king of chefs and the chef of kings," and served on smoked salmon, they make an unbeatable brunch dish or starter—ideal for this majestic sign of the zodiac. They are best served with rounds of hot toast. *Serves 4*

> ½ lb (225 g) wafer-thin slices of smoked salmon
>
> 4 Tb (2 oz; 60 g) butter
>
> 6 medium eggs, lightly beaten
>
> ¼ tsp salt
>
> ⅛ tsp black pepper
>
> 2 Tb (1 oz) light or single cream

Garnish
> Rounds of hot buttered toast

Arrange the smoked salmon equally over 4 plates.

Place 2 tablespoons of butter in a pan over low heat. When it has melted, add the eggs and seasonings, and stir continuously until the eggs have a smooth and creamy consistency. When they are nearly cooked, remove them from the heat, as they will continue to cook in the pan. Blend in the remaining butter and the cream. Spoon an equal amount of scrambled eggs over each plate of smoked salmon. Serve immediately with rounds of hot buttered toast.

Taramosalata

Taramosalata is a Greek pâté made from smoked fish roe (authentically grey mullet). It is an easy dish to make, requiring little time and no cooking. Soft and creamy pink, it looks most attractive garnished with black olives and flecked with vitamin-rich green parsley. *Serves 6*

> 2 slices (about 2 oz; 60 g) of whole wheat bread, crusts removed
>
> 2 Tb milk
>
> ½ lb (225 g) smoked cod roe
>
> 6 Tb (3 oz) olive oil
>
> 2 Tb lemon juice
>
> 1 clove garlic, peeled and pushed through a press
>
> ½ cup plus 2 Tb (5 oz; ¼ Imperial pint) heavy or double cream
>
> 2 Tb chopped fresh parsley
>
> Black pepper to taste

Garnishes
> Paprika
>
> Black olives
>
> Pita bread warmed in the oven

Place the bread in a shallow dish, sprinkle the milk over, and leave to soak. Using a spoon or knife, scrape the cod roe out of its skin and into a food processor or blender. Add the olive oil, lemon juice, garlic, and soaked bread, and purée until smooth. Beat the cream until it thickens but is not stiff. Turn the cod roe mixture into a bowl and fold in the cream and parsley until well mixed. Season with black pepper. Turn into a serving dish, sprinkle with paprika, and garnish with a few black olives. Serve with hot pita bread.

Beef Satay with Peanut Sauce

Beef Satay is a Malaysian dish made up of bite-size pieces of beef, first marinated in spiced coconut milk, then broiled and served on a skewer with a spicy peanut sauce. It is a dish to stimulate the palate at the start of a meal, which will appeal to the Sagittarian sense of fun, adventure, and love of travel. *Serves 4*

Marinade

1 cup (8 oz) canned coconut milk

1 tsp ground ginger

1 tsp ground turmeric

1 tsp ground cumin

1 tsp brown sugar

Salt and black pepper to taste

2 cloves garlic, peeled and pushed through a press

1 lb lean beef, cut into 3/4-inch cubes and trimmed of fat

Peanut sauce

1 small clove garlic, peeled and pushed through a press

1/2 cup (2 oz; 60 g) roasted peanuts, very finely chopped

1/4 tsp chili powder

1/2 cup (4 oz) water

1 tsp brown sugar

1 Tb dark soy sauce

1 tsp lime or lemon juice

Garnish

1/2 small cucumber, wiped clean and cut into 3/4-inch cubes

In a small bowl or jar thoroughly mix the marinade ingredients. Arrange the meat in one layer in a shallow dish and pour the marinade over. Let it marinate for 1 1/2–2 hours. Meanwhile, prepare the sauce.

Place all the sauce ingredients in a pan over moderately low heat, and let bubble for about 5 minutes, stirring and turning continuously, until the liquid has reduced and you have a smooth sauce. Turn into a shallow bowl and set aside to cool.

Preheat the broiler.

Drain the meat, reserving the marinade, and arrange it evenly on eight 4-inch skewers. Place them 3 inches from the broiler element, pour over a little of the marinade, and cook, turning and pouring a little of the marinade over every 2–3 minutes, for 15–20 minutes, or until the meat is cooked. Serve immediately, accompanied by the peanut sauce and cubes of cucumber.

Deep-fried Mushrooms with Tartar Sauce

Succulent, silky-textured mushrooms coated with crisp golden bread crumbs make a tempting way to begin a meal and are satisfyingly complemented by a piquant tartar sauce. *Serves 4*

Tartar sauce
- 1/2 cup mayonnaise (see page 59)
- 1/2 tsp dried tarragon, or 1 tsp chopped fresh
- 2 tsp chopped capers
- 1 finely chopped baby gherkin
- 1 tsp lemon juice
- 2 tsp grated onion
- Salt and black pepper to taste

- 2 medium eggs
- 1 clove garlic, peeled and pushed through a press
- 1 Tb grated Parmesan
- Salt and freshly ground black pepper
- 2/3 cup (3 oz; 85 g) very fine dry bread crumbs
- 1/2 lb (225 g) mushrooms, wiped clean
- Vegetable or sunflower oil

Garnishes
- 1 lemon, cut into 4 wedges
- Thin slices of buttered whole wheat bread

In a small bowl mix together thoroughly the tartar sauce ingredients and set aside.

In a bowl, beat the eggs with the garlic and grated Parmesan, and season to taste with salt and black pepper. Cover a large plate or wooden board with the bread crumbs, dip the mushrooms in the egg mixture, and then roll them in the bread crumbs so they have an even covering on all sides. Pour 1/4 inch oil into a frying pan, place over high heat, and when the oil is hot, lower the heat to moderately high. Add the mushrooms to the pan, and sauté for 5 minutes, turning frequently so they brown evenly on all sides. Transfer them to a paper towel to drain off any excess fat, and then arrange them on a warmed serving dish. Serve hot with tartar sauce, wedges of lemon, and slices of buttered whole wheat bread.

Monkfish and Bacon Kebabs

These kebabs, suggesting the well-aimed arrows of the archer who symbolizes this sign of the zodiac, are a delightful blend of flavors. A good outdoors dish for the hot summer months when the freedom-loving Sagittarian will feel perfectly at home tending to the curling flames of the barbecue. *Serves 5*

1½ lb monkfish, skinned

Marinade
6 Tb (3 oz) olive oil
3 Tb (1½ oz) lemon juice
1 tsp Dijon mustard
1 tsp superfine or castor sugar
2 cloves garlic, peeled and pushed through a press
Salt and black pepper to taste

10 oz (about 10 slices) bacon
20 button mushrooms, wiped clean

Remove the bone from the monkfish and cut the fish into about twenty 1-inch cubes. In a small bowl or jar, mix the marinade ingredients thoroughly together. Place the fish cubes in a shallow dish and pour the marinade over and let sit for 20 minutes. While the fish is marinating, remove the rind from the bacon and cut each slice in half, or into about 4-inch lengths. Break off the stems from the mushrooms and discard or use for another dish. Drain the fish, reserving the marinade, and wrap 1 piece of bacon around each piece of fish. Divide the fish and mushrooms evenly among five 7–8-inch skewers.

Preheat the broiler.

Place the kebabs on the broiler rack, 3 inches

from the element, pour over a little of the marinade, and cook, turning and pouring a little of the marinade over every 2–3 minutes, for 15–20 minutes, or until the bacon begins to sizzle and the fish and mushrooms are cooked. Serve immediately.

Meatballs with Mushroom Sauce

Delicious meatballs with a subtle and creamy sauce make a satisfying dish served with plenty of red Italian wine, a large bowl of noodles or boiled potatoes, and a crisp green salad. *Serves 4 to 6*

Mushroom sauce

    5 Tb (2½ oz) butter
    ¼ lb (115 g) mushrooms, wiped clean
        and chopped
    1 Tb tomato paste
    Pinch of dried sage, or ¼ tsp chopped fresh
    4 Tb (1 oz; 35 g) flour
    1¼ cups (½ Imperial pint) beef stock
    ¾ cup (6 oz) light or single cream
    ½ cup (4 oz) sherry
    Salt and black pepper to taste

Meatballs

    1½ lb ground beef chuck
    2 cups (4 oz; 115 g) soft whole wheat
        bread crumbs
    2 medium eggs, lightly beaten
    1 medium onion, peeled and very finely chopped
    2 cloves garlic, peeled and pushed through a press
    1 Tb chopped fresh parsley
    ½ tsp ground coriander
    ½ tsp ground ginger
    Pinch of nutmeg
    Salt and black pepper to taste

    ½ cup (2 oz; 60 g) very fine dry bread crumbs
    2 Tb butter
    2 Tb sunflower or vegetable oil

First, prepare the mushroom sauce. Melt 2 tablespoons of butter in a small saucepan over moderately low heat. Add the mushrooms, tomato paste, and sage, and sauté, stirring occasionally, until the mushrooms are tender (about 5–6 minutes). Remove from the heat and set aside. Melt the remaining butter over moderately low heat, mix in the flour, and, stirring continuously, cook for 2 minutes. Gradually stir in the beef stock, cream, and sherry, until you have a smooth sauce. Bring to a boil and cook for a few minutes. Stir in the mushroom mixture and add salt and black pepper. Cover and set aside while you prepare the meatballs.

In a large bowl, mix thoroughly the meatball ingredients and season with salt and black pepper. Shape into little balls about 1½ inches in diameter. Spread the bread crumbs over a wooden board and roll the meatballs in them to coat all over. Heat 1 tablespoon each of butter and oil in a frying pan over moderately high heat. Add half of the meatballs, and sauté for 10 minutes, turning often, until they are golden brown and cooked through. Transfer to a paper towel briefly to drain excess fat. Place in a serving dish and keep warm. Cook the remaining meatballs the same way, using the remaining butter and oil.

When all the meatballs are nearly cooked, return the sauce to a moderate heat until it is hot through, then pour it over the meatballs (or into a jug if you would rather have the sauce on the side). Serve hot with a green salad.

Roast Pheasant and Bread Sauce

The pheasant is a magnificent bird, equal in splendor to Jupiter, the king of the gods and Sagittarius' ruling planet. It has a distinctive flavor, which improves if hung for some time before eating, and it is available during the autumn and winter months, making it a most appropriate dish for the hunting sign of the zodiac, symbolized by the archer. Serve this sublime delicacy with Bread Sauce, Brussels Sprouts with Chestnuts (see page 216), and a delicious red wine. *Serves 6*

A brace of pheasants, plucked and drawn

Stuffing
>*1 medium onion, peeled and halved*
>*2 Tb juniper berries, or 4 slices of apple*

>*2 Tb butter*
>*8 slices (1/2 lb; 225 g) streaky bacon, rind removed*
>*Salt and black pepper*
>*1 cup (8 oz) red wine*

Gravy
>*2 Tb flour*
>*3/4 cup (6 oz) water*
>*1/4 cup (2 oz) port or sherry*
>*Salt and black pepper*

>*Bread Sauce (recipe follows)*

Preheat the oven to 375°F (190°C; gas 5).

Stuff each of the birds with half an onion and 1 tablespoon of juniper berries. Skewer to hold the stuffing in and truss to keep the birds intact. Rub them all over with 1 tablespoon of butter each, and cover the breasts with slices of streaky bacon. Season to taste with salt and black pepper and put the birds in a roasting pan just large enough to hold them. Place them in the hot oven and baste every 15 minutes with red wine. Roast for 1–1 1/4 hours, or until no pink juices run out when the birds are pricked with a knife. When the birds are cooked, remove them from the oven onto a platter and keep warm. Meanwhile, prepare the gravy. Skim the fat from the pan juices and discard. Place the roasting pan over moderately low heat. Add the flour, and stir continuously for 2 minutes. Gradually stir in the water and port, bring to a boil, and simmer for a few minutes. Season to taste with salt and black pepper. Turn into a warmed gravy boat and serve with the pheasants and Bread Sauce.

Bread Sauce

Bread Sauce is an ideal accompaniment to most game and poultry dishes and is delicious served with Roast Pheasant. *Serves 6*

>*1 1/2 cups (12 oz) milk*
>*1 medium onion, finely chopped*
>*3 cloves*
>*1 1/2 cups (3 oz; 85 g) soft white bread crumbs*
>*Salt and black pepper*
>*1 1/2 Tb butter*
>*Pinch of cayenne*

Place the milk, chopped onion, and cloves in a saucepan over moderate heat. Bring to a simmer and cook gently for 10 minutes, or until the onion is tender. Turn the heat to very low, mix in the bread crumbs, and cook 15 minutes longer. Season to taste with salt and black pepper. Remove the pan from the heat and mix in the butter and cayenne. Turn into a bowl or pitcher and serve hot.

Paella Formenterra

A dish of paella suggests the heat of a summer day and the pleasure of dining by a sandy beach washed by a caressing sea. This traditional Spanish dish (Spain is ruled by Sagittarius) is ideal for those born under such an expansive sign of the zodiac. They will love the variety and interesting combination of foods that it offers. Serve paella with finger bowls and a bottle of red or white Rioja. *Serves 4*

1/2 lb (225 g) squid
One 4-oz (115-g) green pepper
10 mussels in their shells
4 Tb (2 oz) olive oil
1/2 lb (225 g) pork shoulder, trimmed of fat
   and cut into 1-inch cubes
1 lb chicken legs, skinned and cut into 2-inch
   pieces (with the bone)
1 lb rabbit pieces, skinned and cut into 2-inch
   pieces (with the bone)
1 large ripe tomato, peeled and chopped
2 cloves garlic, peeled and pushed through a press
1¾ cups (14 oz; 400 g) long-grain rice
1 tsp saffron or ground turmeric
3 cups (24 oz) hot chicken stock
1/4 lb (115 g) shelled peas
4–8 Pacific prawns in their shells
4 crab claws, cooked, halved, and cracked
Salt and black pepper

Cut the tentacles and head off the squid and then clean out the sac; remove the bladelike bone and peel off the translucent outer film. Then wash the tentacles and the body in cold water. Chop the tentacles and slice the body

PAELLA FORMENTERRA, CONTINUED

into rings about ½ inch across. Cut the green pepper into fourths lengthwise, remove the stalk, seeds, and whitish membrane, and slice thinly crosswise. Scrub the mussels thoroughly in several changes of cold water and discard any that are open when you finish.

Heat the oil in a very large frying pan or paella pan over moderate heat. Add the pork, chicken, and rabbit, and sauté for 8 minutes, stirring and turning occasionally. Then add the squid, tomato, green pepper, and garlic, and cook 8 minutes longer. Stir the rice and saffron in with the pan ingredients and stir continuously for about 5 minutes. Pour the stock over, bring to a boil, and bubble for 8 minutes, occasionally turning and stirring. Add the mussels, peas, and prawns, and rest the crab claws on the edge of the pan. Cook until the liquid has been absorbed, the prawns turn pink, the mussels have opened, and the rice and peas are cooked. Season to taste with salt and black pepper and serve immediately.

Pizza

Pizzas are best served hot from the oven with a crisp green salad and some Chianti, but they are also delicious cold and can make an excellent dish for a picnic, an activity the outdoors-loving Sagittarian will relish. This pizza has a vegetarian topping that you can vary with pepperoni, anchovies, or a selection of cheeses, as you like.
Serves 4

Dough

> ½ cup plus 2 Tb (5 oz) tepid water
> ½ tsp superfine or castor sugar
> 1 tsp fresh or active dry yeast
> 1½ cups (8 oz; 225 g) flour
> 1 tsp salt
> 1½ tsp olive oil

Topping

> One green pepper (about 4 oz; 115 g)
> 2 cloves garlic, peeled and pushed through a press
> 3 Tb tomato paste
> 1 Tb olive oil
> ½ Spanish onion, peeled and finely chopped
> 7 baby gherkins, sliced in half lengthwise
> ½ lb (225 g) mushrooms, wiped clean and thinly sliced
> 10 oz (285 g) mozzarella, thinly sliced
> 1 Tb chopped fresh marjoram, or 1½ tsp dried
> Salt and black pepper to taste
> 12–15 black olives
> 1 Tb capers

Preheat the oven to 400°F (200°C; gas 6).

First make the pizza dough. Pour the water into a bowl, mix in the sugar, and then sprinkle

Spiced Kidneys

in the yeast. Leave it in a warm place for 5 minutes, until the yeast has dissolved. In a large mixing bowl lightly mix nearly all the flour and salt together. Make a well in the center and fill it with the yeast mixture and oil. Catch the edges of the flour with a fork, until the yeast and oil are all absorbed. Add a little more flour, if necessary, to make a firm dough. Turn the mixture onto a floured wooden board and knead for about 10 minutes, adding a little more flour if necessary, until the dough is elastic. Return the dough to an oiled bowl, cover with plastic wrap, and leave in a warm place for about 1 hour, or until the dough has doubled in size. While the dough is rising, prepare the topping. Cut the green pepper in half lengthwise, remove the stalk, seeds, and whitish membrane, and slice it very thinly cross-wise. Mix the garlic thoroughly with the tomato paste.

When the dough is ready, knead it on a board for a few minutes longer, add more flour if necessary, and then shape it (or roll it) into a 12-inch circle. Place the dough on a lightly greased pizza pan and brush it with the olive oil. Spread a thin layer of the tomato mixture evenly over, and cover it with the onion and then the green pepper slices. Arrange the gherkins and mushrooms over the pepper and completely cover them with the cheese. Season with marjoram and salt and black pepper, and dot with the olives and capers. Place in the oven for 20–25 minutes, or until the cheese has melted and the edges have puffed up and turned golden. Serve hot or cold.

Kidneys in a spicy, creamy tomato sauce make a wonderfully enjoyable and salubrious dish, which should help replenish the Sagittarian's often over-expended energy. Serve hot with a bowl of rice.
Serves 3 to 4

10 lamb kidneys
1/2 medium (about 3 oz; 85 g) green pepper
4 Tb (2 oz) sunflower or vegetable oil
2 medium onions, peeled and finely chopped
1-inch piece of gingerroot, peeled and finely chopped
1 Tb flour
1 Tb tomato paste
3 cloves garlic, peeled and pushed through a press
2 tsp ground coriander
1 tsp ground turmeric
1 tsp ground cumin
1/2 tsp chili powder
3/4 cup (6 oz) water
6 oz (180 g) tomatoes, peeled and chopped
1/4 tsp superfine or castor sugar
1/4 cup (2 oz) plain yogurt
Salt and black pepper

Remove any surrounding fat and the translucent membrane from the outside of the kidneys, cut them into about 1-inch cubes, and snip out the white core. Remove the stalk, seeds, and whitish membrane from the green pepper and chop it very fine. Place 3 tablespoons of oil in a large frying pan over moderately high heat, and when hot, add the kidneys and brown them quickly on all sides, stirring and turning continuously for 1–2 minutes. Remove them to a plate and keep

SPICED KIDNEYS, CONTINUED

warm. Lower the heat slightly and add the remaining oil to the pan juices. When it is hot, mix in the green pepper, chopped onions, and ginger. Sauté, stirring frequently, for about 10 minutes, or until the onion is soft and golden. Add the flour and stir continuously for a few minutes, thoroughly mixing it in. Add the tomato paste, garlic, and spices, and when they are thoroughly blended, slowly pour the water over, stirring continuously until you have a smooth sauce. Simmer for a few minutes. Add the tomatoes and sugar to the pan, mix them in well, and cook 10 minutes longer. Reduce heat to low, and blend in the yogurt. Return the kidneys and any juices to the pan, season to taste with salt and black pepper, and let them simmer gently for 5 minutes.

Rabbit Stew

Rabbits, having the speed of Sagittarius, are a reminder of the swiftness of the archer's arrows that slice the winter air. And the half-horse, half-man Centaur that represents this sign of the zodiac is traditionally associated with archery. Rabbit stew makes a marvelous country dish and warming meal for the cool month of Sagittarius and is a beneficial food for this sign, since both sage (attributed to Jupiter by Culpeper) and thyme are cleansing herbs that aid digestion and act as a liver tonic—often an over-used organ with this high-living sign. *Serves 4*

3/4 lb (340 g) carrots
6 Tb flour
Salt and black pepper
One 2-lb rabbit, skinned, cleaned, and jointed
4 slices (4 oz; 115 g) streaky bacon
3 Tb sunflower or vegetable oil
1 Tb tomato paste
1 clove garlic, peeled and pushed through a press
1½ cups (12 oz) water
½ cup plus 2 Tb (5 oz) red wine
12 pearl onions, peeled
¼ tsp dried sage, or ½ tsp chopped fresh
½ tsp dried thyme, or 1 tsp chopped fresh
Pinch of nutmeg
1 bay leaf
8 oz (225 g) tomatoes, skinned and chopped
½ lb (225 g) shelled lima or broad beans

Preheat the oven to 325°F (165°C; gas 3).

Top, tail, and peel the carrots and cut them into ½-inch disks. Place them in a bowl, cover with cold water, and set aside. Mix 3 tablespoons of flour with 1/2 teaspoon salt and 1/4 teaspoon black pepper. Spread it over a large plate or wooden board and roll the rabbit joints in it so they are evenly coated. Remove the rind from the bacon and cut it into 1 1/2-inch pieces. Place a frying pan over moderately high heat, mix in the bacon pieces, and sauté for 5–6 minutes, or until crisp. Turn the bacon into a casserole and set aside. Drain off most of the fat from the pan, return the pan to the heat, and add 1 1/2 tablespoons of oil. When it is hot add half of the rabbit pieces and sauté quickly on each side until golden, then transfer the rabbit to the casserole. Add the remaining oil to the pan, brown the rest of the rabbit in the same way, and add it to the casserole. Lower the heat slightly, and blend the remaining flour into the pan juices. Cook for 2 minutes, stirring constantly. Mix in the tomato paste and garlic, and blend in the water and wine. Stir continuously until you have a smooth sauce. Turn the sauce into the casserole with the onions, herbs, and drained carrots. Cover, and cook for 1 hour, or until the rabbit is tender. Add the tomatoes and beans to the pan, and season to taste with salt and black pepper; cook 15–20 minutes longer, or until the beans are tender. Serve hot with mashed or boiled potatoes.

Shrimp and Spinach Curry

Spicy curries are strong favorites with this hot and fiery sign of the zodiac. Particularly easy to prepare, Shrimp and Spinach Curry is delicious served with a bowl of rice, papadums, a selection of chutneys, and either chilled beer or white wine. *Serves 2*

> *1 lb fresh spinach, or 1 lb frozen chopped spinach*
> *Salt*
> *3 cloves garlic, peeled*
> *6 Tb sunflower or vegetable oil*
> *2 medium onions, peeled and finely chopped*
> *2 Tb tomato paste*
> *1/2 tsp ground ginger*
> *1/2 tsp ground cumin*
> *1 tsp ground coriander*
> *1/2 tsp ground turmeric*
> *1/2 tsp chili powder*
> *1/2 lb (225 g) shrimp, peeled*
> *Black pepper*

Garnishes
> *Sautéed or broiled papadums*
> *A selection of chutneys*

Wash the spinach thoroughly in several changes of cold water. Discard any rough-looking leaves and trim the stems. Place the spinach in a large pan without any water except what clings to the leaves after washing, with a little salt and 1 clove of garlic. Cover, bring to a simmer, and cook gently for 5–8 minutes, or until the spinach is tender. Thoroughly drain the spinach, discard the garlic, and chop finely.

Place the oil in a frying pan over moderate heat. When it is hot, mix in the onion and cook, stirring and turning, for 8–10 minutes, or until the onion is tender and lightly golden. Mix in the tomato paste, the remaining garlic, pushed through a press, and the spices, and cook 1 minute longer. Add the spinach (if you use frozen spinach, drain it thoroughly before adding it to the pan), and cook, turning and stirring, for 5 minutes. Mix in the shrimp and sauté for 3–5 minutes, or until the shrimp turn pink. Season to taste with salt and black pepper, turn onto a warmed serving platter, and serve hot with papadums, a selection of chutneys, and boiled rice.

SIDE DISHES

Eggplant all'Uovo

Rich, dark purple eggplant (the color of the noble planet Jupiter) is sliced very thinly in this dish, dipped in flour and egg, and then fried quickly. It can be eaten hot or cold and makes a delicious side dish or even lunch dish served with a selection of salads. *Serves 4–6*

1 lb eggplant
Salt
3 medium eggs
2 Tb grated Parmesan
Freshly ground black pepper
1/2 cup (21/2 oz; 70 g) flour
Vegetable or sunflower oil

Rinse the eggplant in cold water and pat it dry. Remove the ends and slice crosswise into about 1/8-inch thickness. Sprinkle the slices with a little salt, place on a large plate or wooden board, and let them sweat for 20 minutes. In a small bowl beat the eggs with the cheese, and season to taste with salt and black pepper. Turn the flour onto a large plate or board. Pat the eggplant dry with a paper towel and turn it in the flour, so the slices are evenly coated on all sides. Film the bottom of a large frying pan with 1/8 inch of oil and place it over high heat. When the oil is hot, reduce heat to moderately high. Place the bowl of egg by the side of the frying pan, and dip the eggplant slices in the egg just before you add them to the pan (cook in batches so you don't crowd the pan). Sauté for 1–2 minutes on each side, or until golden brown. Season to taste with salt and black pepper, then remove to a serving dish and keep warm (if you wish to serve hot). After you have cooked about a third of the eggplant, change the oil and continue cooking in the same way, changing the oil as it begins to burn and as the eggplant absorbs it. Arrange the eggplant on a large serving dish and serve hot or cold.

Brussels Sprouts with Chestnuts

Brussels sprouts and chestnuts, both foods of winter, make a delicious combination of sweet and savory tastes, which relates to the duality of this sign of the zodiac. The dish goes wonderfully well with Roast Pheasant and Bread Sauce (see page 208). *Serves 6*

> *1 cup (6 oz; 180 g) dried chestnuts*
> *1¹/₂ lb brussels sprouts*
> *4 Tb (2 oz; 60 g) butter*
> *2 tsp brown sugar*
> *Salt and black pepper*

Soak the chestnuts overnight in a bowl with several inches of cold water to cover. Transfer them to a fairly large pan with the water they were soaked in, bring to a boil, cover, and simmer for 55 minutes, or until very nearly tender. While the chestnuts are cooking, remove the rough outer leaves from the brussels sprouts, trim, and cut an X into the base. Add them to the boiling chestnuts, cover, and boil for the last 5–10 minutes of the chestnut cooking, or until the brussels sprouts are just tender. When they are nearly ready, melt the butter in a large frying pan over moderate heat. Drain the chestnuts and brussels sprouts and mix them into the butter with the sugar. Sauté for a few minutes, stirring constantly, season to taste with salt and black pepper, and serve.

Chestnut Soufflé

Chestnuts are a highly nutritious fruit of Jupiter, the Roman god of light and air. Transformed into a light and slightly cakey soufflé, they make a most appropriate dessert for this sign of the zodiac and the time of the year that it rules. *Serves 4*

> *2 cups (15¹/₂ oz; 439 g) canned chestnut purée*
> *¹/₄ cup (2 oz; 60 g) light or single cream*
> *6 Tb (3 oz; 85 g) superfine or castor sugar*
> *3 medium egg yolks*
> *5 medium egg whites*

Garnish
> *Cream*

Preheat the oven to 375°F (190°C; gas 5). Butter a 5-cup soufflé dish.

In a large bowl, food processor, or blender, thoroughly mix the chestnut purée with the cream, sugar, and egg yolks. In a separate bowl, beat the egg whites stiff. Spoon the chestnut mixture into the side of the bowl in which the egg whites were beaten and gently fold in the egg whites until they are thoroughly mixed. Turn into the buttered soufflé dish. Bake for 45 minutes, or until the soufflé has risen and is cooked through. Serve immediately with a jug of cream.

Strawberry Tart

Strawberries are a particularly beneficial food for this sign of the zodiac, since they contain the Sagittarian's cell salt, silica, which acts as a cleanser and conditioner and helps to prevent premature aging. Their scarlet color also suggests the fiery nature of this sign. *Serves 6*

Sweet shortcrust pastry to line a 9-inch pie pan (see page 117)

Crème pâtissière

3 medium egg yolks

3 Tb brown sugar

Pinch of salt

2 Tb cornstarch

1 cup (8 oz) milk

1 Tb sherry

3 Tb red currant jelly

3 cups (³/₄ lb; 340 g) strawberries, hulled

Preheat the oven to 425°F (220°C; gas 7).

Roll the pastry out on a floured board to line a 9-inch pie pan, trim the edges, and prick the bottom with a fork. Place it in a hot oven for 12–15 minutes, or until golden. Remove from the heat and set aside to cool. Meanwhile prepare the crème pâtissière. In the top of a double boiler mix the egg yolks with the sugar and salt, and gradually whisk in the cornstarch. Place the bottom of the double boiler over barely simmering water and slowly stir in the milk, stirring constantly until the mixture thickens (if it goes lumpy, remove it from the heat and whisk). Let it cook for a minute after it has thickened. Remove the custard from the heat, mix in the sherry, cover, and set aside to cool.

While the crème pâtissière is cooling, heat 1 tablespoon of red currant jelly in a small pan over low heat. Stir occasionally until it has melted. (Do not allow it to boil or the jelly will not reset.) Using a pastry brush, brush the jelly evenly over the pastry base and set aside to cool.

Spread the crème evenly over the base of the pastry shell. Slice the strawberries into about ¹/₄-inch thickness lengthwise and arrange the slices over the crème so that they overlap in circles and cover the whole surface. Heat the remaining red currant jelly in a small saucepan over low heat and stir until it has melted. Brush the jelly over the fruit so it is evenly coated. Chill for 15 minutes, or until the jelly has set, before serving.

Rummed Maple Pudding

Rummed Maple Pudding is a suitably alcoholic dessert for the thirsty Sagittarian, who will find it hard to resist. *Serves 8*

> 4 Tb water
>
> 1½ Tb gelatin
>
> About 25 ladyfingers
>
> ⅓ cup (2¾ oz) dark rum
>
> One 14½-oz can evaporated milk, chilled
>
> 1 cup (8 oz) maple syrup, or ½–¾ cup
> maple-flavored syrup
>
> ½ cup (1½ oz; 45 g) chopped pecans

Place the water in a medium-size saucepan, sprinkle the gelatin over, and let it soak for 5 minutes. Arrange the ladyfingers in one layer in a shallow dish, pour the rum over so that the ladyfingers are evenly coated, and leave them to soak. Pour the evaporated milk into a bowl and beat it until it is light and fluffy. Then place the gelatin mixture over low heat and stir it gently until it has melted. Mix in the maple syrup and beat the maple mixture into the evaporated milk along with the nuts. Line the bottom of an 8-cup deep dish with half the ladyfingers, breaking them up if necessary to fit the dish. Pour half the maple mixture over, cover with the remaining ladyfingers and then the remaining maple mixture. Leave in the refrigerator for several hours, or until the pudding is firm, then serve.

Ginger Cream Loaf

Gingersnaps soaked in sherry, sandwiched together, and coated with cream make a very easy and quite delicious dessert. Pure white like a snow log, this also makes a charming Christmas dish. *Serves 6*

> 1¼ cups (½ Imperial pint) heavy or double cream
>
> 2 Tb superfine or castor sugar
>
> 6–8 Tb sweet sherry
>
> One 7-oz (200-g) package, or about 20, gingersnaps
>
> 1 Tb grated semisweet chocolate (optional)

Turn the cream into a bowl and beat until it is nearly stiff, then add the sugar as you continue to beat so it is well incorporated. Turn the sherry into a small bowl and dip a few gingersnaps in so that they acquire the flavor of the sherry, but don't become soggy (if you use thick gingersnaps this will take about 30 seconds for each cookie; the thin variety need just a second or two). Shake off any excess liquid. Then spread one side of a biscuit with beaten cream and place it clean-side down on a plate. Spread the remaining biscuits with cream in the same way, and stack them up, bare side to cream. When you have done about four, or enough to stand upright on their edges, place them sideways on an oval platter, and build the remaining biscuits into a loaf. Then spread the remaining cream over all the exposed surfaces of the ginger loaf so it is completely covered. Refrigerate for several hours, or until very cold, sprinkle with grated chocolate if desired, and slice diagonally to serve.

Pears in Zabaglione

Pears, lightly poached in orange juice and served cubed and hidden in a warming, almost intoxicating sauce, make a splendid dessert for two or three. They are a mellow yellow—the color of the mind—which should appeal to the sign of the zodiac that is concerned with intellectual expression and abstract thought. *Serves 2 to 3*

2 ripe Comice pears
1/2 cup plus 2 Tb (5 oz) orange juice

Zabaglione
4 medium egg yolks
2 Tb light brown sugar
1/3 cup (2 1/2 oz) Marsala or sweet sherry

Peel the pears, cut them in half lengthwise, and lay them in a medium-size saucepan with the orange juice. Place over low heat and bring to a simmer. Cover, and cook gently for 10 minutes, or until the pears are tender. Transfer the pears to a wooden board, and when they are not too hot to handle, cut them in half again lengthwise. Cut out the cores and cut the pears into about 3/4-inch pieces. Set aside while you prepare the zabaglione.

Place the egg yolks and sugar in a mixing bowl and beat until they become pale yellow. Then beat in the Marsala. Turn the mixture into the top of a double boiler, place over barely simmering water, and whisk until frothy and thickened; this can take about 10 minutes. Gently fold the pears into the zabaglione, divide equally between 2–3 tall glasses. Serve warm.

Tropical Fruit Salad

Tropical fruit salad is an exotic and pretty combination of soft fruits in effervescent ginger that makes a very refreshing way to end a meal, or even to begin the day. It is best to prepare it just before you eat it, but you can make it in advance if the banana and ginger ale are added at the last minute so the fruit doesn't discolor and the ginger ale go flat. *Serves 4*

>*1 ripe honeydew melon (about 1½ lb; 675 g)*
>
>*1 large banana (about ½ lb; 225 g)*
>
>*2 kiwi fruits*
>
>*½ lb peeled and pitted litchis, or one 15-oz (425-g) can litchis, drained*
>
>*2 Tb lime juice*
>
>*½ tsp ground ginger*
>
>*½ cup (4 oz) chilled ginger ale*

Cut the melon in quarters lengthwise. Scoop out and discard the pips, cut the skin off, and cut the flesh into about 1-inch cubes. Place in a colander to drain off any excess juice while you prepare the remaining ingredients. Peel the banana and kiwi fruits, cut them crosswise into thin slices, and mix them lightly in a bowl with the litchis and melon. Turn the fruits into a glass serving dish and sprinkle with lime juice and ground ginger. Pour the ginger ale over and serve.

CAPRICORN

DECEMBER 22–JANUARY 20

Rules the tenth house, the house of career, public position, and worldly success

RULING PLANET	ELEMENT	QUALITIES
Saturn	Earth	Cardinal, passive
♑	♑	♑

CHARACTERISTICS
Ambitious, cautious, humorous, persevering,
pessimistic, self-disciplined, subtle

♑

OPPOSITE SIGN	BODY AREA	GEMSTONE
Cancer	Knees	Black diamond, onyx
♑	♑	♑

COLOR
Indigo

♑

FLAVOR	METAL	FAUNA
Burned, tart, astringent	Lead	Crocodile, fish, goat, turkey
♑	♑	♑

FLORA
Barley, blackberries, black currants, black figs, cereals,
quinces, red beets, root vegetables, spinach, whole wheat bread

♑

HERBS AND SPICES
Comfrey, cumin, rue, sorrel, turmeric

♑

CELL SALT
Calcium phosphate (Calc. Phos.), found in
almonds, asparagus, barley, cucumber,
figs, fish, legumes, milk, plums

♑

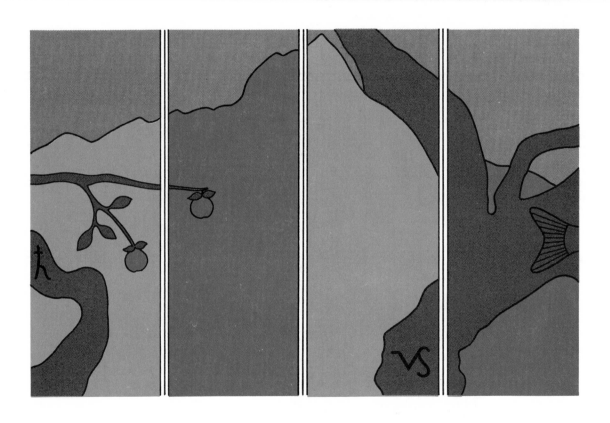

CAPRICORN THE COOK

Capricorns are quite apt to give dinner parties. They like formality, to do things correctly, and they enjoy the pleasures of eating. It is an earthy sign, in tune with the Earth's rich mysteries, and concerned with the feasible and necessary things in life such as food.

Capricorns would much rather eat a little of something good than a lot of something not quite so good; as well as maintaining standards, they are also concerned about their status in the world. This sign of the zodiac is symbolized by the mountain goat, who climbs in a slow, sure-footed way to the top of the mountain. Like the goat that has the ability to survive on practically nothing, Capricorns can make macaroni do endless rounds in different guises, so that when they entertain they can afford to do so in style. They will welcome you with smoked salmon and fine wines, impressing you in an unostentatious way.

This sign of the zodiac is ruled by Saturn, the planet of control and constriction; it has the calm of a dark blue sea, and enforces a discipline that is reflected in a carefully budgeted and well-planned menu. Money is important, not so much for the pleasure that it brings but the power and prestige it accumulates in the bank. The Capricorn's kitchen will run exceptionally smoothly; they make cautious and practical cooks who like to be in complete control. They are bad at delegating and trusting others and they leave nothing to chance, their pessimistic nature anticipating that things would go wrong.

This is a very subtle sign of the zodiac, and the earthy mountain goat that represents Capricorn has a very fishy tail, which indicates duality and a nature that has an intuitive and emotional side. It gives this sign great smoothness and shrewd judgment and the ability to always get what he or she wants, without appearing to. And although Capricorns are fond of practical dishes such as pastas and dried beans and solid earthy foods, they are also great fish lovers, so salmon and sole are more than likely to be on their menu, reflecting the watery nature of the sea goat. Capricorns can also enjoy combinations of sweet and savory, such as a Chinese dish, or a mixture of meat and fruits, such as a chestnut meat loaf, or even a dense rhythmic mousse that reflects the music that dances in their souls.

Dinner at a Capricorn's house should be a stylish occasion; even though this sign of the zodiac has probably moaned and groaned for days about how much the evening has cost, you will still sit down to the finest fish dish and best cuts of meat. Most of your host's money may be invested in gold bricks, but he or she will happily pop the champagne corks when the occasion arises.

RECIPES FOR CAPRICORN

First Courses

Prawns Wrapped in Smoked Salmon
Kipper and Tomato Ring with Crudités
Stuffed Cabbage Leaves
Stilton and Cauliflower Soup
Mixed Bean Salad
Fresh Fig and Goat Cheese Salad
Spinach and Chicken Liver Pâté

Main Courses

Sole Meunière
Salmon Quiche
Lasagne
Turkey Escalopes with Shrimp Sauce
Deviled Chicken Drumsticks
Beef and Chestnut Loaf
Swiss Potato Dish

Side Dishes

Spinach with Yogurt and Nutmeg
Red Beet, Watercress, and Orange Salad

Desserts

Apple Sponge
Amber Crème
Chocolate Pots de Crème
Plum Pudding
Blackberry and Black Currant Fool
Brown Bread Ice Cream

MENU SUGGESTIONS FOR CAPRICORN

Prawns Wrapped in Smoked Salmon
Lasagne
Apple Sponge

VS

Stilton and Cauliflower Soup
Beef and Chestnut Loaf
Blackberry and Black Currant Fool

VS

Mixed Bean Salad
Salmon Quiche
Apple Sponge

VS

Kipper and Tomato Ring with Crudités
Swiss Potato Dish
Chocolate Pots de Crème

VS

Fresh Fig and Goat Cheese Salad
Sole Meunière
Brown Bread Ice Cream

VS

Stuffed Cabbage Leaves
Deviled Chicken Drumsticks
Amber Crème

VS

Spinach and Chicken Liver Pâté
Turkey Escalopes with Shrimp Sauce
Plum Pudding

CAPRICORN THE GUEST

Chances are that your Capricorn friends will say no when you invite them to dinner; they probably have so much work at the office that they can't possibly go anywhere. So if you really want them to come, tempt them with a festive occasion and fine food, and they may not be able to resist. Once they are in the mood, they will probably have a better time than anybody.

Capricorn is a cardinal sign of the zodiac, which suggests an outgoing personality that reflects the energy and vitality of the new year as well as the festivities of Christmas and winter. It is a sign that will quite happily get on with most people even though Capricorns are shrewd judges of character (and are probably most compatible with other earth or water signs, or quite possibly a fire sign). The fiery planet Mars is exalted in this sign of the zodiac, indicating a warmth of feeling that is often not immediately noticeable and that is usually concealed behind the cool and stern face of Saturn (Capricorn's ruling planet).

This fiery side of the Capricorns' nature is reflected in their enjoyment of food, and if you were planning a spicy meal, you needn't worry too much about this earthy sign not enjoying it. It's probably a good idea not to be too heavy-handed with the chili—their sensitive palates are more likely to relish a subtle blending of spices. And don't worry if you accidentally burned the chicken, because Capricorns love burned tastes, and thoroughly enjoy anything caramelized. This is a very diplomatic and easygoing sign of the zodiac who makes a charming guest and who is very good at making the best of situations. He or she will also have a black sense of humor, so if any sign is going to enjoy a culinary disaster it is a Capricorn.

However, if things aren't going too smoothly for you in the kitchen, don't invite your Capricorn friend to help unless you don't mind the idea of him or her taking over; he can be overbearing and quite happily finish cooking the whole meal for you.

Capricorns like to be seen in the right places. Their image is very important to them, as well as their social standing in the world. They also like foods that represent status, and you won't go at all wrong feeding them champagne and caviar. But failing this extravagance, they can be just as happy eating a fishy quiche or a good warming soup that reflects the earthy practicality and shrewdness they respect.

Capricorns like all sorts of foods, so long as they are of good quality and well presented. They set high standards for themselves and expect you to be able to do the same. They will also like the evening to be well organized with the proper conventions of the day observed, such as a table set with linen and silver and a bowl of chocolates to go with their demitasse (they do have a sweet tooth).

Prawns Wrapped in Smoked Salmon

Capricorn is symbolized by the sea goat who has a fish tail. The watery and mysterious side of the goat is not obvious but it is reflected in the Capricorn's love of seafood. Prawns Wrapped in Smoked Salmon is a combination of tastes that this sign of the zodiac should find irresistible.
Serves 4

12 Pacific prawns, peeled
1/2 lb (225 g) wafer-thin slices of smoked salmon

Garnishes

4 leaves of radicchio, washed and dried
4 small leaves of curly endive or lettuce, washed and dried
Mayonnaise (see page 59)
Thin slices of buttered whole wheat bread
1 lemon, quartered
Black pepper

Bring a large pan of salted water to a boil, add the prawns, and simmer about 5–6 minutes, or until the prawns turn pink. Remove from the heat, drain, and set aside to cool. Then divide the salmon into 12 equal slices, lay a prawn at the edge of each slice, and roll it up like a cigar. Garnish a serving dish or 4 individual plates with radicchio and curly endive and arrange the salmon rolls by the side. Serve with a bowl of mayonnaise, thin slices of buttered whole wheat bread, wedges of lemon, and black pepper.

Kipper and Tomato Ring with Crudités

This soft kipper and tomato mousse is served with crisp, raw vegetables, making a colorful and protein-rich starter, which should help to replenish some of Capricorn's overworked energy.
Serves 6 to 8

1 lb kipper fillets, boned
2 cups (16 oz) milk
2 Tb water
1 Tb plus 1 1/2 tsp gelatin
1/2 lb (225 g) tomatoes, peeled and chopped
1 cup (1/2 lb) cream cheese
1 small onion, peeled and grated
1 small clove garlic, peeled and pushed through a press
2 medium egg yolks
2 Tb lemon juice
Black pepper
1/2 cup (4 oz) heavy or double cream
2 medium egg whites

Crudités

1/2 lb (225 g) carrots
2 1/2 cups (1/2 lb; 225 g) cauliflower, broken into florets
A bunch of radishes, with their tops, or half a medium cucumber, cut into 2 1/2–3-inch sticks

Place the kipper fillets in a large frying pan and pour the milk over. Bring to a boil, and simmer for 8 minutes. Drain and set aside to cool. While the fish is cooking, place the water in a small saucepan, sprinkle the gelatin over, and leave it to soak for 5 minutes. Remove the skin from the fish and place it in a food processor or blender with the tomatoes, cream cheese, onion, garlic,

Stuffed Cabbage Leaves

egg yolks, and lemon juice. Purée and season to taste with black pepper (no salt because kippers can be salty). Place the gelatin mixture over low heat, stirring occasionally until it has completely melted (do not let it boil or it will not reset), then blend it thoroughly into the kipper mixture. Turn the cream into a bowl and beat it until just stiff. Fold in the kipper mixture. In a separate bowl and with clean beaters, beat the egg whites stiff. Fold them into the kipper-and-tomato cream, then pour the mixture into a 5-cup (2–Imperial pint) ring mold. Refrigerate for several hours or overnight until set. Prepare the filling just before you wish to eat it.

Peel the carrots, remove the ends, and quarter lengthwise. Cut them into 2½–3-inch lengths. Wash and dry the cauliflower and radishes. Unmold the kipper ring onto a serving dish about 2 inches wider in diameter than the ring by dipping the mold in and immediately out of very hot water. Fill the center of the ring with carrots standing upright around the edge and then a mixture of cauliflower and radishes. Arrange the remaining vegetables around the edge of the dish and serve.

These cabbage leaves are stuffed with a tasty, nutty mixture of ingredients, including pine nuts and barley, which in small doses is also very beneficial to this sign of the zodiac. Barley contains Capricorns' cell salt, calcium phosphate, which helps to strengthen the bones and teeth, often weak areas with this sign of the zodiac. In classical Greece, Chronos, the Greek equivalent of the Latin Saturn, was worshipped as a barley god. Too much barley, however, can induce melancholy, a state that Capricorns have a tendency to suffer from. You can vary this vegetarian stuffing by using some ground meat—Stuffed Cabbage Leaves are a good way of using up leftover meat. *Serves 4*

Salt
2 Tb barley
1 medium cabbage
Sunflower or vegetable oil
1 small onion, peeled and finely chopped
1 clove garlic, peeled and pushed through a press
2 tsp tomato paste
¼ lb (115 g) tomatoes, peeled and chopped
2 oz (60 g) mushrooms, wiped clean and chopped
¼ cup (1¼ oz) pine nuts
½ tsp dried marjoram, or 1 tsp chopped fresh
½ tsp ground cumin
Black pepper
1 Tb chopped fresh parsley
1 cup (2 oz; 60 g) grated Cheddar cheese

Place 2 cups (16 oz) water in a pan and bring to a boil with ½ teaspoon of salt. Stir in the barley, cover, and simmer for 45 minutes, or until tender.

STUFFED CABBAGE LEAVES, CONTINUED

Meanwhile bring a large pan of salted water to a boil. Remove any rough outer leaves from the cabbage and, using a sharp knife, cut a 1-inch-deep circle around the core of the cabbage, to aid cooking. Drop the cabbage into the boiling water, cover, and simmer for 20 minutes. Drain and set aside. When the barley is cooked, drain and set it aside.

Preheat the oven to 350°F (180°C; gas 4).

Heat 2 tablespoons of oil in a frying pan over moderate heat, add the onion, and sauté for 8 minutes, stirring occasionally until soft. Add the garlic, tomato paste, tomatoes, mushrooms, pine nuts, marjoram, and cumin, and season to taste with salt and black pepper. Cook 5 minutes longer, stirring occasionally. Remove from the heat and put the tomato mixture into a mixing bowl. Add the parsley, cheese, and barley and mix thoroughly. Check the seasoning and correct if necessary. Peel 8 outer leaves off the cabbage, taking care not to tear them (use the remaining cabbage as a vegetable dish or in a soup). From the end of each leaf cut out about 1 inch of the thick core at the center. Place 2 tablespoons of the barley mixture in the middle of each cabbage leaf, and wrap the edges of the leaf over so you have a small package. Place the packages seam-side down in a greased shallow ovenproof dish just large enough to hold them in one layer. Brush the tops of the cabbage parcels with a little oil and cover with foil. Cook in a moderate oven for 40 minutes and serve hot.

Stilton and Cauliflower Soup

Stilton and Cauliflower Soup is a delicate, creamy soup—warming for the winter months and a very good way of using up leftover cheese at Christmas, which falls during the month of Capricorn. It can be prepared in advance and even improves in flavor eaten a day after it is made.
Serves 4

> 3 Tb butter
> 1 medium onion, peeled and finely chopped
> 2 ribs of celery, ends and strings removed, chopped
> 2½ cups (8 oz; 225 g) cauliflower, broken into florets
> 2 cups (16 oz) chicken or turkey stock
> 1 cup plus 2 Tb milk
> Salt and black pepper
> 1 Tb cornstarch
> 1 cup (4 oz; 115 g) Stilton, broken into pieces
> ½ cup (4 oz) light or single cream

Garnish
> 4 whole wheat rolls, warmed

Melt the butter in a pan over moderately low heat, add the onion, celery, and cauliflower, and sauté, stirring frequently, for 10 minutes. Pour the stock and 1 cup of milk over and season to taste with salt and black pepper. Bring to a boil, cover, and simmer for 25–30 minutes, or until the cauliflower is soft. Pour the mixture into a food processor or blender, and purée until smooth. Return to the pan over moderate heat. In a small bowl, thoroughly mix the cornstarch with the remaining 2 tablespoons of milk, add it to the soup, and stir continuously until the mixture thickens slightly. Bring to a boil and simmer for a few minutes. Reduce the heat slightly, mix in the Stilton and cream, and stir continuously until the cheese has melted. Check the seasoning, turn into a warmed soup tureen, and serve with warmed rolls.

Mixed Bean Salad

This bean salad is full of nourishing earthy goodness. It combines tender green and red beans—the festive colors of Christmas—with a refreshing mint dressing, to make a delectable combination of tastes and textures for the sign of the zodiac that understands the dark mysteries of the earth. *Serves 6*

1/2 cup (3 1/2 oz; 100 g) red kidney beans
1/2 cup (4 oz; 115 g) flageolets, or small white
    or pea beans
1/2 lb (225 g) fresh or frozen lima beans
    or broad beans
Salt
4 scallions or spring onions
6 slices (6 oz; 180 g) streaky bacon

Dressing
1 1/2 Tb honey
3 Tb (1 1/2 oz) wine vinegar
2 Tb olive oil
1 Tb chopped fresh mint, or 1 1/2 tsp dried
Salt and black pepper to taste

2 Tb chopped fresh parsley
2 ribs of celery, ends and strings removed,
    chopped
2 medium eggs, hard-boiled, peeled, and chopped

Soak the red kidney beans and flageolets overnight in separate bowls, with 2 inches of water to cover. Then drain and turn into 2 separate pans. Cover with 2–3 inches of water, bring the kidney beans to a boil, lower the heat, cover, and simmer for 1 1/2–2 hours, or until tender. Flageolets take less time to cook, so leave them

MIXED BEAN SALAD, CONTINUED

until the red beans have been simmering for about 1 hour, bring the flageolets to a boil, cover, and simmer for 45–50 minutes, or until tender.

When the kidney beans are nearly done, place the lima beans in a pan and just cover with water, add a pinch of salt, partially cover, and bring to a boil. Simmer for 15–20 minutes, or until the beans are tender (if using broad beans, simmer 10–15 minutes). Meanwhile, chop the scallions, remove the rind from the bacon, cut it into ½-inch pieces, and set aside. In a small bowl or jar, mix thoroughly the dressing ingredients. When the beans are tender, drain thoroughly, place in a bowl with the scallions, parsley, celery, and dressing. Mix thoroughly and correct the seasoning with salt and black pepper. Turn the beans into a salad or serving bowl, arrange the chopped egg over, cover, and chill for about 30 minutes, or until you wish to serve. Then place a frying pan over moderately high heat. Add the bacon, and sauté for 5–6 minutes, or until the bacon is crisp. Drain the bacon, toss over the salad, and serve immediately.

Fresh Fig and Goat Cheese Salad

This salad has the sharp tang of goat cheese, which is softened and delightfully complemented by the succulent, sweet fig and crisp croutons. It is a reminder of the mountain goat that symbolizes Capricorn and that artfully makes his way up the steep and barren mountainside until he reaches the summit. *Serves 4*

Dressing

4 Tb (2 oz) olive oil

2 Tb lemon juice

¼ tsp dried marjoram, or ½ tsp chopped fresh

Salt and black pepper to taste

½ clove garlic, peeled and pushed through a press

1 crisp lettuce heart, washed and dried

3 fresh figs, peeled and sliced crosswise

2 oz (60 g) soft goat cheese

Small bunch of mustard greens

One ½-inch slice of bread from a large loaf

3 Tb (1½ oz) olive oil

1 clove garlic, peeled and pushed through a press

In a small jar or bowl, mix thoroughly the dressing ingredients. Shred the lettuce, arrange it in a salad bowl, and place the fig slices on top. Slice the cheese thin or break it up and scatter it over the lettuce and figs with the mustard greens.

Remove the crust from the bread and cut it into ½-inch cubes. Heat the olive oil in a small frying pan over high heat, add the bread cubes and garlic, and sauté for 1–2 minutes on each side, or until golden. Remove from the heat and scatter the croutons over the salad, pour the dressing on, toss, and serve.

Spinach and Chicken Liver Pâté

The extravagant taste of chicken livers and spinach, flavored with brandy and wrapped in bacon, makes a splendid pâté that is elegant enough to grace the grandest of dinner tables with the subtle understatement of Capricorn. Spinach and Chicken Liver Pâté is not difficult to make and can easily be prepared in advance if it is kept cold until it is served. *Serves 6 to 8*

> 1 lb fresh spinach or frozen chopped spinach
> Salt
> 1/2 lb (225 g) chicken livers
> 1/2 lb (225 g) ground pork belly
> 2 cloves garlic, peeled and pushed through a press
> Pinch of nutmeg
> 3 Tb (1 1/2 oz) brandy
> 2 Tb finely chopped fresh parsley
> Black pepper to taste
> 8 slices (1/2 lb; 225 g) streaky bacon, flattened
>   with a spatula

Garnishes
> Trimmed watercress
> Rounds of hot toast
> Butter

Preheat the oven to 325°F (165°C; gas 3).

Wash the spinach in several changes of cold water and remove any tough stems. Then put the leaves in a pan with salt (but no water, because spinach is full of moisture). Cover, place over low heat, and simmer gently for 5–8 minutes, or until the spinach is tender. Thoroughly drain, chop finely (you can do this in a food processor), and put in a mixing bowl. (If using frozen spinach, just drain thoroughly after cooling, then

SPINACH AND CHICKEN LIVER PATÉ, CONTINUED

put in bowl.) Trim any skin or veins from the chicken livers and chop them very fine. Mix all the remaining ingredients thoroughly into the spinach, except for the bacon. Line the base and about 3 inches up the sides of a standard loaf pan with the bacon. Pack the pâté mixture into the pan and cover with foil. Set the loaf pan in a shallow ovenproof dish or pan half full of water. Cook in the oven for 1½ hours. Remove from the heat and leave the pâté to cool, then drain off excess liquid and unmold onto a serving dish. Garnish with watercress and serve with rounds of hot toast and butter, or refrigerate until you wish to serve.

Sole Meunière

Sole is the finest of the flatfish, and cooked in this delicate and simple way it becomes a real luxury. It makes a perfect dish for the sign of the zodiac that likes to enjoy the sublime and quality things in life, which is indicated by their impressive position at the mountain summit. *Serves 2*

3 Tb flour
½ tsp salt
¼ tsp black pepper
12 oz (340 g) filleted and skinned lemon or Dover sole
5 Tb (2½ oz) butter
1 Tb lemon juice

Garnishes
A few sprigs of parsley
2 wedges of lemon

Mix the flour with the salt and black pepper. On a large plate or wooden board roll the fish in the flour so it is lightly coated on all sides and shake off the excess. Place 3 tablespoons of butter in a large frying pan over moderately hot heat, and when it begins to bubble add the fish. Sauté for 3–4 minutes on each side and then transfer the fish to a warm serving dish, sprinkle the lemon juice evenly over, and keep warm. Add the remaining butter to the pan juices, and as it begins to brown, pour it over the fish. Garnish the dish with a few sprigs of parsley and lemon wedges, and serve.

Salmon Quiche

This tempting quiche combines layers of salmon, shrimp, and sliced hard-boiled egg, all hidden beneath a béchamel sauce. It makes a delightful lunch or supper dish and should be served with a green vegetable, such as beans or spinach or a salad, and a very cold white wine. *Serves 6*

> *Shortcrust Pastry to line a 10-inch pie pan*
> *(see page 12)*
> *1/2 lb (225 g) shrimp, peeled*

> *Béchamel sauce*
> *3 Tb (1 1/2 oz; 45 g) butter*
> *3 Tb flour*
> *2 cups (16 oz) milk*
> *Salt and black pepper*

> *Two 7 1/2-oz (213-g) cans salmon, drained, any*
> *bones and skin removed, or 12 oz (340 g) fresh*
> *salmon, cooked, skinned, and boned*
> *6 hard-boiled eggs, peeled and sliced crosswise*
> *Salt and black pepper*

Preheat the oven to 425°F (220°C; gas 7).

Prepare the pastry as described on page 12. Bake it in the oven for 10–12 minutes, or until lightly golden.

While the pastry is baking, prepare the shrimp. Bring 2 cups (16 oz) salted water to a simmer, add the shrimp, and cook for 2–3 minutes, or until the shrimp turn pink. Drain and set aside while you prepare the béchamel sauce.

Melt the butter in a pan over moderately low heat, add the flour, and stir continuously for 2 minutes. Gradually add the milk, stirring constantly until you have a smooth sauce. Bring to a boil and simmer for a few minutes. Season to taste with salt and black pepper. Remove from the heat and set aside.

Lower the oven heat to 350°F (180°C; gas 4).

Flake the salmon over the pastry shell to cover evenly, then place the shrimp over, and lay the eggs on top. Season to taste with salt and black pepper. Pour the béchamel over so all the ingredients are evenly covered and bake for 20 minutes, or until the quiche is hot through. Serve hot.

Lasagne

Ribbons of pasta layered over béchamel and an unusual Bolognese sauce that is made with chicken livers make a very delicious dish that should be served Italian-style with a green salad and some red Italian wine. *Serves 6*

Bolognese sauce

1/4 lb (115 g) chicken livers

3 Tb (1 1/2 oz) butter

1 medium onion, peeled and finely chopped

4 slices (1/4 lb; 115 g) streaky bacon

1 large carrot, peeled and finely chopped

1 rib of celery, strings removed, wiped clean, and finely chopped

1/2 lb (225 g) ground or minced beef

2 Tb tomato paste

3/4 cup (6 oz) beef stock

1/2 cup (4 oz) white wine

Pinch of nutmeg

Salt and black pepper

Béchamel sauce

4 Tb (2 oz) butter

5 Tb (1 1/2 oz; 45 g) flour

3 cups (24 oz) milk

Pinch of nutmeg

Salt and black pepper

About 10 sheets (12 oz; 340 g) lasagne

1/4 cup (1 oz; 30 g) grated Parmesan

Preheat the oven to 350°F (180°C; gas 4).

Prepare the Bolognese sauce first. Rinse the chicken livers in cold water and pat them dry with a paper towel. Trim any skin or veins from the livers, chop them into about 1/2-inch pieces, and set aside.

Heat the butter in a pan over moderately low heat. When it begins to bubble, add the onion and sauté, stirring occasionally, for about 5–8 minutes, or until soft. While the onion is cooking, remove the rind from the bacon and cut the bacon into small pieces. Add it to the pan along with the carrot, celery, and beef, and cook, stirring to break up any meat lumps, for about 10 minutes, or until beef has browned. Mix in the tomato paste, chicken livers, stock, wine, and nutmeg, and season to taste with salt and black pepper. Cover, and simmer for 30 minutes.

While the Bolognese sauce is simmering, prepare the béchamel. Melt the butter in a pan over moderately low heat, add the flour, and stir continuously for 2 minutes. Gradually pour in the milk and stir continuously until you have a smooth sauce. Add a pinch of nutmeg and season to taste with salt and black pepper. Remove from the heat, cover, and set aside.

Cook the lasagne in a large pot of boiling water until done *al dente*. Drain. Butter a shallow ovenproof dish, about 8 by 10 inches. Cover the bottom of the dish with one-third of the Bolognese (about 1 1/3 cups; 11 oz), then spread one-quarter of the béchamel evenly over. Cover it with a layer of lasagne, overlapping the edges of the lasagne slightly so there are no gaps. Continue to build the dish up in this way, finishing on top with a layer of béchamel. Sprinkle the Parmesan over and place in the oven for 30 minutes. Remove the lasagne from the oven and let it sit for 10 minutes before serving hot.

Turkey Escalopes with Shrimp Sauce

Turkeys are seasonally associated with Capricorn, the sign of the zodiac that begins with the winter solstice. Slices of turkey breast, dipped in egg and bread crumbs, then fried and served with a shrimp sauce, make a very delicious and elegant dinner party dish served with a crisp green salad, boiled potatoes, and a cold white Burgundy. *Serves 4*

Shrimp sauce
> 2 Tb butter
> 2 Tb flour
> 3/4 cup (6 oz) milk
> 1 tsp ground turmeric
> 1/2 lb (225 g) peeled shrimp
> 1/2 cup (4 oz) sour cream
> Salt and black pepper

> 2 medium eggs
> 2 cloves garlic, peeled and pushed through a press
> Salt and black pepper to taste
> 1 cup (6 oz; 180 g) very fine dry bread crumbs
> 1 1/2 lb turkey breast, cut into 1/4-inch-thick slices
> Vegetable or sunflower oil

Prepare the sauce first. Place the butter in a saucepan over moderately low heat. When it has melted, add the flour and cook, stirring continuously, for 2 minutes. Gradually stir in the milk until you have a smooth sauce. Bring to a boil, mix in the turmeric and shrimp, and simmer for 3–5 minutes, or until the shrimp turn pink. Remove from the heat, stir in the sour cream, season to taste with salt and black pepper, cover, and set aside.

In a bowl, beat the eggs with the garlic and season lightly with salt and black pepper. Cover a large plate or wooden board with the bread crumbs. Dip the turkey breasts into the egg mixture and then roll them in the bread crumbs so they have an even coating on each side. Pour enough oil into a large frying pan to fill 1/4 inch, place over high heat, and when the oil is hot, lower heat to moderately high. Sauté the turkey in batches, so you do not crowd the pan, for 3–4 minutes on each side, or until lightly browned on the outside and cooked in the middle. Transfer the turkey slices to a paper towel to drain excess oil, and then to a warmed serving dish, and keep warm.

Place the sauce over low heat and rewarm it without boiling, or the cream will curdle. Pour the sauce evenly over the turkey slices and serve.

Deviled Chicken Drumsticks

Deviled Chicken Drumsticks, cooked in an unusual combination of spices and mango chutney, make a delicious supper dish, served with a green salad or Spinach with Yogurt and Nutmeg (see page 239) and baked potatoes—one that should be a favorite with this outgoing sign of the zodiac in which the fiery planet Mars is exalted.

Serves 3 to 4

Deviled sauce

    4 Tb mango chutney

    2 Tb tomato paste

    3 cloves garlic, peeled and pushed through a press

    1 tsp English mustard

    1 tsp superfine or castor sugar

    1 tsp ground ginger

    1/2 tsp ground turmeric

    1/4 tsp chili powder

    1/2 cup (4 oz) white wine

    Salt and black pepper to taste

    2 Tb flour

    1/2 tsp salt

    1/4 tsp black pepper

    8 chicken legs

    1 Tb sunflower or vegetable oil

    1 Tb butter

Preheat the oven to 350°F (180°C; gas 4).

In a bowl, thoroughly mix together all the sauce ingredients and set aside while you prepare the chicken.

Mix the flour with the salt and pepper on a large plate or wooden board. Roll the chicken legs in it so they are evenly coated on all sides and shake off any excess. Place the oil and butter in a frying pan over high heat. When it is hot, lower the heat slightly and add the chicken legs (do them in batches so you don't crowd the pan). Sauté for a few minutes on each side, or until golden. As you cook the drumsticks transfer them to an ovenproof dish just large enough to hold them in one layer. When they are all browned, pour the sauce over so that they are evenly coated. Cover the dish with foil and cook in the oven for 20 minutes. Then remove the foil and cook 20 minutes longer, or until the meat is no longer pink near the bone. Serve hot.

Beef and Chestnut Loaf

This meat loaf has a luxurious and unique taste that is complemented by the purée of leeks and peas that surrounds it. It makes an unusual and warming dish for the winter months and should be served with a fruity red wine. *Serves 4*

Chestnut meat loaf

 1/2 cup (3 oz; 85 g) dried chestnuts

1/4 cup (1 1/2 oz; 45 g) golden raisins or sultanas

1 lb ground beef

1 medium onion, peeled and finely chopped

2 cloves garlic, peeled and pushed through a press

1 medium egg

3 Tb chopped fresh parsley

Pinch of nutmeg

Salt and black pepper to taste

1/4 cup (2 oz) red wine

Leek and pea purée

1 cup (7 oz; 200 g) dried split peas

2 Tb sunflower or vegetable oil

1 lb leeks, tough green tops removed, sliced crosswise, and washed

1/2 cup (4 oz) heavy or double cream

Salt and black pepper

Soak the chestnuts overnight in a bowl with several inches of cold water to cover. Then transfer them to a pan with the water they were soaked in, bring to a boil, cover, and simmer for 45 minutes, or until nearly tender. Drain and chop into about 1/4–1/2-inch pieces.

Place the peas for the purée in a pan with 2–3 inches of water to cover, bring to a boil, cover, and simmer for 45 minutes, or until tender.

While the peas are cooking prepare the meat loaf.

Preheat the oven to 350°F (180°C; gas 4). Butter a 5-cup (2–Imperial pint) loaf pan.

Place the raisins in a bowl, cover with boiling water, and leave to soak for 5 minutes. Then drain the raisins and turn them into a mixing bowl with the chestnuts and all the remaining meat loaf ingredients. Mix thoroughly and then press into the buttered loaf pan. Bake for 45 minutes.

While the meat loaf is cooking, prepare the leek and pea purée. Heat the oil in a pan over moderately low heat, turn the leeks in the oil, cover, and cook gently for 20 minutes, or until tender. When the peas are tender, thoroughly drain and put into a food processor or blender with the leeks and cream, and purée. Season to taste with salt and black pepper. Return the purée to a pan, cover, and keep warm.

When the meat loaf is cooked, unmold it onto a serving dish. Spoon the puréed vegetables along each side of the loaf, and serve hot.

Swiss Potato Dish

This Swiss peasant dish is a meal for Capricorn when he or she is in a parsimonious mood. It is inexpensive to prepare, but utterly delicious to eat. The onions top the dish and their juices run down into the cheese, potato, and macaroni curls, which recall the horns of the sea goat. Serve it with a green salad and a chilled German or Swiss white wine. *Serves 4*

Heat the butter and oil in a large saucepan over moderately low heat. Add the onions and turn them in the fat. Season to taste with salt and black pepper, cover, and let them sweat for 30 minutes, stirring occasionally, or until they are soft. Bring a pan of salted water to a boil, add a few drops of oil and the macaroni, stir occasionally, and boil for 10–12 minutes, or until the macaroni is cooked *al dente*. Meanwhile, peel the potatoes, rinse them in cold water, and cut them into cubes about 3/4–1 inch. Turn the potato cubes into a pan of boiling salted water and cook for 5–10 minutes, or until the potatoes are tender. Thoroughly drain and mix evenly with the macaroni. Turn into an 8-cup (64-oz) ovenproof dish. Season to taste with salt and black pepper. Cover with the grated cheese, and then turn the onions and their pan juices over the layer of cheese. Keep warm in the oven until you wish to serve, or eat immediately.

4 Tb (2 oz) butter

1 Tb oil

1½ lb onions, peeled and sliced

Salt and black pepper

A few drops of sunflower or vegetable oil

1 cup (5 oz; 140 g) macaroni

1 lb potatoes

1½ cups (4 oz; 115 g) grated Gruyère or
    Emmenthal cheese

Spinach with Yogurt and Nutmeg

Dark, leafy green spinach is rich in iron and full of the goodness of the earth. Flavored with nutmeg and yogurt, it makes a tasty side dish that goes very well with Deviled Chicken Drumsticks (see page 236). *Serves 4*

> 1 lb spinach
>
> 3 Tb (1½ oz) olive oil
>
> 1 small onion, peeled and finely chopped
>
> 1 Tb tomato paste
>
> 2 cloves garlic, peeled and pushed through a press
>
> ½ cup (4 oz) plain yogurt
>
> ⅛ tsp grated nutmeg
>
> Salt and black pepper

Wash the spinach thoroughly in several changes of cold water, then dry and shred it. Heat the oil in a large frying pan over moderately low heat. Add the onion and sauté, stirring occasionally, for 10 minutes, or until soft. Mix in the tomato paste and garlic and then half the spinach, increase the heat slightly, and stir continuously for 1–2 minutes. When the spinach has cooked down a bit add the rest of it and sauté 5 minutes longer, or until all the spinach is tender, stirring frequently. Turn the heat to low and add the yogurt and nutmeg. Mix thoroughly and season to taste with salt and black pepper. Turn into a warm dish and serve.

Red Beet, Watercress, and Orange Salad

A sweet and refreshing salad that makes a good accompaniment to Beef and Chestnut Loaf (see page 237) and is also excellent with pork dishes. *Serves 4*

> ¾ lb (340 g) beets
>
> 2 large oranges
>
> 1 large bunch of watercress, well trimmed

Dressing

> 3 Tb (1½ oz) sunflower or vegetable oil
>
> 1 Tb lemon juice
>
> 2 Tb orange juice (saved from the oranges as you slice them)
>
> 1 tsp superfine or castor sugar
>
> Salt and black pepper to taste

Cut the leaves and all but 1 inch of the stalk off the beets, leaving the roots intact. Wash in plenty of cold water without scrubbing, or the beets will bleed. Place them in a saucepan with 1–2 inches of water to cover. Boil gently for 45–60 minutes, or until the beets are tender. Drain and cool slightly by rinsing in cold water. Peel off the skins and remove the roots and tops and set aside.

Peel the oranges with a sharp knife so that you remove the pith as well. Slice into segments, removing the translucent skin and any pith, and cut the flesh into ½-inch cubes. (Reserve any juice that escapes for the dressing.) On a wooden board slice the beets thinly crosswise and arrange them in a circle around the edge of a shallow round dish. Mix together the watercress and orange and arrange like a nest in the center. Thoroughly mix together the dressing ingredients, pour over the salad, and serve.

Apple Sponge

The apple is a poetic tree of immortality and an appropriate fruit for the sign of the zodiac that seems to get younger as it gets older. Apple sponge is a pudding that has a sponge cake base soaked in a fruit brandy, then a thick layer of apple and a cream topping that suggests the snowy white peaks of a mountain. *Serves 6 to 8*

> Victoria sponge cake to line an 8-inch cake pan (see page 98), or store-bought sponge cake
>
> 1/4 cup (2 oz) cherry or other fruit brandy or Kirsch
>
> 3 lb cooking apples
>
> 5 Tb (2 1/2 oz) butter
>
> 1 cup (5 oz; 140 g) brown sugar
>
> 1/2 tsp cinnamon
>
> 4 Tb (2 oz) cider
>
> Pinch of salt
>
> 1 cup (8 oz) heavy or double cream
>
> 1 Tb grated semisweet chocolate

Make the Victoria sponge cake as directed. When it has cooled, break it into largish pieces and fit into the bottom of a fairly deep 6-cup (2 1/2-pint) dish. Sprinkle the fruit brandy over and set aside. Peel, quarter, and core the apples. Place them in a large saucepan with the butter, brown sugar, cinnamon, cider, and salt, cover, and simmer, stirring occasionally, for 15 minutes, or until the apples are soft. If you have any excess liquid, remove the lid, increase the heat slightly, and let the apples bubble for a few minutes to reduce it. Remove the apples from the heat and mash any largish pieces, leaving them with a slightly rough texture. Set aside to cool slightly. Spread the apples evenly over the sponge. Pour the cream into a bowl and beat it until stiff. Spread it over the apples and then cover the top with grated chocolate. Refrigerate for 1 hour, or until you wish to serve.

Amber Crème

This silky-smooth custard has the refreshing and aromatic taste of citrus fruits and cinnamon, which is contrasted with a glassy amber-gold caramel. It recalls the era in mythology when Saturn ruled, which was a Golden Age when men were happy and festive and enjoyed the abundant fruits of the earth. Amber Crème makes an unusual dessert that is easy to prepare in advance, as long as the caramel is added at the last minute so it will not get soft. *Serves 4*

2½ cups (1 Imperial pint) milk
¼ cup (2 oz) superfine or castor sugar
1 stick cinnamon
1 vanilla bean
About 3 strips of lemon peel (from ¼ lemon)
About 4 strips of orange peel (from ¼ orange)
3 Tb cornstarch
3 medium egg yolks

Caramel
½ cup (4 oz; 115 g) superfine or castor sugar
¼ cup (2 oz) water

Heat 2 cups (16 oz) milk in a saucepan with the sugar, cinnamon stick, vanilla bean, and lemon and orange peels over moderately low heat. Bring the milk to the simmering point, then remove from the heat. Let it stand for 15 minutes so it can infuse. Pour the remaining milk into a small bowl and whisk in the cornstarch and egg yolks. Pour the egg yolk mixture through a sieve into the top of a double boiler, then add the flavored scalded milk. Place over simmering water and stir continuously until the mixture thickens. Cook a few minutes so the cornstarch cooks, remove from the heat, and turn into 4 ramekins. Refrigerate for several hours or overnight, until very cold.

Prepare the caramel. Place the sugar and water in a pan over low heat, stirring occasionally until the sugar has melted. Increase the heat to moderate and let the mixture bubble, without stirring, for about 6–8 minutes, until it is a caramel color. Remove from the heat. Pour the hot caramel over the top of the custards, so the whole surface is covered, just before serving.

Chocolate Pots de Crème

A dark, soft, and dense chocolaty dessert for the sign of the zodiac that is ruled by the dark, earthy planet Saturn. Chocolate pots can be made in minutes well in advance of a dinner party and refrigerated until you wish to serve them. *Serves 4*

> 7 oz (200 g) semisweet chocolate, broken into pieces, or semisweet chocolate chips
>
> 1¼ cups (½ Imperial pint) light or single cream
>
> 3 Tb (1½ oz) whisky
>
> 1 medium egg

Topping

> ½ cup (4 oz) heavy or double cream
>
> 1 Tb superfine or castor sugar
>
> 2 Tb (½ oz) toasted slivered almonds

Place the chocolate and cream in a pan over moderate heat and stir continuously until the chocolate is completely melted and incorporated into the cream, and the mixture has reached the simmering point. Remove from the heat and pour into a bowl. Whisk in the whisky and then the egg and divide the mixture equally among 4 ramekins. Refrigerate for several hours or overnight, until thick. Turn the heavy cream into a bowl and beat it until just stiff, fold in the sugar, and spread it over the tops of the chocolate pots. Sprinkle the almonds over and serve.

Plum Pudding

Christmas pudding is the perfect dish for the tradition-loving Capricorn, who will adore the festive flames of the brandy as well as the opportunity to discover hidden money. *Makes two 5-cup (2–Imperial pint) puddings, which can be enough for 2 years*

> 6½ cups (1 lb; 450 g) soft white bread crumbs (about 1 large loaf)
>
> 1 tsp allspice or mixed spice
>
> 2½ cups (¾ lb; 340 g) shredded suet
>
> 2½ cups (1 lb; 450 g) turbinado or demerara sugar
>
> ⅝ cup (3 oz; 85 g) chopped almonds
>
> 1¾ cups (10 oz; 285 g) muscatel (or very large) raisins, seeds removed
>
> 1½ cups (8 oz; 225 g) dark raisins
>
> 2¼ cups (12 oz; 340 g) golden raisins or sultanas
>
> 1 cup (5 oz; 140 g) candied peel, finely chopped
>
> Juice of 1 lemon (4 Tb)
>
> Grated rind of 1 lemon
>
> 7 medium eggs, lightly beaten
>
> ⅜ cup (3 oz) Guinness stout
>
> ⅓ cup (2¾ oz) brandy
>
> Sterilized coins (optional)

Garnishes

> A sprig of holly
>
> ¼ cup (2 oz) brandy
>
> A bowl of rum or brandy butter (recipe follows)

In a very large bowl mix the bread crumbs with the allspice, suet, and sugar. Add the almonds, dried fruits, and peel, and mix thoroughly. Stir in the lemon juice and rind and then gradually stir in the eggs, Guinness, and brandy until they are thoroughly mixed in. Mix in a selection of coins if you wish. Cover with a cloth and let stand overnight.

Butter two 5-cup (2-Imperial pint) pudding molds and fill them to the top with the pudding mixture. Cut 2 pieces of wax paper to lie on top of the puddings and just touch the edges of the mold. Then take 2 large pieces of foil, fold a pleat in the center of each, and lay them over the pudding molds with 3 inches to spare all around (this gives the pudding room to expand). Wrap a piece of string tightly around the foil-covered mold. Fill the bottom of a steamer three-fourths full of water and bring it to a simmer. Place the puddings (or one at a time if your steamer is not big enough) in the top of the steamer over the water. Cover, and steam for 8 hours, checking occasionally to see that the water has not evaporated. Remove from the heat, allow to cool (unless you wish to eat it straight away), remove the greaseproof paper and foil, and re-cover with a clean piece of greaseproof paper and a lid or cloth with 3 inches to spare all around; tie tightly around the mold with a piece of string. Store in a cool, dry place.

To serve a pudding, steam it for 2 hours (as directed above), then turn onto a serving dish and garnish with a sprig of holly on top. Place the brandy in a small pan and when it is hot, pour it over the pudding, ignite, and serve flaming with rum or brandy butter.

Rum Butter

Very quick and easy to make, Rum Butter is delicious served with Plum Pudding. It can also be made with brandy instead of rum, if you omit the lime juice.

> 5 Tb (2½ oz; 75 g) soft unsalted butter
> 1 cup (8 oz; 225 g) superfine or castor sugar
> 3 Tb rum
> 1 tsp lime juice

In a food processor or mixing bowl, beat the butter until it is pale and creamy. Gradually add the sugar until the mixture resembles bread crumbs, and then add the rum and lime juice. Mix well and turn into a serving dish. Refrigerate for several hours, or until you wish to serve it.

Blackberry and Black Currant Fool

Black fruits are used here because black is the color of Saturn—Capricorn's ruling planet—and because their dark musky scent suggests the strong sexual drive of this sign of the zodiac, which is indicated by the association of Capricorn with the lustful fertility goat-god Pan. *Serves 6*

> *3 cups (1 lb) blackberries*
> *1 cup (1/2 lb) black currants*
> *5/8 cup (5 oz; 140 g) granulated sugar*
> *1 1/4 cups (1/2 Imperial pint) heavy or double cream*
> *1–2 Tb superfine or castor sugar*

<u>*Garnish*</u>
> *A plate of ladyfingers*

Hull the blackberries and top and tail the black currants. Place the fruits in a fairly large pan with the granulated sugar over low heat. Cover, and simmer very gently, stirring occasionally, for 2 minutes, so that the sugar has melted but the fruits are only just tender. Turn the contents of the pan into a food processor or blender and purée. Then, using the back of a spoon, push the fruit purée through a sieve into a mixing bowl. Beat the cream in a separate bowl until it is just stiff. Fold the cream into the blackberry mixture and sweeten to taste with superfine sugar. Turn into a glass bowl, or individual glass dishes, and refrigerate several hours or overnight until very cold. Serve accompanied by ladyfingers.

Brown Bread Ice Cream

Brown Bread Ice Cream is a pale creamy-golden color, dotted with crunchy caramelized bread crumbs and flavored with brandy. It makes an unusual and delicious dessert that was very popular with the Victorians. *Serves 4 to 6*

> 1½ cups (3 oz; 85 g) soft whole wheat
>   bread crumbs
> ¾ cup (3 oz; 85 g) brown sugar
> 1¼ cups (½ Imperial pint) heavy or double cream
> 1¼ cups (½ Imperial pint) light or single cream
> 2 medium eggs, separated
> ¼ cup (2 oz) brandy

Grease a baking tin. Preheat the oven to 400°F (200°C; gas 6).

In a bowl, mix the bread crumbs and sugar together, arrange them evenly in a thin layer over a greased baking sheet, and place them in the oven for about 20 minutes, or until the bread crumbs are crisp and caramelized, turning them occasionally so that they brown evenly. Remove from the heat and set aside to cool slightly. In a large bowl, beat the heavy cream until it is just stiff. Then beat in the light cream, egg yolks, and brandy, and fold in the bread crumb mixture. In a separate bowl and with clean beaters, beat the egg whites until stiff but not dry. Gently fold them into the cream mixture and turn into an ice tray. Chill in the freezer for 3 hours, or until half frozen. (Or if you have an ice cream maker, make the ice cream following the manufacturer's directions.) Remove the ice cream from the freezer and whisk it with a fork so that the crystallized edges are mixed into the center and the bread crumbs are evenly distributed. Return to the freezer and leave at least 4 hours or overnight before serving. Remove the ice cream from the freezer and place it in the refrigerator a few hours before you wish to serve it so it can soften. Serve it in scoops in a glass bowl.

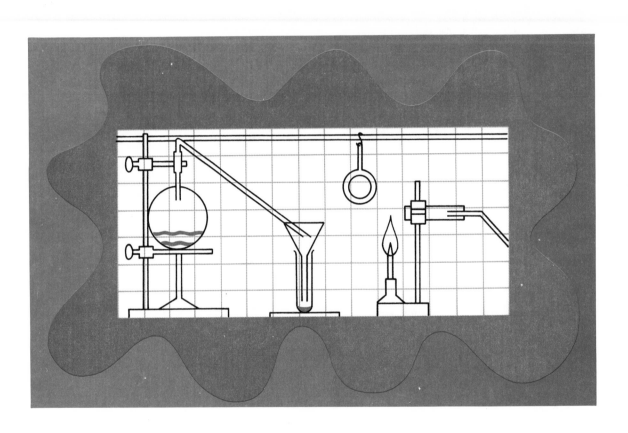

AQUARIUS

JANUARY 21–FEBRUARY 19

Rules the eleventh house, the house of hopes, friends, and wishes

RULING PLANETS	ELEMENT	QUALITIES
Uranus and Saturn	Air	Fixed, active
≈	≈	≈

CHARACTERISTICS
Detached, eccentric, futuristic, humanitarian,
independent, inventive, original, unconventional

≈

OPPOSITE SIGN	BODY AREA	GEMSTONE
Leo	Ankles	Aquamarine
≈	≈	≈

COLOR
Violet

≈

FLAVOR	METAL	FAUNA
Salty, cold, fresh	Uranium	Birds, ducks, geese
≈	≈	≈

FLORA
Anchovies, bread, coconuts, olives, rice, root vegetables,
spinach, tea, water chestnuts, watercress

≈

HERBS	CELL SALT
Dill, fennel leaves, parsley, winter savory	Sodium chloride (Nat. Mur.), found in
≈	apples, cabbage, carrots, chestnuts,
	cucumbers, lettuce, radishes, strawberries
	≈

AQUARIUS THE COOK

Go prepared for the unusual when you visit an Aquarian's household, because this sign loves to experiment and invent new dishes, and some of the combinations arrived at can be quite eccentric. Aquarians' kitchens are their laboratories, where they analyze and experiment with food, sometimes producing a masterpiece and sometimes a failure.

This sign of the zodiac strives to break new ground, often in unorthodox ways. Their (more recently discovered) ruling planet Uranus is the planet of the future, the great awakener who urges Aquarians to rebel against convention and tradition and produce new forms of expression. So dinner should take you where you have never been before—into the future. Uranus is a dark and mysterious planet whose influence can turn conventions and beliefs upside down. He is the magician who has the ability to transform the mediocre into the exceptional, often in quite ruthless ways; he enables this sign of the zodiac to divorce feeling from intellect and not let their emotions interfere with their judgment. Aquarians will quite happily toss dinner in the bin and start again if they feel it is necessary, but are often saved from doing this by their great intuition and occasional flashes of inspiration.

This sign is one of the friendliest and most social of the zodiac. It rules the eleventh house, which is concerned with group activities and friendship, and Aquarians draw people to them as well as being drawn to others. It is an air sign that loves to exchange ideas and intellectualize, thoroughly enjoying a chance to invite people to their homes. They won't mind at all if you wish to join them in the kitchen, since they will be keen to learn what they can from you. Just don't try to carry on a conversation; in the throes of creation, your Aquarian friends tend to work with such intensity that the kitchen could burn down around them and they probably wouldn't even notice.

At the same time, Aquarians are very absent-minded; they could get to chatting with you and forget that they have a pie in the oven or leave out the most vital ingredient. So if you want to eat well, it might be a good idea to let them be, until you are sure dinner is ready.

All sorts of food are possible in this household, but you are more likely to be fed a delicate soufflé or a roasted bird (which reflects the Aquarian's airy nature) than a practical stew, although an unusual vegetable pie or a spinach tart that suggests the earthy influence of Saturn (the more traditional ruler of this sign) is a possibility. Simple foods and foods that reflect their own individuality are what interest Aquarians. They are not particularly concerned with money, except for the freedom that it buys, so they will quite happily spend on things of pleasure. Above all, dinner with this sign of the zodiac should be an adventure.

RECIPES FOR AQUARIUS

MENU SUGGESTIONS FOR AQUARIUS

First Courses

Palm Hearts in Batter
Watercress and Almond Soup
Avocado, Melon, and Mozzarella Salad
Croque Monsieur
Artichoke Heart Soufflés
Tomatoes Stuffed with Cold
    Scrambled Eggs
Angels on Horseback

Main Courses

Zarzuela
Spinach and White Stilton Tart
Chicken Satay with Peanut Sauce
Roast Duck with Orange and Olives
Mixed Vegetables in Cheese Pastry
Chicken Liver Risotto
Stir-fried Beef with Water Chestnuts

Side Dishes

Greek Salad
Brussels Sprouts Mayonnaise

Desserts

Queen Anne's Pudding
Jellied Fruit Salad
Coconut Cheesecake
Choux Pastry Ring with Apple
Marsala Soufflé
Strawberry Charlotte

Palm Hearts in Batter
Chicken Liver Risotto
Strawberry Charlotte

≈

Artichoke Heart Soufflés
Stir-fried Beef with Water Chestnuts
Choux Pastry Ring with Apple

≈

Watercress and Almond Soup
Chicken Satay with Peanut Sauce
Queen Anne's Pudding

≈

Avocado, Melon, and Mozzarella Salad
Roast Duck with Orange and Olives
Coconut Cheesecake

≈

Tomatoes Stuffed with Cold Scrambled Eggs
Mixed Vegetables in Cheese Pastry
Marsala Soufflé

≈

Croque Monsieur
Zarzuela
Jellied Fruit Salad

≈

Angels on Horseback
Spinach and White Stilton Tart
Jellied Fruit Salad

AQUARIUS THE GUEST

You are more than likely going to know a few Aquarians, because this is one of the friendliest and most social signs of the zodiac and they love to be invited out; and even if you don't, they are quite easy to spot because their individuality makes them stand out from the crowd.

Aquarius is like a white cloud on a still day. High above the ground it appears motionless, as it peeps into tomorrow, and often this detached sign of the zodiac seems to be somewhere else. Aquarians are dreamers, but they are realistic dreamers who do tend to know what they like and how to go about getting it.

Don't invite an Aquarian to dinner if it's a romantic, candlelit evening that you had in mind; this sign of the zodiac finds displays of emotion embarrassing and would much rather spend the evening mingling with a crowd and talking concepts than revealing his or her feelings. Freedom and independence are extremely important to Aquarians, and they don't enjoy committing themselves. However, it is worth nailing them down for dinner, because they do make intelligent guests who have great personal charm, which is suggested by the identification of this sign of the zodiac with Ganymede, the beautiful mortal who so charmed Zeus that he made him his cupbearer and gave him immortality.

Aquarians not only mix well with all sorts of people, they are interested in humanity as a whole. (They are symbolized by the man who holds a pitcher of water with which he offers spiritual enlightenment to mankind.) Open-minded and unprejudiced, they will be more than willing to try out whatever new ideas you have been cooking up, and are never too difficult to please.

This is a fixed sign of the zodiac, which reflects a time of year that is cold and white, as if the season will never change. And true to this image, Aquarians will quite happily eat the same dish time and time again so long as it's a favorite. But remember that this sign is fond of chilled dishes, such as a cold soup or a tart that echoes the cool of the winter, and food from the rivers or the sea, such as duck or goose or fish, which relates to their symbol of the waterman. Their aesthetic nature also appreciates an attractive-looking dish, but keep it simple because elaborate frills are not for this truth-seeking and idealistic sign.

If you invite an Aquarian to dinner, the evening may be unpredictable, but it should have a little bit of magic. Cater well because left to their own devices this sign of the zodiac can forget to eat altogether.

FIRST COURSES

Palm Hearts in Batter

Palm Hearts in Batter makes an exotic and different way of starting a meal that will appeal to the sign of the zodiac that strives for original ideas and different forms of expression. Serve this delicious vegetable with a bowl of mayonnaise as a starter, or on its own as a side dish to a game bird such as pheasant or grouse. *Serves 4*

> *2 medium eggs*
> *1 Tb grated Parmesan*
> *Salt and black pepper to taste*
> *One 14-oz (425-g) can of palm hearts*
> *1/4 cup (1 1/4 oz; 35 g) flour*
> *Vegetable or sunflower oil for frying*

<u>Garnishes</u>
> *A few lettuce leaves, washed and dried*
> *Mayonnaise (see page 59)*

In a small bowl, beat the eggs with the Parmesan and salt and black pepper. Drain the palm hearts and cut them lengthwise into approximately 1/4-inch slices. Turn the flour onto a large plate or wooden board and evenly coat the palm hearts with the flour. Shake off any excess. Pour enough oil into a large frying pan to fill 1/2 inch, and place over high heat. When the oil is hot, reduce the heat to moderately high. Place the bowl of eggs by the side of the frying pan and dip the palm heart slices in the egg just before you add them to the pan. Cook in batches so you don't crowd the pan. Sauté for 2–3 minutes on each side, or until golden brown, then drain and transfer to a hot serving dish and keep warm. After you have cooked about half of the palm hearts, drain the oil and add fresh oil. Garnish the edges of the dish (or individual dishes) with lettuce and serve with mayonnaise.

Watercress and Almond Soup

This delicious creamy soup is flecked with the dark green of watercress—an appropriate food for the sign of the zodiac that is represented by the water carrier. It can be served hot or cold (although you will need to add a little more milk if you serve it cold). Make it the night before you wish to serve and it will even improve in flavor. *Serves 4*

> ¾ lb (340 g) potatoes
> 4 Tb (2 oz; 60 g) butter
> 1 medium onion, peeled and finely chopped
> 1 small clove garlic, peeled and pushed through a press
> ½ cup (2 oz; 60 g) ground almonds
> Salt and black pepper
> 1¾ cups (14 oz) chicken stock
> 1 cup (8 oz) milk
> 2 bunches of watercress, trimmed
> ¼ cup (2 oz) light or single cream

Garnish

> 4 rolls, warmed in the oven

Peel the potatoes, rinse them in cold water, and cut them into about 1-inch cubes. Place the butter in a fairly large saucepan over moderately low heat. Add the potato cubes, onion, garlic, and almonds, and turn them in the fat. Season to taste with salt and black pepper. Cover, and sauté, stirring occasionally, for 10 minutes. Add the stock and milk, cover, and cook 10 minutes longer, or until the potatoes are just tender. Add the watercress and simmer 5 more minutes. Pour the soup into a food processor or blender, and purée. Return it to the pan, check the seasoning, and reheat. While the soup is reheating, pour the cream into a small pan and heat it through. Turn the soup into a warmed soup tureen, swirl in the cream, and serve with warm rolls.

Avocado, Melon, and Mozzarella Salad

This dish combines the pretty yellow-greens of avocado and melon, thinly sliced and broken up, with creamy white slices of mozzarella and black olives. Coated with a dressing that is lightly flavored and colored with dill, it makes a refreshing way to begin a meal. *Serves 4 to 6*

Dressing

3 Tb (1½ oz) sunflower or vegetable oil

1 Tb lemon juice

1 tsp superfine or castor sugar

½ tsp chopped fresh dill, or ¼ tsp dried

Salt and black pepper to taste

1 small honeydew (or other) melon
  (about 1 lb; 450 g)

5 oz (140 g) mozzarella

1 medium avocado

1 Tb lemon juice

Garnishes

6 black olives

Thin slices of buttered whole wheat bread

In a small bowl or jar, mix together thoroughly the dressing ingredients. Cut the melon in quarters lengthwise and scoop out and discard the seeds. Slice off the skin and cut the melon lengthwise into 12 slices of about ½-inch thickness and set aside. Cut the mozzarella into 12 slices about 3 inches by 1 inch. Then cut the avocado in half lengthwise, remove the pit, and lay the avocado flesh-side down on a plate or wooden board. Using a sharp knife, pierce the skin down the center from the top to the bottom and peel it off. Slice thinly lengthwise into 12 slices.

Sprinkle the avocado with lemon juice. Alternate slices of avocado with melon and mozzarella either on one large serving dish or equally among 4 individual dishes. Pour the dressing over, garnish with black olives, and serve with thin slices of buttered whole wheat bread.

Croque Monsieur

This French café dish is ideal for the Aquarian, who likes good food but is far too preoccupied with "higher things" to spend much time in the kitchen. It is a very good way for using up left-over ham and makes a marvelous snack dish or appetizer if it is sliced into small triangles. *Serves 2 to 8*

> 4 Tb (2 oz) soft butter
>
> 8 slices of bread from an average loaf, crusts removed
>
> 2 tsp Dijon mustard
>
> 6 oz (180 g) Gruyère or Emmenthal cheese, sliced into 4 pieces
>
> 12 stuffed green olives
>
> 4 slices (about 4 oz; 115 g) cooked ham
>
> Black pepper to taste
>
> 1 tsp red wine vinegar

Garnishes

> Slices of tomato
>
> A bunch of watercress, trimmed

Preheat the oven to 350°F (180°C; gas 4).

Butter each slice of bread and then spread ½ tsp mustard over 4 of the slices. Lay a slice of cheese over each piece of bread covered with mustard. Slice the olives and distribute an equal amount over each piece of cheese. Remove any surrounding fat from the ham slices, and arrange them equally over the cheese and olives. Season with black pepper (you probably won't need any salt because ham can be salty), and cover each with a slice of bread. Sprinkle a few drops of vinegar over each bread package.

Arrange the bread packages on a rack in a moderate oven and cook for 10 minutes, or until the cheese has melted and the bread is crisp. Remove to a wooden board and cut in half diagonally (and half again if you are serving as an appetizer). Arrange on a flat, warmed dish garnished with a few slices of tomato and sprigs of watercress, and serve immediately.

Artichoke Heart Soufflés

Puffs of delicately piquant soufflé served in individual dishes make a light and very inviting way to begin a meal. Easy to prepare, they make an ideal dish for this airy sign of the zodiac. *Serves 4 or 5*

One 14-oz (400-g) can artichoke hearts
Lemon juice
3 medium eggs, separated
Salt and black pepper

Béchamel sauce
1 Tb butter
1 Tb flour
1/2 cup (4 oz) milk

Preheat the oven to 375°F (190°C; gas 5). Butter four 3/4-cup (6-oz) ramekins, or 5 slightly smaller dishes.

Drain the artichokes, rinse, and pat them dry. Meanwhile, prepare the béchamel sauce. Place the butter in a small pan over moderately low heat, and when it has melted, add the flour and stir continuously for 2 minutes. Gradually pour in the milk and stir until you have a smooth sauce. Simmer for a few minutes and remove from the heat. Turn the artichoke hearts, 1 tablespoon of lemon juice, the béchamel sauce, and the egg yolks into a food processor or blender and purée. Season to taste with salt and black pepper. In a bowl beat the egg whites stiff. Pour the artichoke mixture down the side of the bowl in which the egg whites were beaten, and gently fold the egg whites in until they are thoroughly mixed. Divide the mixture among the ramekins and bake for 20 minutes, or until the soufflés have risen and are golden. Serve immediately.

Tomatoes Stuffed with Cold Scrambled Eggs

Sweet scarlet tomatoes are filled with creamy scrambled eggs and garnished with anchovies to make a colorful and very unusual starter. This is a good dish for a dinner party, which can be made in advance to leave the sociable Aquarian free to entertain his or her guests. *Serves 6*

6 large tomatoes (about 1¾ lb)
4 Tb (2 oz; 60 g) butter
6 medium eggs, lightly beaten
¼ tsp salt
⅛ tsp black pepper
2 Tb light or single cream

Garnishes

One 1¾-oz (50-g) can of anchovies, drained
Hot buttered toast

Place the tomatoes in a bowl, cover them with boiling water, and leave them for 30 seconds. Drain off the water and peel away their skins. Using a sharp knife, cut a fairly deep 1½-inch-diameter circle around the top of the tomato and scoop out the seeds and inside flesh, leaving about ¼ inch of tomato case. Place the tomatoes upside down on a paper towel to drain, while you prepare the eggs.

Place 2 tablespoons of butter in a pan over low heat. When it has melted, add the eggs and seasoning, and stir continuously until the eggs have a smooth consistency. When they are nearly cooked, remove them from the heat as they will continue to cook in the pan. Blend in the remaining butter and the cream, and spoon an equal amount of egg into each tomato case.

Set aside to cool (not in the refrigerator) for about 30 minutes, or until you wish to serve them. Garnish the top of each tomato with 2 anchovy fillets, crossing them over each other, and serve with triangles of hot buttered toast.

Angels on Horseback

Angels on Horseback recall the flight of Ganymede, the boy with the beauty of angels whom Zeus abducted. He was made immortal and became Zeus' cupbearer, pouring nectar from a golden bowl, and is responsible for showering Earth with heavenly rain. He is identified with the zodiac sign Aquarius, who is depicted as the man who holds a pitcher of water with which he offers spiritual rebirth to mankind. *Serves 4*

12 prunes
2 cups (16 oz) cold tea
6 slices (6 oz; 180 g) streaky bacon
4 medium slices of bread from an average loaf
4 Tb sunflower or vegetable oil

Preheat the broiler.

Place the prunes in a bowl, cover with cold tea, and leave to soak overnight. Drain them, then, using a sharp knife, cut a slit along one side and remove the pits. Pat the prunes dry with a paper towel. Remove the rind from the bacon, cut the slices in half crosswise (you need about 4–5-inch lengths), and roll one piece of bacon around each prune. Thread the bacon rolls onto four 5-inch skewers (or two 10-inch). Place on a rack covered with foil, 3 inches from the broiler element. Turn every 3–4 minutes and cook for 10–15 minutes, or until the bacon begins to brown and crisp. While the bacon rolls are cooking, remove the crusts from the bread and cut each slice in half diagonally. Place the oil in a large frying pan over moderately high heat. When it is hot, add the bread slices. Sauté for 1–2 minutes on each side, or until the bread is golden brown. (Remove the fried bread to a paper towel and keep warm if the bacon is not quite cooked.) Put 2 pieces of bread on each serving dish, arrange 3 bacon rolls on top, and serve.

MAIN COURSES

Zarzuela

Zarzuela is a Catalan dish that combines a delicious mixture of seafood cooked in a garlicky tomato and wine sauce. It is very messy and time-consuming to eat, so serve it on a lazy day, with finger bowls, lots of hot crusty bread, a green salad, and some Spanish Rioja wine. *Serves 2*

One 6–8-oz (180–225-g) squid

6 mussels

2 slices (10 oz; 285 g) swordfish, boned, or a thick fish that has been boned

2–3 Tb flour

3 Tb (1½ oz) olive oil

1 Spanish onion, peeled and thinly sliced

8 raw Pacific prawns

2 crab claws, cooked and broken in half

2 Tb chopped fresh parsley

2 large cloves garlic, peeled and pushed through a press

½ cup (4 oz) tomato paste

½ tsp superfine or castor sugar

1 cup (8 oz) fish or chicken stock

1 cup (8 oz) dry white wine

Salt and black pepper

Preheat the oven to 350°F (180°C; gas 4).

Cut the tentacles and head off the squid and then clean out the body; remove the bladelike bone and peel off the translucent outer film. Wash the tentacles and body in cold water. Chop the tentacles and slice the body into ½-inch-thick rings and set aside. Scrub the mussels clean in several changes of cold water. If any mussels are open when you have finished, throw them out. Turn the squid and swordfish in the flour and shake off any excess. Place the oil in a frying pan over high heat. When it is hot, add the swordfish and squid, and sauté for 1 minute on each side to seal in the juices, turning the squid so it cooks evenly. Turn into a 2-quart (about 3–Imperial pint) deep ovenproof dish (or 2 smaller ovenproof dishes). Lower the heat to moderately high, add the onion and sauté, stirring continuously for 5 minutes. Turn the onions into the dish with the prawns, mussels, crab, and parsley. In a bowl thoroughly mix together the garlic, tomato paste, sugar, stock, and wine, and pour over the fish. Season to taste with salt and black pepper. Place in the oven and cook for 40 minutes, or until the prawns have turned pink, the mussels have opened, the fish is cooked, and the dish is piping hot. (It will take less time if you use 2 dishes.) Serve hot from the oven with crusty bread and a green salad.

Spinach and White Stilton Tart

Dark, leafy spinach suggests the influence of the earthy planet Saturn, which is touched by the mysterious inspiration of Uranus (the modern ruler of Aquarius), giving this tart a little bit of magic. *Serves 4*

Shortcrust pastry to line a 10-inch pie pan (see page 12)

3 Tb (1½ oz) sunflower or vegetable oil

1 Spanish onion, peeled and thinly sliced

1½ lb fresh or frozen spinach

3 cloves garlic, peeled

5 medium eggs

½ cup (4 oz) light or single cream

¼ lb white (or blue) Stilton

1 tsp Dijon mustard

Salt and black pepper

Prepare the pastry as described on page 12.

While the pastry is chilling, prepare the filling. Heat the oil in a frying pan over moderately low heat, add the onion, and sauté for 20 minutes, stirring occasionally until the onion is soft. Meanwhile, wash the spinach in several changes of cold water, discarding any rough leaves and tough stems. Place it in a large pan with 1 clove of garlic. Cover, place over low heat, and simmer gently for 5–8 minutes, or until the spinach is tender. Drain thoroughly and turn into a food processor or onto a board, and chop quite finely. Put in a bowl (if it is not already in one) and thoroughly mix in the eggs, cream, 2 cloves of garlic pushed through a press, Stilton, and mustard, and season to taste with salt and black pepper.

Preheat the oven to 375°F (190°C; gas 5).

Roll the pastry out on a floured board into a circle to line a 9–10-inch quiche pan. Ease it into the pan, trim the edges, and fill with the spinach mixture. Bake for 30–35 minutes, or until the pastry is golden and the filling has risen slightly and is firm. Remove from the oven and serve hot or cold.

Chicken Satay with Peanut Sauce

Small cubes of chicken are marinated in a spicy coconut sauce, broiled, and served with a peanut sauce to make a deliciously different dish. Serve hot with a green salad or Greek Salad (see page 266), a bowl of egg noodles or rice, and a very cold, crisp white wine. *Serves 4*

Marinade

    1$\frac{1}{2}$ cups coconut milk

    1$\frac{1}{2}$ tsp ground ginger

    1$\frac{1}{2}$ tsp ground turmeric

    1$\frac{1}{2}$ tsp ground cumin

    1$\frac{1}{2}$ tsp brown sugar

    Salt and black pepper to taste

    2 large cloves garlic, peeled and pushed through a press

    1$\frac{1}{2}$ lb boned and skinned chicken breast, cut into about $\frac{3}{4}$-inch cubes

Peanut sauce

    1 clove garlic, peeled and pushed through a press

    1 cup (4 oz; 115 g) roasted peanuts, very finely chopped

    $\frac{1}{2}$ tsp chili powder

    1 cup (8 oz) water

    2 tsp brown sugar

    2 Tb soy sauce

    2 tsp lime or lemon juice

Garnishes

    $\frac{1}{2}$ medium cucumber, wiped clean and cut into $\frac{3}{4}$-inch cubes

    A bunch of scallions or spring onions

In a bowl or jar, mix thoroughly the marinade ingredients. Arrange the chicken in one layer in a shallow dish, and pour the marinade over. Leave it to marinate for 1$\frac{1}{2}$–2 hours. While the chicken is marinating, prepare the sauce.

Place all the sauce ingredients in a pan over moderately low heat, bring to a simmer, and let bubble for about 15–20 minutes, stirring occasionally, until the liquid has reduced and you have a smooth sauce. Turn into 2 small shallow bowls and set aside to cool.

Preheat the broiler.

Drain the chicken, reserving the marinade, and divide the chicken evenly among eight 6-inch skewers. Place them 3 inches from the broiler element, pour over a little of the marinade, and cook, turning and pouring a little of the marinade over every 2–3 minutes, for 8–10 minutes, or until the chicken is just cooked. Transfer to a warm, flat serving dish, garnish with cucumber cubes and scallions. Serve hot with the peanut sauce.

Roast Duck with Orange and Olives

Hapi, the Egyptian god of the Nile, was identified with Aquarius, the sign of the zodiac whose double zigzagging symbol represents a stream. All food from rivers and streams, especially water birds, are appropriate for this sign. Duck rubbed with cinnamon, roasted with orange and olives, and served with a delicious sauce that has a subtle bouquet of oranges, makes an exotic and festive dish—and it's no trouble to prepare. (For 6 people, cook 2 ducks and make twice as much sauce.) Serve with a red Burgundy wine, a green vegetable, and roast potatoes. *Serves 3*

One 5-lb duck, cleaned (with the giblets reserved)
1 clove garlic, peeled and pushed through a press
Salt
1 tsp cinnamon
Black pepper
1 orange, halved
6 pitted black olives

Stock
1 small onion, peeled
Bouquet garni
1½ cups (12 oz) water

Orange sauce
1 Tb flour
10 pitted black olives, sliced thinly crosswise
½ cup (4 oz) orange juice
1 Tb Cointreau

Thoroughly dry the duck inside and outside with a paper towel. Reserve the giblets for the stock. Prick the skin all over with a skewer or needle and leave it in a dry, airy place for a few hours. Pat the duck dry again in the same way.

Preheat the oven to 350°F (180°C; gas 4).

Rub the duck skin with the garlic, salt, and ground cinnamon. Season generously with black pepper. Stuff the duck with the 2 orange halves and black olives, and skewer to hold the stuffing in. Arrange the duck on a rack over a roasting pan. Roast for 1¾–2¼ hours for medium rare to well done, drawing off the fat every 30–40 minutes as it accumulates in the pan.

Meanwhile place the giblets and the other stock ingredients in a pan, cover, and simmer for 1 hour. Remove from the heat and set aside.

Transfer the duck to a platter and keep it warm while you prepare the sauce. Drain all but

ROAST DUCK WITH ORANGE AND OLIVES, CONTINUED

1 tablespoon of fat from the roasting pan, leaving the juices. Place the pan over moderately low heat. Add the flour and olives, and stir continuously for 2 minutes. Gradually stir in ½ cup (4 oz) stock and the orange juice, bring to a boil, and simmer for a few minutes. Remove from the heat, stir in the Cointreau, turn into a gravy boat, and serve the sauce with the duck.

Mixed Vegetables in Cheese Pastry

This dish combines an attractive mixture of nourishing vegetables in a curried sauce, all hidden by a delicious cheese pastry. It makes a beautifully simple supper dish that is wholesome and warming on a cold winter day. You can vary the filling according to what is seasonally available, but it is a good idea to use vegetables that need about the same time cooking and that give a splash of color. *Serves 4*

Cheese pastry

    1 cup plus 2 Tb (6 oz; 180 g) flour
    ¼ tsp salt
    6 Tb (3 oz; 85 g) butter
    2 cups (4 oz; 115 g) grated Cheddar cheese
    3 Tb (1½ oz) cold water

    1 medium (½ lb; 225 g) zucchini or courgettes
    Salt
    10 oz (285 g) rutabaga or swede
    2 medium (6 oz; 180 g) carrots
    1 tsp light brown sugar
    1½ cups (6 oz; 180 g) cauliflower florets
    ¼ lb (115 g) shelled fresh or frozen peas
    3 Tb (1½ oz; 45 g) butter
    3 Tb flour
    2 tsp curry powder
    1 clove garlic, peeled and pushed through a press
    Black pepper

Preheat the oven to 375°F (190°C; gas 5).

First prepare the pastry. Toss the flour and salt in a large bowl, cut in the butter, and mix lightly, then with your fingertips work the flour and butter together until the mixture has the consistency of bread crumbs. Add the cheese and water, mixing with a fork until the water is all absorbed and the cheese well mixed. Or alternatively, you can make this pastry in a food processor. First mix the flour, salt, and butter together until they resemble large bread crumbs, add the cheese, and then the water, through the funnel, mixing to a dough. Remove and shape into one round piece. Wrap the dough in plastic wrap and leave to chill for 20–30 minutes. While the pastry is chilling, prepare the filling.

Remove the ends of the zucchini, wash, pat dry, and cut crosswise into about 1/2-inch slices. Place on a large plate, sprinkle with salt, and leave to sweat for 20 minutes. Peel the rutabaga, rinse it in cold water, and cut into 3/4-inch cubes. Remove the ends from the carrots and cut them into 1/2-inch slices. Bring a large pan with a few inches of salted water to a boil, add the sugar, rutabaga, and carrots, cover, and boil for 5 minutes. Add the remaining vegetables, bring back to a boil, and cook 3 minutes longer, or until the vegetables are only just tender. Drain, reserving 1 1/4 cups (1/2 Imperial pint) of the water, and set aside.

Place the butter in a pan over moderately low heat. Add the flour and stir continuously for 2 minutes. Gradually add the reserved vegetable water, stirring continuously, until you have a smooth sauce. Add the curry powder and garlic and season to taste with salt and black pepper. Remove from the heat and gently mix in the vegetables. Turn into a 5 1/2-cup (2 1/4–Imperial pint) deep ovenproof pie plate. Place a shallow cup in the middle. Roll the pastry out on a floured board into a circle large enough to cover

the top generously, fold it in half, and lay it over the dish with the seam in the center. Unfold and crimp the edges. Cut two 2-inch slits on either side of the center, so that the steam can escape, and bake for 30 minutes, or until the pastry is golden brown. Serve immediately with a salad and crusty bread.

Chicken Liver Risotto

Rice relates to this humanitarian sign of the zodiac, because it feeds hundreds of millions of people in many Eastern countries and because it grows submerged in water. According to a certain myth, it was a food of the heavens that was brought to Earth by the daughter of the highest god. *Serves 4*

1 lb chicken livers

6 Tb (3 oz; 85 g) butter

1/2 lb (225 g) mushrooms, wiped clean and sliced

1/4 lb (115 g) shelled fresh or frozen peas

2 medium onions, peeled and chopped

1 cup (7 oz; 200 g) short-grain rice, preferably Italian Arborio

2 1/4 cups (18 oz) hot chicken stock

Salt and black pepper

Rinse the chicken livers in cold water and pat them dry with a paper towel. Trim any skin, veins, or greenish areas from the livers, and cut them into about 1-inch pieces. Heat 3 tablespoons of butter in a frying pan over moderate heat. Add the chicken livers, mushrooms, and peas, and sauté, stirring continuously, for 5–7 minutes, or until the livers are browned on the outside but still pink in the middle. Put on a plate and keep warm. Heat the remaining butter in the pan, add the onions, and sauté for 10 minutes, or until the onions are soft but not browned. Add the rice and stir to coat it in the butter and onions. Then mix in about 1/2 cup of the hot stock, and stir continuously until it has been absorbed. Continue to add the stock a little at a time, stirring until it is all absorbed, then add more. When the rice is tender and has absorbed all the liquid, mix in the chicken livers, mushrooms, and peas, and heat through. Season to taste with salt and black pepper, turn into a warmed serving dish, and serve hot with a green salad.

Stir-fried Beef with Water Chestnuts

Stir-fried Beef with Water Chestnuts has the taste of the Orient. Very quick and easy to prepare, it makes a different and excellent dish for the Aquarian, who likes to experiment in his or her laboratory—the kitchen. It is delicious served with a colorful stir-fried vegetable, such as broccoli, and noodles. *Serves 4*

1 lb sirloin or flank steak or fillet of beef

Marinade

1 Tb tomato ketchup

2 Tb dark soy sauce

1 Tb Shaosing wine or dry sherry

Black pepper to taste

1/2 tsp grated fresh gingerroot

1 tsp light brown sugar

2 Tb ground nut or corn oil

2 cloves garlic, peeled and pushed through a press

1-inch piece of gingerroot, peeled and finely chopped

3 scallions or spring onions, finely chopped crosswise

1/4 lb mushrooms, wiped clean and thinly sliced

1/2 lb bean sprouts

One 8-oz (227-g) can of water chestnuts, drained and sliced

Salt and black pepper

Garnish

Soy sauce

Trim any fat from the beef and cut it into 2-inch-long slices, 1/4–1/2 inch in thickness. In a small bowl or jar, thoroughly mix together the marinade ingredients. Arrange the beef in a shallow dish, pour the marinade over, and leave it in the refrigerator for 1 hour.

Drain the meat, reserving the marinade, and pat it dry. Place 1 tablespoon of the oil in a wok or large nonstick frying pan over moderately high heat. When it is hot, add the garlic and gingerroot, stir-fry for 30 seconds, then add the beef and stir-fry for 2–3 minutes longer, depending on how well done you like your meat. Transfer to a warmed serving dish and keep warm. Turn the pan juices into the reserved marinade and set aside. Heat the remaining oil in the wok or frying pan over the same heat. Add the scallions, mushrooms, bean sprouts, and water chestnuts, and stir-fry for 1 minute. Add the marinade to the pan and cook 2 minutes longer. Season to taste with salt and black pepper, arrange in the serving dish with the beef, and serve with soy sauce.

Greek Salad

Serve this colorful salad as a light summer lunch dish with some pita bread, Taramosalata, and Hummus (see pages 203 and 8), and Demestica wine, or to accompany a main course such as Chicken Satay with Peanut Sauce or Moussaka (see pages 260 and 37). *Serves 4*

1 small crisp head of lettuce

1/2 medium cucumber

3 medium tomatoes

6 scallions or spring onions

*1 1/4 cups (6 oz; 180 g) feta cheese,
    cut into 1/2-inch cubes*

3/4 cup (3 1/2 oz) black olives

Dressing

6 Tb olive oil

3 Tb lemon juice

Salt and black pepper

*1 Tb chopped fresh parsley (preferably
    Italian or flat-leaf)*

Trim the end of the lettuce and remove any damaged outer leaves. Wash and dry the leaves, shred, and arrange in a salad bowl. Peel the cucumber, quarter it lengthwise, and slice it into about 1–1 1/2-inch lengths. Wipe the tomatoes clean and quarter them. Chop the scallions finely crosswise. Arrange all the vegetables, cheese, and olives over the lettuce. In a small bowl or jar, mix together the dressing ingredients and season to taste with salt and black pepper. Pour over the salad, sprinkle with the parsley, toss, and serve.

Brussels Sprouts Mayonnaise

Brussels sprouts improve in flavor with the frosts of winter and are especially good when they are picked with the frost on them, making a suitable vegetable for the sign of the zodiac that rules midwinter. Small sprouts are best for this salad dish, which combines their sweet taste with grated carrot and chopped dates and a sharp mayonnaise dressing. Brussels Sprouts Mayonnaise goes well with Spinach and White Stilton Tart (see page 259), particularly if it is served cold. *Serves 6*

2 lb brussels sprouts

4 Tb (2 oz) mayonnaise (see page 59)

1/4 cup (2 oz) lemon juice

1/2 lb (225 g) carrots

3/4 cup (4 oz; 115 g) dates

Salt and black pepper

Garnish

1 small bunch of watercress, trimmed

Remove the rough outer leaves from the sprouts, trim the ends, and halve any large sprouts lengthwise. Cut an X into the bases. Place the sprouts in the top of a steamer over boiling water. Cover and steam for 10 minutes, or until the sprouts are just tender. Meanwhile, mix the mayonnaise with the lemon juice, trim the ends from the carrots, peel, and grate them. Pit the dates and chop them. Then add the sprouts to all the ingredients in a mixing bowl. Season to taste with salt and black pepper and transfer to a serving bowl. Refrigerate for several hours or overnight. Garnish the edges of the dish with watercress and serve.

Queen Anne's Pudding

King William thinks all,
Queen Mary talks all,
Prince George drinks all,
Princess Anne eats all.

Aquarian Princess Anne later became Queen of England, and was certainly fond enough of her food to have this dessert named after her; it is a simple dish of baked custard, sprinkled with Cointreau and then covered with a soft meringue topping. Very delicious and easy to make, it suggests the hazy genius of this air sign. *Serves 6*

> *3 medium egg yolks*
> *3 medium eggs*
> *1/4 cup (2 oz; 60 g) superfine or castor sugar*
> *Pinch of salt*
> *3 cups (1 1/4 Imperial pints) milk*
> *3 Tb (1 1/2 oz) Cointreau*

<u>Meringue topping</u>
> *4 medium egg whites*
> *4 Tb (2 oz) superfine or castor sugar*
> *Grated rind of 1 orange*

Preheat the oven to 300°F (150°C; gas 2). Butter a 5-cup ovenproof dish that is about 2 1/2 inches deep.

In a mixing bowl, beat the egg yolks with the whole eggs and sugar. Then mix in the salt and milk. Pour into the ovenproof dish and set in a pan of cold water. Bake for 75–80 minutes, or until a knife plunged into the center of the custard comes out clean. (While the custard is cooking, make sure that the water surrounding it does not reach the boiling point, or the custard will separate.) Remove the custard from the oven. Sprinkle the top with Cointreau and let the custard completely cool. Just before you wish to serve it, prepare the meringue.

Preheat the oven to 300°F (150°C; gas 2).

Put the egg whites in a bowl and beat, gradually adding the sugar, until stiff. Spread this meringue evenly over the top of the custard and sprinkle the orange rind over. Bake for 10–15 minutes, or until the meringue is lightly golden. Serve at room temperature.

Jellied Fruit Salad

Colorful fruits in a fresh orange jelly ring make a very refreshing and attractive way to end a meal, particularly good after a rich dish such as Roast Duck with Orange and Olives or Zarzuela (see pages 261 and 258). Vary the fruits as you like, although it's worth noting that the vivid green and black seeds of the kiwi fruit look delightful against the pale orange jelly. *Serves 6 to 8*

Orange jelly

    1 cup (8 oz) water
    3 Tb plus 2 tsp gelatin
    3 cups (24 oz) fresh orange juice
    1/4 cup (2 oz) lemon juice
    1/4 cup (2 oz; 60 g) superfine or castor sugar

    2 kiwi fruit, peeled and sliced crosswise
    1 1/4 cups (8 oz; 225 g) white grapes
    1 pear
    2 tangerines, peeled

Garnish

    Mixed peeled fruits for the center of the ring
        (optional)

Put the water in a small pan, sprinkle the gelatin over, and leave to soak for 5–10 minutes. Place over moderately low heat and stir occasionally until the gelatin has melted. Do not let it boil or the gelatin will not set. Turn the orange and lemon juice, sugar, and melted gelatin into a bowl, and mix thoroughly. Film the bottom of a 6-cup (2 1/2–Imperial pint) ring mold with the orange jelly and cover with about half the kiwi fruit, so that their edges just touch. Refrigerate for about 10–15 minutes, or until set. While the jelly is setting, peel the grapes, slice them in half lengthwise, and remove the seeds. Peel the pear, quarter it lengthwise and remove the core, then cut into 3/4-inch squares. Peel the membrane off each tangerine section. Mix all the remaining fruits into the liquid jelly. Pour or spoon into the ring mold, and refrigerate for several hours or overnight, until it is completely set. Unmold onto a serving dish, just before you serve, by dipping the ring in and immediately out of very hot water. Garnish the center of the ring with a selection of fresh fruits, if you wish, and serve.

Coconut Cheesecake

Coconut Cheesecake is a truly Aquarian creation. Coconuts are associated with Juno, goddess of light and air, whose special month was February. Rich, perfectly combining the taste of coconut and soft cheese, with just a hint of rum, this cheesecake is delicious enough for a very special occasion. *Serves 8*

Crumb crust

- 7 oz (200 g; about 13) graham crackers or digestive biscuits
- 2 Tb superfine or castor sugar
- 7 Tb (3½ oz; 100 g) melted butter

- 1 cup plus 2 Tb (5 oz; 140 g) creamed coconut, broken into pieces
- ½ cup boiling water
- 3 Tb cold water
- 4 tsp gelatin
- 2 medium eggs, separated
- ½ cup (4 oz; 115 g) superfine or castor sugar
- ½ cup (4 oz) heavy or double cream
- 1 cup (½ lb; 225 g) cream cheese
- 4 Tb (2 oz) white rum

In a food processor or with a rolling pin, crush the crackers. Pour the sugar and melted butter through the funnel of the food processor and mix thoroughly. Press the mixture into the bottom of a 9–10-inch pie or quiche pan and refrigerate.

Place the coconut in a bowl, pour the boiling water over, and let it soak for about 5 minutes. Turn the cold water into a pan, sprinkle the gelatin over, and let it soak for 5 minutes. Meanwhile, in the top of a double boiler, mix the egg yolks with the sugar. Place the bottom of the double boiler over barely simmering water, and slowly stir in the cream, stirring constantly until the mixture thickens slightly. Remove the custard from the heat and set aside. Stir the coconut so it dissolves and you have a smooth paste. Place the gelatin mixture over moderately low heat and stir occasionally until the gelatin has melted; do not boil or it will not set. Turn the coconut, custard, cream cheese, gelatin, and rum into a food processor or blender and mix thoroughly. In a clean bowl beat the egg whites until stiff. Gently but thoroughly fold them into the cheesecake mixture and turn into the crumb crust. Refrigerate for several hours or overnight. Serve chilled.

Choux Pastry Ring with Apple

This choux pastry ring is filled with a tasty mixture of cooked apple, golden raisins, and almonds. The top is sprinkled with confectioners sugar, which suggests the soft white snows of winter and the time of the year ruled by Aquarius. *Serves 6*

Choux pastry

   1/2 cup (4 oz) water
   Pinch of salt
   4 Tb (2 oz; 60 g) butter
   3/4 cup plus 2 Tb (4 oz; 115 g) flour
   2 medium eggs
   A few drops of vanilla

   2 lb (900 g) cooking apples
   3 Tb (1 1/2 oz; 45 g) butter
   2/3 cup (4 oz; 115 g) brown sugar
   1/4 tsp cinnamon
   3 Tb (1 1/2 oz) cider
   Pinch of salt
   1/4 cup (1 1/2 oz; 45 g) golden raisins or sultanas
   1/4 cup (1 oz; 30 g) toasted slivered almonds
   1 Tb confectioners or icing sugar

Garnish
   Thick cream

Preheat the oven to 375°F (190°C; gas 5).

Place the water and salt in a saucepan over moderate heat. Add the butter, and when it has melted, pour in all the flour. Stir continuously until the dough forms a ball. Remove from the heat and put in a bowl or food processor. Thoroughly beat in the eggs and vanilla or mix them in the food processor. Leave to cool slightly. On a buttered baking sheet form the dough into a 6 1/2-inch-diameter ring, 1 1/4 inches thick. Bake for 40–45 minutes. Remove from the oven and let it cool.

While the ring is cooling, peel and quarter the apples and cut out the cores. Place them in a pan with the butter, brown sugar, cinnamon, cider, salt, and raisins. Cover and simmer for 15 minutes, or until the apples are soft, stirring occasionally. If you have any excess liquid, remove the lid, increase the heat slightly, and let the apples bubble for a few minutes to reduce it. Remove the apples from the heat, and mash them a little so that they retain a slightly rough texture. Set aside to cool. Slice the top off the pastry ring. Mix the almonds into the apple mixture and spread into the bottom half of the ring, mounding the filling up in the middle so that it will fill

Marsala Soufflé

the hollow in the top half. Set the top half over the filling, sieve the confectioners sugar evenly over the surface, and serve with a bowl of thick cream.

Marsala Soufflé is a cold, light, and creamy soufflé that is delicately flavored with this sweet and very delicious Italian dessert wine. If Marsala is unavailable you can also use a sweet sherry or Madeira. Make this soufflé several hours or the night before you wish to serve it so it has time to set. *Serves 6*

> 1/2 cup (4 oz) Marsala, Madeira, or sweet sherry
> 1 Tb plus 1/2 tsp gelatin
> 5 medium eggs, separated
> 1/4 cup (2 oz; 60 g) superfine or castor sugar
> 11/4 cups (1/2 Imperial pint) heavy or double cream

Pour the Marsala into a small saucepan, sprinkle the gelatin over, and let soak for 5 minutes. Meanwhile, place the egg yolks and sugar in a bowl and beat them until they are pale and creamy. Turn the cream into a separate bowl and, using the same beaters, beat it until it is stiff. Place the Marsala mixture over low heat, and stir occasionally until the gelatin has melted. Do not boil or the gelatin will not set. Fold the egg yolk mixture and Marsala into the cream and mix lightly. Then, in a separate bowl, with clean beaters, beat the egg whites until they are stiff. Fold them into the cream, turn into a 6-cup (48-oz) dish, and refrigerate for several hours or overnight, until set, before serving.

Strawberry Charlotte

Strawberry Charlotte is an impressive-looking dessert that makes a very good dinner party dish. The light, delicious mousse filling is particularly appropriate for this sign of the zodiac since strawberries contain Aquarians' cell salt, sodium chloride (common salt), which distributes and regulates the moisture content of the body and helps circulation problems—a common complaint of this sign of the zodiac. *Serves 6*

4–6 Tb (3–4 oz) cherry brandy

4 tsp gelatin

About 20 ladyfingers

1 lb strawberries

1¼ cups (½ Imperial pint) heavy or double cream

6 Tb (3 oz; 85 g) superfine or castor sugar

2 medium egg whites

Place 3 tablespoons of the cherry brandy in a small saucepan, sprinkle the gelatin over, and let soak for a few minutes. Meanwhile arrange the ladyfingers in one layer in a shallow dish, pour the remaining cherry brandy over, and let them soak. Hull the strawberries, reserving 6–8 for decoration, and turn the rest into a food processor or blender, and purée. Place the gelatin mixture over low heat and stir occasionally until the gelatin has melted. Do not let it boil or the gelatin will not set. Mix the gelatin thoroughly with the strawberry purée. Turn the cream into a bowl and beat it until stiff, then fold in the sugar and the strawberry mixture. Turn the egg whites into a separate bowl and with clean beaters beat them stiff. Gently fold the egg whites into the strawberry mixture until they are thoroughly blended. Line the edges of a 7-cup (3–Imperial pint) glass bowl with the ladyfingers. Turn the strawberry filling into the bowl and refrigerate for several hours or overnight, until set. Garnish the top of the charlotte with the reserved strawberries and serve.

PISCES

FEBRUARY 20–MARCH 20

Rules the twelfth house, the house of the higher imagination

RULING PLANETS
Neptune and Jupiter
♓

ELEMENT
Water
♓

QUALITIES
Mutable, passive
♓

CHARACTERISTICS
Adaptable, artistic, compassionate, expansive,
impressionable, intuitive
♓

OPPOSITE SIGN
Virgo
♓

BODY AREA
Feet
♓

GEMSTONE
Amethyst, pearl
♓

COLOR
Crimson
♓

FLAVOR
Subtle, sweet-and-sour
♓

METAL
Aluminum
♓

FAUNA
Seafood, fish, fowl
♓

FLORA
Almonds, chestnuts, chicory, cucumber, endive,
fennel, figs, limes, maple, seaweed, sugarcane
♓

HERBS AND SPICES
Aniseed, chervil, cinnamon,
nutmeg, tarragon
♓

CELL SALT
Phosphate of iron (Ferr. Phos.), found in
almonds, beans, carrots, chicken, cocoa,
cucumber, egg yolk, fish, fresh fruits, leeks,
lettuce, liver, mustard greens, parsley, peas,
radishes, seaweed, spinach, watercress

PISCES THE COOK

If you happen to know any Pisceans, you are sure to be invited to their homes for a meal. This is a very sociable sign, which loves to entertain and is particularly sensitive to the likes and dislikes of others. Just what the Piscean is going to conjure up will remain a secret until it is time to eat, for the Piscean is fond of mystery and will not want to reveal exactly what went into the pot to create such a fascinating and subtle taste. The truth is that they probably won't remember themselves. So don't be surprised if your Piscean hosts present you with a plate of seaweed as a first course—apart from their obvious preference for seafood, they love to experiment and they rank among the most adventurous cooks in the zodiac.

Pisces is a water sign, suggesting an emotional, artistic, and imaginative nature. As a cook the Piscean will work impulsively and intuitively, making wonderfully decorative dishes. Recipe books will be gaily tossed aside as the Piscean lets creativity flow, transforming a relatively tidy kitchen into a disaster area as he or she becomes inspired. These are the most theatrical and flamboyant cooks of the zodiac, and you would be well advised to stay out of the kitchen when they are creating.

Pisces is ruled by two planets—Jupiter, the traditional ruler, and the more recently discovered Neptune. The influence of the expansive Jupiter is one of joviality, but it is also the planet that rules long-distance travel and communication. This suggests that the meal prepared by the Piscean will be both exotic and abundant. The quality of the dish may occasionally be lost because the impulsive Piscean refuses to work within the confines of a recipe, but happily the good fortune of Jupiter will enable this boundless creativity to be rewarded with culinary success, however unorthodox.

The effect that Neptune has on this sign is much more subtle and elusive. It rules the higher mind and the ability for complete spiritual awareness; it is responsible for the flash of genius in the kitchen that produces the perfect finishing touch to a dish—that yearning for perfection that is unobtainable in life—and suggests through its rulership of the sea a preponderance of seafood, tasty soups, and shimmering mousses, which echo the reflective surface of water.

Wine is likely to flow in the Piscean household, partly because of the generous and fun-loving nature of Jupiter and also because Neptune rules states of consciousness that reveal themselves under the influence of drink or drugs. Pisces, like its element, water, is nonmaterial, and consequently, will not begrudge spending on delicious bottles of wine; Pisceans have a preference for slightly sweet white wines, or an Alsatian wine or champagne, which echoes the effervescence of the Piscean personality.

RECIPES FOR PISCES

First Courses

Fresh Figs Wrapped in Smoked Salmon
Avocado with Crab and Walnuts
Almond and Fennel Fish Soup
Leeks with Lemon and Coriander Dressing
Rolled Seaweed Bex
Cucumber Ring with Chicken Filling
Chicken Livers in Aspic

Main Courses

Belgian Endive with Ham and Cheese
Trout with Mushrooms and Watercress
Wine-Glazed Beef Roll
Creamed Noodles with Liver
    and Soy Sauce
Neapolitan Leek Tart
Sweet-and-Sour Shrimp with
    Green Pepper and Cashew Nuts
Poached Chicken with Mussel Sauce

Side Dishes

Spinach, Cress, and Water Chestnut Salad
Stir-fried Bean Sprouts

Desserts

Poached Pears in Orange with
    Chocolate Sauce
Raspberry Trifle
Strawberry, Banana, and Kiwi Fruit Tart
Lime Soufflé
Highland Fling
Madame Banchet's Chestnut Pudding

MENU SUGGESTIONS FOR PISCES

Almond and Fennel Fish Soup
Wine-Glazed Beef Roll
Madame Banchet's Chestnut Pudding

)(

Avocado with Crab and Walnuts
Creamed Noodles with Liver and Soy Sauce
Strawberry, Banana, and Kiwi Fruit Tart

)(

Rolled Seaweed Bex
Sweet-and-Sour Shrimp with Green Pepper
and Cashew Nuts
Highland Fling

)(

Fresh Figs Wrapped in Smoked Salmon
Poached Chicken with Mussel Sauce
Lime Soufflé

)(

Cucumber Ring with Chicken Filling
Belgian Endive with Ham and Cheese
Highland Fling

)(

Leeks with Lemon and Coriander Dressing
Trout with Mushrooms and Watercress
Raspberry Trifle

)(

Chicken Livers in Aspic
Neapolitan Leek Tart
Poached Pears in Orange with
Chocolate Sauce

PISCES THE GUEST

If the Piscean can be persuaded to stop dreaming for a moment and join you for dinner, you won't be disappointed. Those born under this sign of the zodiac are natural comedians who treat life as a masquerade and, when called upon, can keep an entire dinner party entertained with amusing stories and anecdotes. Pisceans love convivial gatherings and they possess a natural ability to involve others. While they are extremely partial to food and drink, they will undoubtedly relish whatever delicacy you provide on such an occasion.

Pisces is a mutable sign, indicating a versatile nature and one that has the ability to capture the spirit of the moment and adapt to it. But it also has a darker side, indicated by its dual nature and rulership by two planets, Jupiter and Neptune, suggesting an aptitude for sudden change. Like Neptune, the god of the sea who is both merciless and playful, Pisces is capable of extreme moods, often without warning.

Pisceans, like the fish that symbolize the sign, are able to change their coloring to blend in with their surroundings and to harmonize with them, taking things very much as they come. So don't panic if your quiche has frayed, brown edges—the Piscean guest, who inwardly suspects that it might upset rather than excite the gastric juices, will be sure to convince you that this is truly delicious. In the right mood, people under this sign can convince themselves (and you) that a simple meal is really a banquet; this is the magician in them at work.

As dining companions, Pisceans have the ideal temperament—they are amenable and charming and will get on with most people. Blessed with an easygoing nature, they are inclined to gloss over rather than confront difficulties and will no doubt chat freely, listen sympathetically, and generously give people the benefit of the doubt. However, if you are worried that your party may not go with a swing, remember that they are most compatible with other water and earth signs.

When cooking for a Piscean, choose one colorful dish, as this will appeal to the aesthetic side of his or her nature. You are free to experiment with this sign, so try a Chinese or Oriental dish, beautifully arranged, or one that combines sweet-and-sour flavors—a contrast they love. Other foods that will appeal to the Piscean include fish and seafood; liquid foods such as soups, stews, and casseroles; foods with a shimmering or reflective quality, such as aspic, jelly, or mousse; and slippery foods, such as pasta and noodles. Iron is an important ingredient in the Piscean diet, and any foods that contain their cell salt, phosphate of iron, are also ideal.

Fresh Figs Wrapped in Smoked Salmon

This delicious appetizer, a combination of sweet and savory tastes, is best served with champagne or an Alsatian wine. The contrasting flavors appeal to the dual nature of Pisces and show the influence of the ruling planets—figs for Jupiter, fish for Neptune. Make the most of this dish in midsummer, when rich, ripe figs are available. *Serves 4*

8 slices (*1/2* lb; 225 g) smoked salmon

8 fresh, ripe figs, peeled

Garnishes

4 thin slices of whole wheat bread, buttered and halved

1 lemon, quartered

Mustard greens

Watercress, trimmed

Wrap a slice of smoked salmon around each fig and arrange these on a serving dish. Serve with thin slices of whole wheat bread, lightly buttered, and lemon quarters. Garnish with mustard greens and watercress.

Avocado with Crab and Walnuts

Avocado cases, enclosing a rich and creamy crabmeat filling, make a very special appetizer. Serve with thin slices of bread and butter and wedges of lemon. *Serves 4*

1 cup (6 oz; 180 g) fresh crabmeat

2 Tb crushed shelled walnuts

1 cup (2 oz; 60 g) grated Cheddar cheese

2 Tb heavy or double cream

2 Tb lemon juice

2 Tb chopped fresh parsley

2 Tb chopped fresh chives

Salt and black pepper

2 ripe avocados

Preheat the broiler.

In a mixing bowl or food processor, thoroughly mix all the ingredients, except the avocados, and season to taste with salt and pepper. Slice the avocados in half lengthwise and remove the pits. Fill the cavities with the crab mixture, mounding the filling so that all the avocado is covered. Then place them so their tops are 3 inches from the broiler element, and cook for 5 minutes, until the top is golden brown and bubbling. Serve hot.

Almond and Fennel Fish Soup

Pisceans will love this unusual and replenishing soup, which is full of ingredients beneficial to this sign of the zodiac—almonds, and cod rich in protein and nourishing liquid to match the shadowy and boundless nature of Pisces' ruling planet, Neptune, the god of the sea. *Serves 4*

4 Tb (2 oz; 60 g) butter
1 medium onion, peeled and finely chopped
1 cup (4 oz; 115 g) chopped fennel (about 1/2 a
    large bulb)
1/2 cup (2 oz; 60 g) ground almonds
Salt and black pepper
1 1/2 cups (12 oz) milk
1 1/4 cups (10 oz) water
1 lb cod fillet (from the thin end so there are
    no bones), skinned
2 Tb Pernod
3/8 cup (3 oz) light or single cream

Garnishes
A few chopped fennel leaves
4 rolls, warmed

Place the butter in a fairly large saucepan over moderately low heat. Add the onion, fennel, and almonds and turn them to coat. Season to taste with salt and black pepper. Cover, and sauté, stirring occasionally, for 10 minutes. Pour the milk and water over, cover, and increase the heat just slightly. Simmer for 10 minutes. Turn the soup into a food processor or blender, and purée. Return to the pan, bring to a simmer, and add the fish. Cover, and cook for 8–10 minutes longer, or until the fish is cooked and has broken into pieces. Remove from the heat, stir in the Pernod and cream, check the seasoning, and turn into a warmed soup tureen. Garnish with chopped fennel leaves and serve with warmed rolls.

Leeks with Lemon and Coriander Dressing

A harmonious way to begin a meal. Pisceans, fond of dressings, will be charmed by the delicate and subtle flavor of this pleasing first course. The leeks supply the Piscean cell salt, phosphate of iron, as well as a Martian nature, to strengthen their spirit. (Water signs are sympathetic to Mars because of the fiery motion water has of breaking down and demolishing solids.) *Serves 4*

> 2–2½ lb (8 medium) leeks

Dressing
> 6 Tb (3 oz) olive oil
> 3 Tb (1½ oz) lemon juice
> 2 tsp superfine or castor sugar
> 1 Tb ground coriander
> Salt and black pepper

Garnish
> Buttered slices of whole wheat bread

Cut the roots and tough green ends off the leeks, leaving about 1½ inches of green part, and cut a 2½-inch X down the remaining green of each leek. Then place them in a heavy-bottomed pan with about ½ inch of water, just enough so that the leeks will not burn. Cover, and simmer for 10–15 minutes, adding a little more water if necessary, until the leeks are tender.

While the leeks are cooking, mix the dressing ingredients in a small bowl or jar, and season to taste with salt and black pepper. Then when the leeks are cooked, drain any water from them and arrange in a shallow serving dish. Pour the dressing over while the leeks are still hot and leave them to chill before serving with buttered slices of whole wheat bread.

Rolled Seaweed Bex

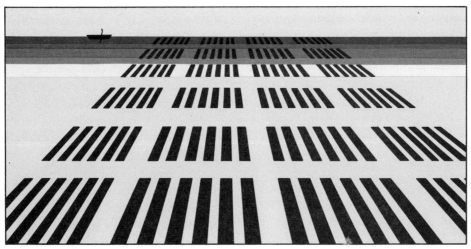

This is as unusual in taste as it is in concept. Echoing the secrecy and genius of the sea, embodied in the astrological sign of Pisces, Japanese Nori, which is grown on nets in tidal waters, has a sweet and delicate nutty taste; rich in iodine, it is also particularly beneficial for this sign of the zodiac, and a necessity for the correct functioning of the Piscean's metabolism. *Serves 4*

4 Tb soft whole wheat bread crumbs

2 Tb milk

3 Tb vegetable oil

2 small onions, peeled and finely chopped

3 cloves garlic, peeled and pushed through a press

3/8–1/2 cup (about 1/4 lb or 2 small) finely chopped tomatoes

2/3 cup (2 oz; 60 g) finely chopped mushrooms

1/2 cup (2 oz; 60 g) finely chopped mixed nuts

Pinch of dried basil, or 1/4 tsp chopped fresh

1 Tb finely chopped fresh parsley

Salt and black pepper

8 sheets of Nori or green laver seaweed, 4 by 8 inches

In a small bowl, soak the bread crumbs in the milk. Then heat 2 tablespoons of the oil in a medium-size frying pan and gently sauté the onions for 8 minutes, or until translucent. Stir in the garlic, tomatoes, mushrooms, mixed nuts, and bread crumbs, add the basil and parsley, and cook gently for 10 minutes; season with salt and pepper to taste. Then divide the mixture into eight equal amounts. On a wooden board place a strip of seaweed, spoon one portion of the stuffing at one end, then roll the seaweed up so it resembles a sausage. Repeat.

Heat the remaining tablespoon of oil in the frying pan, and over medium heat cook the seaweed rolls for about 5 minutes, turning them frequently. Correct the seasoning, if necessary. Remove the seaweed rolls, and drain any excess oil on paper towels before serving.

Cucumber Ring with Chicken Filling

This refreshing dish even tastes as if it is good for you. The cucumber ring can easily be made in advance, while the filling can transform leftover chicken into something quite special. A most appropriate starter (or even light lunch dish, served with a salad) for Pisces, the most fluid of all the water signs, who will naturally respond to the rhythmic curves suggested by this shimmering form. *Serves 6 to 8*

> 2 large cucumbers, peeled and finely grated
>
> 1 small onion, peeled and finely grated
>
> 4 Tb (2 oz) lemon juice
>
> 1 Tb chopped fresh parsley
>
> 1 Tb chopped fresh tarragon, or 1½ tsp dried
>
> 3 Tb medium-dry sherry
>
> 2 Tb plus 1 tsp gelatin
>
> 2 cups (16 oz) chicken stock
>
> Salt and black pepper

Filling

> 1¼ cups (6 oz) cooked, skinned, boned, and shredded chicken
>
> 1 cup (3 ribs) chopped celery
>
> 1 scallion or spring onion, finely chopped
>
> 2 Tb lemon juice
>
> 3 Tb mayonnaise (see page 59)
>
> Salt and black pepper

Garnishes

> Watercress, trimmed
>
> Rounds of toast or hot crunchy bread

In a large mixing bowl, thoroughly mix the cucumbers, onion, lemon juice, parsley, and tarragon. Pour the sherry into a medium-size bowl, sprinkle in the gelatin, and allow it to soften for a few minutes. Then pour the stock into a saucepan, bring it to a boil, and pour it over the gelatin. Stir constantly until the gelatin has completely dissolved, and then turn it into the cucumber mixture. Mix together thoroughly, season to taste with salt and black pepper, and turn the mixture into a 5-cup (2–Imperial pint) ring mold. Let it chill until it has set, and prepare the filling.

In a bowl, thoroughly mix the chicken with the celery, scallion, lemon juice, and mayonnaise, and season to taste with salt and black pepper. Turn the cucumber ring out onto a serving dish (to unmold, dip the mold in and immediately out of very hot water). Fill the center with the chicken mixture, garnish the ring with watercress, and serve with rounds of toast or hot crunchy bread.

Chicken Livers in Aspic

This rich and decorative first course is an unusual way to start a meal and can be prepared the night before. Serve garnished with lettuce and watercress, and with a bottle of light, fruity red wine and rounds of toast. *Serves 6 to 8*

> 1 lb chicken livers
>
> 2 Tb butter
>
> 1/2 cup (about 6) finely chopped scallions or spring onions
>
> 2 tsp Dijon mustard
>
> Salt and black pepper
>
> 1/2 cup (4 oz) brandy
>
> 2 Tb port or Marsala
>
> 1 Tb plus 1/2 tsp gelatin
>
> 1 cup (8 oz) chicken stock

Garnishes

> Lettuce, washed and dried
>
> Watercress, stems trimmed

First trim any skin or veins from the livers. Then in a medium-size frying pan, melt the butter over low heat and sauté the scallions gently for 10 minutes. Add the livers, increase the heat slightly, and sauté for 2–3 minutes longer, turning occasionally. Stir in the mustard, season with salt and pepper to taste, and pour the brandy over. Cover, and simmer for 10 minutes—the livers should be slightly pink in the center. Then remove them to a board and allow them to cool, reserving their juices.

Next, pour the port or Marsala into a medium-size mixing bowl, sprinkle in the gelatin, and leave it to soak for a few minutes. Then pour the stock into the reserved liver juices, bring to a boil, and pour into the gelatin. Stir continuously until all the gelatin has dissolved. Pour a 1/4-inch layer of the stock mixture into a 41/2-cup (11/2–Imperial pint) mold and chill for about 30 minutes, or until it has set. Arrange the livers in the mold and pour over the remaining stock and leave to chill until set.

Turn the aspic out onto a serving dish lined with lettuce leaves (to unmold, dip the mold in and immediately out of very hot water), garnish with watercress, and serve.

Belgian Endive with Ham and Cheese

An ideal light lunch or supper dish for the Piscean who loves sauces. The main ingredient, Belgian endive, is a beneficial plant for this sign, since it clears congestion, a complaint from which the Piscean tends to suffer. Serve with green beans or Spinach, Cress, and Water Chestnut Salad (see page 291) and new potatoes. *Serves 4*

2 lb (or 8 pieces) Belgian endive
1 Tb lemon juice

Cheese sauce
2 Tb butter
3 Tb flour
2 cups (16 oz) milk
1 cup (2 oz; 60 g) grated Cheddar cheese
1 cup (2 oz; 60 g) grated Gruyère cheese
2 tsp Dijon mustard
Salt and black pepper
Pinch of nutmeg
1 lb (or 8 slices) cooked ham

Topping
1 cup (2 oz; 60 g) soft whole wheat bread crumbs
2 Tb butter

Trim and clean the endive and place it and the lemon juice in a large pan of boiling salted water. Cover, and simmer for 20 minutes, or until tender. While the endive is cooking, make the cheese sauce.

Melt the butter in a medium-size saucepan and stir in the flour. Cook them together for 1–2 minutes before gradually stirring in the milk. Bring to a boil, and simmer for 2–3 minutes, then stir in the cheeses and mustard, and season to taste with salt, pepper, and nutmeg.

Preheat the broiler.

Drain the endive well and transfer it to a wooden board. Roll one piece of ham around each piece of endive and lay in an ovenproof dish, seam-side down. Then pour the cheese sauce over, sprinkle with bread crumbs, and dot with butter. Place the dish about 2 inches from the broiler, and cook for 3–4 minutes, or until the top is bubbling and golden.

Trout with Mushrooms and Watercress

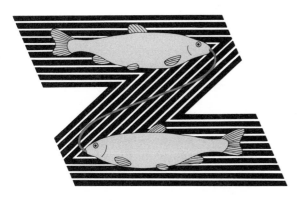

Pisces is graphically symbolized by the two fish who swim in opposite directions and yet are joined by a silver cord. They represent the yearning the Piscean has for the unobtainable—this is the mystic in Pisces—and the confusion this sign often experiences in having to cope with everyday reality. *Serves 2*

2 trout, gutted and washed
2 Tb flour
2 Tb butter
1 Tb vegetable oil
1 Spanish onion, peeled and thinly sliced
3 scallions or spring onions, sliced
1 clove garlic, peeled and pushed through a press
1/4 lb (115 g) mushrooms, wiped clean and sliced
2 Tb chopped, trimmed watercress
Salt and black pepper
1 1/2 Tb Pernod
Pinch of chervil
1 1/2 Tb heavy or double cream

Roll the trout in the flour and shake off any excess. Then gently melt the butter in a frying pan large enough to hold both fish. Over moderate heat, sauté the fish for 5 minutes on each side. Remove them to a serving dish and keep warm while you prepare the vegetables.

Heat the oil in the same frying pan over moderate heat, and add the onions and garlic. Cook them gently for 10 minutes, until the onions are translucent. Mix in the mushrooms and watercress, and cook for 10 minutes longer, stirring occasionally. Season to taste with salt and pepper, and stir in the Pernod and chervil. Simmer a moment, then turn the heat to very low and blend in the cream. Remove the pan from the heat, spoon the vegetables and sauce over the trout, and serve.

Wine-Glazed Beef Roll

A dish to excite the appetite but soothe the stomach. Neptune's influence is in evidence here, transforming ordinary ingredients into an exotic culinary creation. Glowing, wine-dark, and green, the reflective quality of the jelly surrounding this beef roll will appeal to the aesthetic side of the Piscean nature, while the parsley provides a decorative source of phosphate of iron, the Piscean's cell salt. Beef roll is an adaptable dish that can also be served hot from the oven, to please any less watery sign the Piscean may wish to entertain. *Serves 4*

    1 lb ground beef

    1 small onion, peeled and finely chopped

    3 cloves garlic, peeled and pushed through a press

    1 cup (2 oz; 60 g) soft whole wheat bread crumbs

    1 tsp dry mustard

    2 medium carrots, peeled and grated

    1/2 cup (2 oz; 60 g) clean, finely
        chopped mushrooms

    1 Tb tomato paste

    1 medium egg

    1 1/2 tsp dried mixed herbs, or 1 Tb finely
        chopped fresh mixed herbs

    Salt and black pepper to taste

    4 pieces (4 oz) unsmoked, streaky bacon

Wine glaze

    Red wine

    1 Tb gelatin

    4 Tb finely chopped fresh parsley

Preheat the oven to 350°F (180°C; gas 4).
    Thoroughly mix all the ingredients in a large bowl, except for the bacon and wine glaze, then firmly shape them into a rounded oblong loaf. Remove the rind from the bacon and lay two strips along the bottom of the meat loaf and two along the top. Place in a shallow pan (there is no need to grease it since the bottom of the loaf is covered with bacon). Bake the meat loaf for 45 minutes. Remove the loaf from the oven and wrap it in foil. Let it cool for a few hours, and when the meat is cold, prepare the glaze.

Place 2 Tb of red wine in a small bowl, then sprinkle in the gelatin and allow it to soak for a few minutes. Heat 3/4 cup (6 oz) of wine in a saucepan, and when it begins to simmer, pour it into the gelatin. Stir so that the gelatin completely dissolves, and then mix in the parsley. Chill until the gelatin begins to thicken. Unwrap the beef and place it on a cake rack. Then, using a pastry brush, brush the meat with the glaze, turning it so that it is completely coated. Chill the meat for 10–15 minutes, until the coating of jelly has set, and then repeat this procedure, giving it 3–4 coats. If the jelly becomes too solid to work with, warm it gently in a small saucepan. Do not allow it to boil or it will not set. Serve when the final glaze has set, with a spinach salad and hot crusty bread.

Creamed Noodles with Liver and Soy Sauce

This nourishing meal is a tonic for any Piscean, and is as versatile a dish as the sign to which it is allocated. Serve without the liver as a vegetarian first course or as a main dish with a hot crusty loaf and a chervil, endive, and radish salad, all beneficial foods for this sign of the zodiac. *Serves 4*

*5/8 cup (3 1/2 oz; 95 g) dried white kidney beans
  or butter beans*

Salt

1/4 lb (115 g) zucchini

2 medium leeks

3 Tb (1 1/2 oz) vegetable oil

2 cloves garlic, peeled and pushed through a press

1 Tb tomato paste

1 cup (8 oz; 225 g) shelled cooked peas

1 1/2 tsp dried basil, or 1 Tb chopped fresh

2 tsp dried oregano, or 1 1/2 Tb chopped fresh

2 Tb soy sauce

1/2 cup (4 oz) light or single cream

Salt and black pepper

1/2 lb (8 oz; 225 g) Chinese egg noodles

1/2 lb lamb's liver, thinly sliced

Butter

Soak kidney beans overnight in 3 inches of water to cover. Drain the kidney beans and place them in a medium-size saucepan with 1/4 teaspoon of salt and cover them with 2–3 inches of cold water. Cover them with a lid and bring them to a boil, then cook for about 1 hour, or until they are tender. While the beans are cooking, slice the zucchini crosswise, discard the ends, and sprinkle with salt. Leave the zucchini to sweat for about 30 minutes.

Chop the leeks, discard the roots and ragged green ends, and rinse well in cold water. Pat them dry using a paper towel. Heat the oil in a large frying pan and gently sauté the leeks, over moderate heat, for 10 minutes. Pat the zucchini dry with a paper towel, stir them into the leeks with the garlic and tomato paste, and cook 5–10 minutes longer, stirring occasionally. Mix in the kidney beans, peas, herbs, and soy sauce, and heat through. Then turn the heat to very low, stir in the cream, and season to taste with salt and pepper. Cover the pan to keep the vegetables warm while you prepare the liver and noodles.

Place the noodles in a large pan of boiling salted water and cook them rapidly, until they are done *al dente*. While the noodles are cooking melt 1 tablespoon of butter in a medium-size frying pan and gently sauté the liver for 1–2 minutes on each side, season to taste with salt and black pepper, and remove it to a wooden board. Cut the liver into thin strips and mix it into the vegetables. Drain the noodles and turn them into a large, warmed serving dish with a knob of butter, toss with the vegetables and liver, and serve immediately.

Neapolitan Leek Tart

This unusual and delicately flavored tart makes a tasty lunch or dinner party dish. Serve it with a crisp green salad, potato salad, and some Chianti.
Serves 4

> Shortcrust pastry to line a 10-inch pan
> (see page 12)
> 2 lb (or 6–8) leeks
> 4 Tb (2 oz) sunflower oil
> 1/2 tsp dried oregano, or 1 tsp chopped fresh
> Salt and black pepper to taste

Neapolitan sauce

> 2 Tb olive oil
> 2 small onions, peeled and finely chopped
> 2 cloves garlic, peeled and pushed through a press
> 1 Tb tomato paste
> 1 lb tomatoes, peeled and chopped
> 1/2 lb (225 g) mushrooms, wiped clean and sliced
> 1 medium carrot, peeled and grated
> 1/4 tsp dried basil, or 1/2 tsp chopped fresh
> 1 tsp sugar
> Salt and black pepper
> 1 Tb chopped fresh parsley

White sauce

> 2 Tb butter
> 2 Tb flour
> 1 cup (8 oz) milk
> 1 tsp Dijon mustard
> Pinch of nutmeg
> Salt and black pepper

> 1 Tb grated Parmesan

Preheat the oven to 425°F (220°C; gas 7).

Roll out the pastry to line a 10-inch tart or quiche pan, prick the bottom with a fork, and bake for 10 minutes. Remove and lower the heat to 375°F (190°C; gas 5).

Chop the leeks and rinse them well in cold water, then dry them. Heat the sunflower oil in a large saucepan and add the leeks, turning them in the oil. Stir in the oregano, season with salt and black pepper to taste, cover, and let the leeks cook gently for 20 minutes over a medium heat, while you prepare the Neapolitan sauce.

Heat the olive oil in a large frying pan, add the onions, and sauté them over moderately high heat for about 6 minutes. Stir in the garlic and tomato paste, mixing well before adding the tomatoes, mushrooms, carrot, basil, sugar, and parsley; season to taste with salt and black pepper, and leave to simmer for 30 minutes, stirring occasionally, while you prepare the white sauce.

Melt the butter in a medium-size saucepan and stir in the flour to form a roux. Cook gently for 1–2 minutes before gradually pouring in the milk. Stir continuously until you have a smooth sauce, and when it has come to a boil, lower the heat and simmer for 2–3 minutes. Season to taste with mustard, nutmeg, salt, and pepper. Remove from the heat and cover.

Then uncover the leeks and let them simmer for a few minutes, to reduce any liquid. Turn the leeks into the pastry shell. Reduce the liquid from the Neapolitan sauce by fast boiling for about 10 minutes. Pour the white sauce over the leeks, then cover with the Neapolitan sauce. Sprinkle with Parmesan and cook in the oven for 30–35 minutes.

Sweet-and-Sour Shrimp with Green Pepper and Cashew Nuts

Pisceans will adore this Chinese dish that combines the dual tastes of sweet and sour, perfect for this mutable and most dual sign of the zodiac. It goes particularly well with Stir-fried Bean Sprouts (see page 291) and noodles and soy sauce. Serve with a cold white wine. *Serves 4*

Sweet-and-sour sauce

> 2 Tb (1¹/₂ oz) wine vinegar
>
> 3 Tb brown sugar
>
> 3 Tb (1¹/₂ oz) Shaosing wine or sweet sherry
>
> 2 Tb (1¹/₂ oz) soy sauce
>
> 1 Tb tomato ketchup
>
> 2 tsp cornstarch

> 1 medium green pepper
>
> 2 Tb sesame or corn oil
>
> 4 large scallions or spring onions
>
> 1¹/₂-inch piece of gingerroot, peeled and finely chopped
>
> 4 cloves garlic, peeled and pushed through a press
>
> ¹/₂ cup (2 oz) raw cashew nuts, broken into large pieces
>
> 1 lb raw shrimp or prawns, peeled
>
> 1 Tb toasted sesame seeds

In a small bowl or jar mix together the sauce ingredients. Then prepare the green pepper: cut it in half lengthwise, remove the stalk, seeds, and whitish membrane, and chop it.

Heat the oil in a wok or frying pan over high heat and quickly stir-fry the green pepper, scallions, ginger, garlic, nuts, and shrimp for 2 minutes. Pour over the sauce, and cook 2–3 minutes longer, turning the shrimp in the sauce. Then, when the shrimp turn pink, remove the pan from the heat, sprinkle the sesame seeds over, and serve.

Poached Chicken with Mussel Sauce

Sensitive to the altered states that alcohol can induce, the Piscean will be delighted by the generous and seductive flavor of the wine and mussel sauce covering this poached chicken. Truly a Neptune-inspired dish, this is delicious served with rice and petits pois. *Serves 4*

2¹/₂–3 lb chicken, cut into 8 pieces

1 bay leaf

About 3 cups (24 oz) water

1 quart (2 lb) mussels

1 medium onion, peeled and finely chopped

5 cloves garlic, peeled and finely chopped

1 cup plus 2 Tb (10 oz) dry white wine

3 large egg yolks

¹/₂ cup (4 oz) heavy or double cream

1 Tb cornstarch

3 Tb chopped fresh parsley

Salt and black pepper

Preheat the oven to 400°F (200°C; gas 6).

Arrange the chicken pieces and bay leaf in a casserole, and just cover with the water. Cover, and cook in the oven for 40–45 minutes, or until the chicken is done.

While the chicken is cooking, scrub the mussels clean in a basin of cold water. If any mussels are open when you have finished, throw them out. Place the onion, garlic, and wine in a saucepan, cover, and bring to a boil. Simmer for 5 minutes, then add the mussels, cover, and cook 5 minutes longer, until the mussel shells have steamed open. Remove the pan from the heat, transfer the mussels to a bowl, and strain the mussel liquor through cheesecloth or muslin,

reserving 1¹/₄ cup (10 oz). When the mussels have cooled enough to handle, discard their shells.

In the top of a double boiler, mix the egg yolks with the cream, then gradually whisk in the cornstarch. Place the pan over barely simmering water, and stir in the reserved mussel liquor. Stir until the mixture thickens, then mix in the mussels and parsley, and allow them to heat through for a few minutes. Season to taste with salt and black pepper, cover the sauce, and keep it warm while you check the chicken.

When the chicken is cooked, drain it, discard the bay leaf, then arrange the pieces on a warmed serving dish, pour over the mussel sauce, and serve.

Spinach, Cress, and Water Chestnut Salad

Serves 4

> 3 scallions or spring onions
> 1/3 cup (2²/3 oz) olive oil
> 2 Tb soy sauce
> Black pepper
> 1/2 lb (225 g) trimmed spinach
> 1 cup (225 g) canned water chestnuts, drained
> 1 small bunch of trimmed watercress
> 1¹/2 Tb toasted sesame seeds

Thinly slice the scallions. Then in a jar or small bowl, thoroughly mix the olive oil and soy sauce, and season to taste with black pepper. Wash the spinach thoroughly in cold water and dry it. Arrange the spinach in a salad bowl. Then slice the water chestnuts and scatter them over the spinach with the watercress, scallions, and sesame seeds. Pour the dressing over, toss, and serve.

Stir-fried Bean Sprouts

These beans have a high protein content and are a good complement to sweet-and-sour prawns. They are also very easy to do. *Serves 3 to 4*

> 1 Tb sesame or corn oil
> 1 small onion, peeled and finely chopped
> 3 cups (12 oz) bean sprouts
> 1 tsp lemon juice
> 2 tsp superfine or castor sugar
> 1 tsp soy sauce

Heat the oil over high heat, then add the chopped onion and bean sprouts, and cook for 1 minute, stirring. Add the lemon juice, sugar, and soy sauce, stir-fry for 1–2 minutes longer, and serve.

Poached Pears in Orange with Chocolate Sauce

A most attractive dessert, combining the contrasting pale yellow of the pears with the richness of orange chocolate. Here the cocoa combined with the orange increases the absorption of iron in the bloodstream, helping to oxygenate it and alleviate any nervous stress, insomnia, or catarrh —all possible Piscean complaints. This is delicious served alone or with vanilla or orange ice cream. *Serves 4 to 6*

> 6 ripe Comice pears
> Juice of about 8 fresh oranges (3 cups; 24 oz)

> Chocolate sauce
> > 2 Tb cocoa
> > 4 Tb brown sugar
> > Pinch of salt
> > ½ cup (4 oz) orange juice (reserved from juice the pears were cooked in)
> > 1 Tb butter
> > 2 Tb Grand Marnier or Cointreau

Peel the pears, but leave their stalks intact. Then slice their bottoms so they can stand upright and set them in a medium-size saucepan. Pour the orange juice over, bring to a boil, cover, and simmer gently for 10 minutes, or until the pears are tender. Drain, reserving ½ cup (4 oz) of orange juice. Arrange the pears upright on a serving dish.

In a small saucepan mix together the cocoa, sugar, and salt, gradually stir in the reserved orange juice, and place the pan over medium heat. Bring to a boil, stir in the butter, and cook for about 5 minutes, or until the mixture has thickened slightly. Then remove the pan from the heat, stir in the Grand Marnier, pour the sauce over the pears, and serve.

Raspberry Trifle

Rich in whisky and sherry, this typical English dessert is the perfect dish to serve a Piscean.
Serves 4

Victoria sponge cake to line a 9-inch glass bowl (see page 98), or store-bought sponge cake

³/8 cup (3 oz) medium-sweet sherry

2 Tb (1 oz) whisky

4 Tb raspberry jam

2 bananas

¹/2 lb (8 oz) raspberries, washed and hulled

¹/4 cup (1 oz) toasted slivered almonds

Custard

4 large egg yolks

3 Tb brown sugar

2 Tb cornstarch

2 cups (16 oz) milk

2 Tb sweet sherry

1¹/4 cups (10 oz) heavy or double cream

A few drops of vanilla

First break the sponge cake roughly into about 1- or 2-inch squares and lay it over the bottom of a glass bowl. Then pour the medium-sweet sherry and the whisky evenly over the cake, and spread the raspberry jam over it to make a thin and even covering. Peel and slice the bananas thinly crosswise, and arrange them over the sponge with the raspberries and half of the nuts. Now prepare the custard.

In the top of a double boiler mix the egg yolks with the sugar, and then whisk in the cornstarch. Place the top of the double boiler over barely simmering water, add the milk, and stir until the mixture thickens to a custard. Lift off the top of the double boiler, remove it from the heat, and stir in the sweet sherry. Pour the custard over the fruit and nuts and leave it to chill for about an hour. When the custard has set, beat the cream with a little vanilla and spread it over the custard. Sprinkle the remaining nuts over the top and serve.

Strawberry, Banana, and Kiwi Fruit Tart

This attractive, eye-catching dish makes a palette of tastes and matches Pisces, the artist, who has a heightened awareness of beauty. Venus is exalted in this sign of the zodiac, and here the fruits of Venus will excite the Piscean appetite and act as a gentle digestive. Strawberries will also have a cooling effect on the blood and liver, Piscean weak spots. This goes especially well with a sweet white wine, such as a Sauternes, and plenty of cream. *Serves 6*

Sweet shortcrust pastry to line a 9-inch pie pan (see page 117)

Crème pâtissière
3 medium egg yolks
1/4 cup (1 3/4 oz) light brown sugar
Pinch of salt
2 Tb cornstarch
1 cup (8 oz) milk
1 Tb sweet sherry

1 pint (8 oz) strawberries, hulled
2 medium bananas
2 kiwi fruit, peeled and thinly sliced
2 Tb apricot jam
1 tsp water

Preheat the oven to 425°F (220°C; gas 7).

Roll the pastry out on a floured board to line a 9-inch pie pan, trim the edges, and prick the bottom with a fork. Place it in the oven for 12–15 minutes, or until golden. Remove from the heat and set aside to cool. Meanwhile prepare the crème pâtissière. In the top of a double boiler mix the egg yolks with the sugar and salt, and gradually whisk in the cornstarch. Place over barely simmering water and slowly stir in the milk, stirring constantly until the mixture thickens (if it goes lumpy, remove it from the heat and whisk). Let it cook for a minute after it has thickened. Remove the custard from the heat, mix in the sherry, cover, and set aside to cool. Now spread the custard evenly over the base of the pastry, and leave to chill.

Slice the strawberries into about 1/4-inch thickness lengthwise. Peel and slice the bananas and arrange along with the strawberries and kiwi fruit decoratively over the custard. In a small saucepan gently melt the apricot jam with the water, without boiling. Cool slightly, and using a pastry brush, brush the jam over the fruit. Chill the tart 10–15 minutes before serving.

Lime Soufflé

This subtle-tasting dessert relates to the secret and subtle strength of this sign. While its lightness suggests the Piscean receptivity to higher levels, Jupiter-ruled limes are combined here with nourishing and iron-rich egg yolks and almonds, producing a light and refreshing end to a meal. Lime Soufflé is particularly good served with whipped cream. *Serves 4*

> 2 Tb butter
> 2 Tb flour
> 1/2 cup (4 oz) milk
> Juice of about 5 limes (2/3 cup; 51/2 oz)
> 5 medium eggs, separated
> 1/4 cup (1 oz) toasted slivered almonds
> Grated peel of 1 lime
> 5 Tb superfine or castor sugar

Preheat the oven to 325°F (165°C; gas 3). Butter a 1½-quart soufflé dish.

In a medium-size saucepan, melt the butter and stir in the flour to form a roux. Cook for 1–2 minutes, then gradually pour in the milk. Stir continuously until smooth, then slowly add the lime juice and bring to a boil. Cook for a few minutes before removing from the heat.

In a large mixing bowl, lightly beat the egg yolks. When the sauce has cooled slightly, stir it into the egg yolks with the almonds and lime peel. (Make sure the sauce has cooled enough so you don't curdle the egg yolks.)

Beat the egg whites in a large bowl until they are stiff, and then, using a metal spoon, fold them into the lime mixture along with the sugar. Turn into the buttered soufflé dish and bake for 35–40 minutes, or until the soufflé has risen and cooked through. Serve immediately.

Highland Fling

An effortless, quick, and intoxicating dessert, a must for the Piscean cook, who can make this either five minutes before a dinner party or the day before. Combining the fragrant and enticing taste of honey with the hidden strength of whisky, Highland Fling directly suggests the duality and concealed power of this sign. *Serves 4*

> 1 cup (8 oz) heavy or double cream
>
> 4 Tb (2 oz) whisky
>
> 4 Tb (2 oz) clear honey
>
> 1 cup (8 oz) plain yogurt
>
> 2 Tb brown sugar (optional)

In a large mixing bowl beat the cream stiff, then beat in the whisky and honey until the mixture regains its firmness. Fold in the yogurt and turn the mixture into a glass serving dish or individual glass dishes.

For a sweet top, sprinkle the sugar over, and leave it to chill overnight before serving.

Madame Banchet's Chestnut Pudding

A simple, velvety dish that is no trouble to make and looks impressive. *Serves 4 to 6*

> 2 cups (15¹/₂ oz; 439 g) canned chestnut purée
>
> 5 Tb superfine or castor sugar
>
> 1¹/₄ cups (¹/₂ Imperial pint) heavy or double cream
>
> A few drops of vanilla

Meringue
> 3 large egg whites
>
> 1¹/₂ Tb superfine or castor sugar
>
> 1¹/₂ Tb confectioners or icing sugar

Preheat the broiler.

In a food processor or mixing bowl beat the chestnut purée with the superfine sugar. Place the mixture in a shallow ovenproof dessert dish, approximately 8 by 10 inches, and spread it evenly over the base.

In a fresh mixing bowl, with clean beaters, beat the cream with the vanilla until it is stiff and spread it over the chestnut purée. Then, again using a clean bowl and beaters, beat the egg whites, adding the sugars, until they form peaks. Pour the meringue over the cream so the cream is completely covered, and place the dish about 2 inches below the broiler. Cook for 1–3 minutes, until the meringue is lightly browned, and then serve.

Index

almond(s)
    and fennel fish soup, 279
    ground, in carrot torte, 144
    slivered in
        apfel strudel, 168
        figs with rum, 169
        Polynesian pork, 115–16
    toasted
        with cherry ice cream with
            cherry brandy, 50
        with French beans, 165
        in Nelly's shape, 48
        in shrimp fricassee, 68
    and watercress soup, 252
amber crème, 241
anchovy fillets
    in egg mousse, 81
    in quail eggs in pastry, 129
    in salade Niçoise, 134
    in Singapore sole, 13
angels on horseback, 257
apfel strudel, 168
apple(s)
    and bacon with chicory salad,
        155
    and beef stew, 89
    Bramley, in apfel strudel, 168
    brulée, toasted, 51
    with choux pastry ring, 270–1
    Granny Smith
        in Bute Street salad, 132
        in lamb kebabs, 16
        in mixed spiced vegetables, 21
    McIntosh, in apfel strudel, 168
    sponge, 240
apricot(s)
    fool, 74
    with gingered chicken, 113–14
    jam and cream-baked custard, 96

apricot(s) (continued)
    sauce with mixed melon
        and mango, 145
Aquarius
    characteristics of, 247
    the cook, 248
    the guest, 250
    menu suggestions and recipes for, 249
arborio rice in chicken liver risotto, 264
Aries
    characteristics of, 3
    the cook, 4
    the guest, 6
    menu suggestions and recipes for, 5
armagnac in flamed chicken
        with cherries, 160–1
arroz con pollo, 187–8
artichoke(s)
    bottoms with Parma ham, 130
    globe with hollandaise, 60
    heart soufflés, 255
asparagus
    with chicken, 45
    and chicken salad, 202
    soufflé, 63
    steamed, with hollandaise, 11
    wrapped in Parma ham, 177
aspic
    chicken livers in, 283
    eggs in, 179
aubergine. See eggplant(s)
avocado(s)
    in crab salad, 133
    with crab and walnuts, 278
    in guacamole, 154
    kiwi fruit, and radicchio salad, 33
    melon, and mozzarella salad, 253
    in salad Saint-Tropez, 60
    with tropical smoked salmon, 154

bacon
    and apple with chicory salad, 155
    in corn soup, 131
    in mixed bean salad, 229–30
    and monkfish kebabs, 206
    with mushrooms and horseradish, 182
    in spinach and chicken liver pâté, 231–2
    in stuffed tomatoes, 61
baked Alaska, 192–3
baked custard with apricot jam and cream, 96
baked spinach creams, 35–6
banana(s)
    flambé, 193
    strawberry, and kiwi fruit tart, 294
    in tropical fruit salad, 220
barley in stuffed cabbage leaves, 227–8
basil dressing, 108
bay leaves in cod with tomatoes and olives,
        112
beans (dried)
    chick-peas. See chick-peas
    flageolets
        in bean salad with lemon and
            yogurt dressing, 44
        in mixed bean salad, 229–30
    haricot beans in pork pot with hot pepperoni,
        88
    kidney (red)
        in bean salad with lemon and yogurt dressing,
        44
        in chili con carne, 15
        in mixed bean salad, 229–30
    kidney (white) in creamed noodles with liver
        and soy sauce, 287
    lentil salad with yogurt and parsley, 165
    navy, in pork pot with hot pepperoni, 88
    salad with lemon and yogurt dressing, 44
beans (dried and fresh)
    mixed salad, 229–30

beans (fresh)
    broad, in rabbit stew, 212
    green
        French, with toasted almonds, 165
        mixed, in vinaigrette, 36
        in salade Niçoise, 134
        with stir-fried vegetables and monkfish, 136
    lima
        in mixed bean vinaigrette, 36
        in rabbit stew, 212
        in spring stew, 40–1
bean sprouts, stir-fried, 291
Beard, James, 30
béchamel sauce, 37–8
    in artichoke heart soufflés, 255
    in egg mousse, 81
    for lasagne, 234
    for salmon quiche, 233
beef
    and apple stew, 89
    and chestnut loaf, 237
    chopped, in hamburgers with cheese and nuts,
        67
    consommé in eggs in aspic, 179
    fillet steaks with mushroom and scallop sauce,
        42–3
    ground, in Bolognese sauce
        for lasagne, 234
    ground chuck, in chili con carne, 15
    meatballs with mushroom sauce, 207
    roll, wine-glazed, 286
    satay with peanut sauce, 204
    steak and kidney pie, 140
    stir-fried with water chestnuts, 265
beet(s)
    in orange sauce, 116
    red, watercress, and orange salad, 239
Belgian endive with ham and cheese, 284
black-and-white salad, 58

blackberry/ies
    and black currant fool, 244
    cream, 23
    jam in queen of puddings, 22
    in layered fruit sponge, 98
Bolognese sauce, 234
Bombay monkfish, 105
brandy
    in baked Alaska, 192–3
    cherry, with cherry ice cream, 50
    in crêpes Suzette, 119
bread
    brown, ice cream, 245
    fried, with Maria's sardines, 9
    garlic, 20
breaded lamb chops, 159
broccoli in garlic sauce, 190
brown bread ice cream, 245
brulée
    crème, 122
    toasted apple, 51
Brussels sprouts
    with chestnuts, 216
    mayonnaise, 266
Bute Street salad, 132
butter, rum, 243

cabbage
    leaves, stuffed, 227–8
    red, sweet-and-sour, 93
    white, in coleslaw with caraway, 141
    white, in pork pot with hot pepperoni,
        88
cake
    cheese
        chocolate, 195
        coconut, 269
        ginger, 24

cake (*continued*)
    sponge
        layered fruit, 98
        Victoria, 98
    strawberry cream, 73
Cancer
    characteristics of, 75
    the cook, 77
    the guest, 79
    menu suggestions and recipes for, 78
cantaloupe in melon, cucumber, and mango salad, 80
capers
    and lemon poached with skate, 66
    in salmon tartare, 109
Capricorn
    characteristics of, 221
    the cook, 223
    the guest, 225
    menu suggestions and recipes for, 224
caramel
    in amber crème, 241
    rice, 146
caramelized oranges, 119
caraway with coleslaw, 141
carrot(s)
    baby
        in spring chicken, 18
        in spring stew, 40–1
    cashew nut and dill soup, 57
    in kipper and tomato ring with crudités, 226–7
    in pork pot with hot pepperoni, 88
    torte, 144
cashew nut(s)
    carrot, and dill soup, 57
    and green pepper with sweet-and-sour shrimp, 289
    with pork and orange, 183–4
cauliflower
    in mixed spiced vegetables, 21
    in mixed vegetables in cheese pastry, 262

cauliflower (*continued*)
 and Stilton soup, 228–9
caviar
 in chilled consommé Maria, 80
 in eggs in aspic, 178
 pie, 106
 in smoked haddock mousse, 62
celery
 in gazpacho, 10
 hearts with mozzarella and tomato sauce, 85
cell salt. *See under individual astrological signs*
charlotte
 coffee-hazelnut, 72
 strawberry, 272
cheddar cheese
 in asparagus soufflé, 63
 in avocado with crab and walnuts, 278
 in Belgian endive with ham and cheese, 284
 in chicken, zucchini, and shrimp tart, 92
 in fennel in cheese sauce, 69
 in leeks in cheese sauce, 180
 in mixed vegetables in cheese pastry,
  262–3
 in onion and cheese tart, 17
 in semolina gnocchi, 128
 in stuffed cabbage leaves, 227–8
 in stuffed peppers, 178
 in stuffed tomatoes, 61
cheese
 croque monsieur, 254
 and ham with Belgian endive, 284
 and nuts with hamburgers, 67
 and onion tart, 17
 pastry with mixed vegetables,
  262–3
 salami croissants, 155
 sauce
  with fennel, 69
  with leeks, 180

cheese (*continued*)
 See also under cheddar, cream, Emmenthal, feta,
  Gloucester, goat, Gruyère, mozzarella,
  parmesan, Stilton
cheesecake
 chocolate, 195
 coconut, 269
 ginger, 24
cherry-chili sauce with roast duck, 91
cherry/ies
 flamed with chicken, 160–1
 ice cream with cherry brandy, 50
 in layered fruit sponge, 98
chestnut(s)
 and beef loaf, 237
 with Brussels sprouts, 216
 pudding, Madame Banchet's, 296
 soufflé, 216
chicken
 arroz con pollo, 187–8
 with asparagus, 45
 and asparagus salad, 202
 drumsticks, deviled, 236
 filling in cucumber ring, 282
 flamed with cherries, 160–1
 gingered with apricots, 113–14
 legs in paella formenterra, 209
 liver(s)
  in aspic, 283
  with Marsala, 182–3
  pâté, 33
  risotto, 264
  and spinach pâté, 231–2
 pear and cress salad, 37
 poached, with mussel sauce, 290
 satay with peanut sauce, 260
 spring, 18
 soup with vermicelli, 83
 zucchini, and shrimp tart, 92

chick-peas
    in bean salad with lemon and yogurt dressing, 44
    in hummus, 8
chicory salad with apple and bacon, 155
chili-cherry sauce with roast duck, 91
chili con carne, 15
chilled consommé Maria, 80
chocolate
    cheesecake, 195
    mousse, 94
    pots de crème, 242
    sauce
        with choux pastry ring, 120
        with figs in rum, 169
        with poached pears in orange, 292
choux pastry ring
    with apple, 270–1
    with chocolate sauce, 120
chowder, fish, 201
cinnamon pastry, 49
coconut cheesecake, 269
coconut milk
    in beef satay with peanut sauce, 204
    in chicken satay with peanut sauce, 260
cod
    in almonds and fennel fish soup, 279
    in fish chowder, 201
    in fish pie, 41–2
    roe, smoked, in taramosalata, 203
    in spiced fish, 19
    in sweet-and-sour fish, 65
    with tomatoes and olives, 112
coffee
    hazelnut charlotte, 72
    marshmallow mousse, 27
cognac
    in flambé bananas, 193
    in flamed chicken with cherries,
        160–1

Cointreau
    in crêpes Suzette, 119
    in custard sauce, 97
    in orange cream, 74
coleslaw with caraway, 141
Comice pears. See under pear(s)
coquilles St. Jacques, 157
coriander and lemon dressing with leeks, 280
corn
    soufflé, sweet, 161
    soup, 131
courgette. See zucchini
court bouillon, 185
crab
    claws
        in paella formenterra, 209–10
        in zarzuela, 258
    ring with mussels, 162–3
    roast, with ginger and scallions, 87
    salad, 133
    and walnuts with avocado, 278
cream(s)
    and apricot jam baked custard, 96
    blackberry, 23
    ginger loaf, 218
    orange, 74
    peach, and grape salad, 171
    spinach, baked, 35–6
    See also crème
cream cheese
    in chilled consommé Maria, 80
    in chocolate cheesecake, 195
    in coconut cheesecake, 269
    in ginger cheesecake, 24
creamed noodles with liver and soy sauce,
    287
crème
    amber, 241
    brulée, 122

crème (*continued*)
    chocolate, pots de, 242
    See also cream(s) *and* custard
crème pâtissière, 217, 294
crêpes Suzette, 119
cress
    pear, and chicken salad, 37
    spinach, and water chestnut salad, 291
    See also under watercress
croissants, cheese-salami, 155
croque monsieur, 254
crown of lamb, 111
crudités with kipper and tomato ring,
      226–7
crumb crust
    gingersnap, 195
    graham cracker or digestive biscuit, 99, 166
cucumber(s)
    in gazpacho, 10
    in Greek salad, 266
    with lemon sole and dill, 135
    melon, and mango salad, 80
    and radish salad, minted, 20
    ring with chicken filling, 282
    salad with yogurt and mint, 142
Culpeper, Nicholas, 23, 112, 212
currant(s)
    black, and blackberry fool, 244
    black, in layered fruit sponge, 98
    black and red, in summer pudding, 191
curry/ied
    parsnip soup, 34
    powder in Maria's sardines on fried bread, 9
    shrimp and spinach, 214
custard
    amber crème, 241
    apple brulée, toasted, 51
    apricot jam and cream, baked, 96
    blackberry cream, 23

custard (*continued*)
    crème brulée, 122
    floating islands, 143
    with lemon snow, 97
    sauce
      Cointreau, 97
      sherry, 194, 293
    See also cream, crème, pudding

dandelion leaves in salad Saint-Tropez, 60
deep-fried mushrooms with tartar sauce, 205
deviled chicken drumsticks, 236
dill
    carrot and cashew nut soup, 57
    and cucumber with lemon sole, 135
Dover sole in sole meunière, 232
dressing
    basil, 108
    coriander and lemon, 280
    lemon and yogurt, 44
    vinaigrette
      garlic, 134
      honey, 80
      hot, 133
      lemon, 117
      mint, 36
      orange, 239
duck
    roast, with chili-cherry sauce, 91
    with orange and olives, 261–2

eel, poached with parsley sauce, 185–6
egg(s)
    in aspic, 179
    in floating islands, 143
    mousse, 81
    pipérade, 114–15

egg(s) (*continued*)
  quail, in pastry, 129
  scrambled
    cold, stuffed in tomatoes, 256
    with smoked salmon, 203
eggplant(s)
  all'uovo, 215
  in moussaka, 37–8
  spiced, 188–9
  stuffed with pine nuts, 82
  and zucchini au gratin, 90
Emmenthal cheese
  in croque monsieur, 254
  with onion soup, 181
  in Swiss potato dish, 238
endive
  Belgian, with ham and cheese, 284
  curly, in lobster salad, 186–7

fennel
  and almond fish soup, 279
  in cheese sauce, 69
  with roast poussin, 64
feta cheese in Greek salad, 266
fig(s)
  fresh, and goat cheese salad, 230
  fresh, wrapped in smoked salmon, 278
  with rum in chocolate sauce, 169
fillet steak with scallop and mushroom sauce,
    42–3
fish
  chowder, 201
  pie, 41–2
  soup with fennel and almond, 279
  spiced, 19
  sweet-and-sour, 65
  See also under anchovy, cod, Dover sole, eel,
    flounder, haddock, halibut, kipper, lemon sole,

fish (*continued*)
    monkfish, plaice, salmon, sardines, shark,
    skate, smoked fish, sole, squid, swordfish,
    trout, tuna fish, turbot
flageolet beans. *See under* beans (dried)
flambé bananas, 193
flamed chicken with cherries, 160–1
floating islands, 143
flounder in Singapore sole, 13
fool
  apricot, 74
  blackberry, and black currant, 244
  rhubarb, 190
French beans with toasted almonds, 165
fresh fig and goat cheese salad, 278
fresh figs wrapped in smoked salmon, 278
fruit
  salad
    jellied, 268
    tropical, 220
  sponge, layered, 98
  See also under the names of individual fruits

game
  roast grouse, 139
  roast pheasant and bread sauce,
    208–9
garlic
  bread, 20
  mushrooms, 8
  and mussels with spaghetti, 86
  sauce with broccoli, 190
gazpacho, 10
Gemini
  characteristics of, 53
  the cook, 54
  the guest, 56
  menu and recipe suggestions for, 55

ginger
  cheesecake, 24
  cream loaf, 218
  pudding, steamed, 26
  and scallions with roast crab, 87
gingered chicken with apricots,
    113–14
gingerroot
  in mixed spiced vegetables, 21
  in spiced eggplant, 188–9
  in stir-fried vegetables with monkfish,
    136
globe artichokes with hollandaise, 60
Gloucester cheese in leeks and cheese sauce,
    180
gnocchi
  potato, 35
  semolina, 128
goat cheese and fresh fig salad, 230
gooseberry/ies
  crumble, 51
  in summer pudding, 191
grape(s)
  in black-and-white salad, 58
  with halibut and peanuts, 39
  in jellied fruit salad, 268
  and peach cream salad, 171
  white seedless, in ham Véronique,
    138
Greek salad, 266
green beans. *See under* beans (fresh)
green pepper and cashew nuts with sweet-and-sour
    shrimp, 289
  For additional green pepper recipes, see under
    pepper(s)
grouse, roast, 139
Gruyère cheese
  in Belgian endive with ham and cheese, 284
  in cheese-salami croissants, 155

Gruyère cheese (*continued*)
  with chicory salad with apples and bacon,
    155
  in croque monsieur, 254
  in eggplant and zucchini au gratin, 90
  with onion soup, 181
  in potatoes au gratin, 189
  in seafood pancakes, 83–4
  in Swiss potato dish, 238
guacamole, 154

haddock
  in fish chowder, 201
  mousse, smoked, 62
  in spiced fish, 19
  in sweet-and-sour fish, 65
halibut
  with peanuts and grapes, 39
  in salmon tartare, 109
ham
  and cheese with Belgian endive, 284
  parma
    with artichoke bottoms, 130
    asparagus wrapped in, 177
    with melon, 108
  Véronique, 138
hamburgers with cheese and nuts, 67
haricot beans in pork pot with hot pepperoni,
    88
hazelnut-coffee charlotte, 72
herbs and spices. *See under individual herbs and*
    also under individual astrological signs
herring fillets, pickled, in Bute Street salad,
    132
Highland fling, 296
hollandaise
  basic sauce, 11
  with globe artichokes, 60

honeydew
    in avocado, melon, and mozzarella salad,
        253
    in gazpacho, 10
    in melon, cucumber, and mango salad, 80
    in tropical fruit salad, 220
horseradish with mushrooms and bacon, 182
hummus, 8

ice cream
    brown bread, 245
    cherry, with cherry brandy, 50
    pistachio, 170
    rose petal, 170
    vanilla, in baked Alaska, 192–3

jellied fruit salad, 268
Jerusalem artichokes in spring stew, 40–1

Kaori's oven-baked spareribs, 111
kebabs
    lamb, 16
    monkfish and bacon, 206
kidney(s)
    in pastry shells, 12
    spiced, 211–12
    stew, 163
kipper and tomato ring with crudités,
        226–7
kiwi
    banana, and strawberry fruit tart, 294
    fruit, avocado, and radicchio salad, 33
    fruit with tropical smoked salmon, 154
    in jellied fruit salad, 268
    in tropical fruit salad, 220
kirsch in peach and grape cream salad, 171

ladyfingers
    in Lady Scott's lemon pudding, 147
    in rhubarb fool, 190
Lady Scott's lemon pudding, 147
lamb
    chops, breaded, 159
    crown of, 111
    ground, in moussaka, 37–8
    kebabs, 16
    kidneys
        in lamb kebabs, 16
        in pastry shells, 12
        spiced, 211–12
        stew, 163
    minced, in stuffed vine leaves,
        106–7
    shoulder of, in spring stew,
        40–1
lasagne, 234
layered fruit sponge, 98
leek(s)
    in cheese sauce, 180
    with lemon and coriander dressing,
        280
    and pea purée, 237
    tart, Neapolitan, 288
    in vichyssoise with pecans, 110
lemon
    and capers poached with skate, 66
    and coriander dressing, 280
    curd, 147
    lovely, 71
    pudding, Lady Scott's, 147
    snow with custard, 97
    and yogurt dressing, 44
lemon sole
    with cucumber and dill, 135
    in Singapore sole, 13
    in sole meunière, 232

lentil salad with yogurt and parsley, 165
Leo
    characteristics of, 101
    the cook, 102
    the guest, 104
    menu suggestions and recipes for, 103
Libra
    characteristics of, 149
    the cook, 150
    the guest, 152
    menu suggestions and recipes for, 151
lima beans
    in mixed bean vinaigrette, 36
    in rabbit stew, 212
    in spring stew, 40–1
lime soufflé, 295
litchis
    in layered fruit sponge, 98
    in tropical fruit salad, 220
liver
    calf's, with creamed noodles and soy sauce, 287
    chicken
        in aspic, 283
        with Marsala, 182–3
        pâté, 33
        risotto, 264
        and spinach pâté, 231–2
loaf
    beef and chestnut, 237
    cream ginger, 218
lobster
    salad, 186–7
    thermidor, 112–13

Madame Banchet's chestnut pudding, 296
Madeira soufflé, 271

mango
    melon, and cucumber salad, 80
    and melon, mixed, with apricot sauce, 145
maple pudding, rummed, 218
Maria's sardines on fried bread, 9
marmalade in Nelly's shape, 48
Marsala
    with chicken livers, 182–3
    soufflé, 271
    in zabaglione, 70
marshmallow
    coffee mousse, 27
    raspberry pudding, 166
mayonnaise, 58
    Brussels sprouts, 266
    by processor, 58
meat. See under beef, ham, lamb, pork, rabbit
meatballs with mushroom sauce, 207
mélange of seafood in white wine sauce, 7
melon
    avocado, and mozzarella salad, 253
    cucumber salad, 80
    and mango, mixed, with apricot sauce, 145
    with parma ham, 108
meringue
    in baked Alaska, 192–3
    in Madame Banchet's chestnut pudding, 296
    raspberry pyramid, 121
mint(ed)
    cucumber and radish salad, 20
    and pea soup, 156
    and yogurt with cucumber salad, 142
mixed bean salad, 229–30
mixed bean vinaigrette, 36
mixed melon and mango with apricot sauce, 145
mixed spiced vegetables, 21
mixed vegetables in cheese pastry, 262–3

monkfish
    and bacon kebabs, 206
    Bombay, 105
    in a mélange of seafood in white wine sauce,
        7
    in seafood pancakes, 83–4
    with stir-fried vegetables, 136
moussaka, 37–8
mousse
    chocolate, 94
    egg, 81
    marshmallow-coffee, 27
    smoked haddock, 62
mozzarella
    melon, and avocado salad, 253
    in pizza, 210–11
    in red, white, and black salad, 108
    and tomato sauce with celery hearts, 85
mushroom(s)
    in chicken liver risotto, 264
    in coquilles St. Jacques, 157
    deep-fried, with tartar sauce, 205
    garlic, 8
    with horseradish and bacon, 182
    in lamb kebabs, 16
    Montreal, 58
    pâté, 132
    in rolled seaweed Bex, 281
    sauce with meatballs, 207
    and scallop sauce with fillet steak,
        42–3
    in shrimp fricassee, 68
    in spiced eggplant, 188–9
    in steak and kidney pie, 140
    in stuffed tomatoes, 61
    and watercress with trout, 285
mussel(s)
    in black-and-white salad, 58
    with crab ring, 162–3

mussel(s) (continued)
    and garlic with spaghetti, 86
    in a mélange of seafood in white wine sauce, 7
    in paella formenterra, 209–10
    sauce with poached chicken, 290
    smoked, in fish chowder, 201
    in zarzuela, 258

navy beans in pork pot with hot pepperoni, 88
Neapolitan leek tart, 288
Nelly's shape, 48
noodles, creamed, with liver and soy sauce,
    287
nutmeg and yogurt with spinach, 239
nuts and cheese with hamburgers, 67

olives
    black, in Greek salad, 266
    black, in red, white, and black salad,
        108
    and orange roast with duck, 261–2
    with spaghetti and tuna fish, 14
    with tomatoes and cod, 112
omelet. See pipérade
onion(s)
    and cheese tart, 17
    in gazpacho, 10
    soup, 181
    Spanish, in pipérade, 114–15
orange(s)
    caramelized, 119
    cream, 74
    and olives roast with duck, 261–2
    pastry, 95
    with pork and cashew nuts, 183–4
    sauce with beets, 116
    watercress, and red beet salad, 239

orange jelly in jellied fruit salad, 268
oysters
    with hot tomato sauce, 153
    smoked
        in fish chowder, 201
        and palm heart salad, 117

paella formenterra, 209–10
palm heart(s)
    in batter, 251
    and smoked oyster salad, 117
pancakes, seafood, 83–4
papaya in mixed melon with mango and apricot
        sauce, 145
parma ham
    with artichoke bottoms, 130
    asparagus wrapped in, 177
    with melon, 108
parmesan cheese
    in lasagne, 234
    in pork costoletta, 69
    in semolina gnocchi, 128
parsley
    sauce with poached eel, 185–6
    and yogurt with lentil salad, 165
parsnip(s)
    in mixed spiced vegetables, 21
    sauce with Singapore sole, 13
    soufflé, 137
pastry
    cheese, 262–3
    choux ring
        with apple, 270–1
        with chocolate sauce, 120
    cinnamon, 49
    orange, 95
    quick flaky, 158
    salmon wrapped in, 158

pastry (continued)
    shells with kidneys, 12
    shortcrust, 12, 129
    shortcrust, sweet, 117–18
    whole wheat, 17
pâté
    chicken liver, 33
    mushroom, 132
    smoked trout, 177
    spinach and chicken liver,
        231–2
pea(s)
    in arroz con pollo, 187
    in chicken liver risotto, 264
    and leek purée, 237
    and mint soup, 156
    in mixed vegetables in cheese pastry,
        262–3
    in Polynesian pork, 115–16
    snow, in spring chicken, 18
    in spiced mixed vegetables, 21
peach and grape cream salad, 171
peanut(s)
    with halibut and grapes, 39
    sauce
        with beef satay, 204
        with chicken satay, 260
pear(s)
    Comice
        cress, and chicken salad, 37
        poached, in orange with chocolate sauce,
            292
        in port, 167
        in zabaglione, 219
    in jellied fruit salad, 268
pecans
    chopped, in rummed maple pudding,
        218
    with vichyssoise, 110

pepper(s)
  green
    in gazpacho, 10
    stuffed, 178
    with sweet-and-sour shrimp, 289
  red, in pipérade, 114–15
  yellow, in pipérade, 114–15
pepperoni, hot, with pork pot, 88
pheasant, roast, and bread sauce,
    208–9
pie
  caviar, 106
  fish, 41–2
  pumpkin, 95
  rhubarb, 25
  steak and kidney, 140
pineapple
  in lamb kebabs, 16
  in Singapore sole, 13
pine nuts
  in stuffed cabbage leaves, 227
  stuffed in eggplant, 82
  in stuffed peppers, 178
pipérade, 114–15
Pisces
  characteristics of, 273
  the cook, 275
  the guest, 277
  menu and recipe suggestions for, 276
pistachio ice cream, 142
pizza, 210–11
plaice in Singapore sole, 13
plum
  pudding, 242
  tart, 49
poached chicken with mussel sauce, 290
poached eel with parsley sauce, 185–6
poached pears in orange with chocolate sauce,
    292

poached skate with capers and lemon, 66
Polynesian pork, 115–16
pork
  chipolatas in beef and apple stew, 89
  costoletta, 69
  ham. See ham
  with orange and cashew nuts, 183–4
  Polynesian, 115–16
  pot with hot pepperoni, 88
  sausages. See sausages
  shoulder in paella formenterra, 209–10
  spareribs, Kaori's oven-baked, 111
port with pears, 167
potato(es)
  dish, Swiss, 238
  gnocchi, 35
  au gratin, 189
  in moussaka, 37–8
  new
    in black-and-white salad, 58
    in Bute Street salad, 132
    in chicken and asparagus salad, 202
    in pork pot with hot pepperoni, 88
    in spring chicken, 18
    in spring stew, 40–1
  in vichyssoise with pecans, 110
poultry. See under chicken, poussin, Rock Cornish
    hens, squab, turkey. See also game
poussin, roast, with fennel, 64
prawns
  in paella formenterra, 209–10
  wrapped in smoked salmon, 226
  in zarzuela, 258
prune(s)
  in angels on horseback, 257
  whip, 194
pudding(s)
  apple sponge cake, 240
  Lady Scott's lemon, 147

pudding(s) (*continued*)
  Madame Banchet's chestnut, 296
  plum, 242
  Queen Anne's, 267
  queen of, 22
  raspberry-marshmallow, 166
  rhubarb with strawberries, 99
  rice caramel, 146
  rummed maple, 218
  steamed ginger, 26
  summer, 191
  See also custard
pumpkin pie, 95
purée, leek and pea, 180

quail eggs in pastry, 129
Queen Anne's pudding, 267
queen of puddings, 22
quiche, salmon, 233
quick-fried turnips with soy sauce and yogurt, 94

rabbit
  pieces in paella formenterra, 209–10
  stew, 212–13
radicchio
  kiwi fruit, and avocado salad, 33
  in lobster salad, 186–7
  in palm heart and smoked oyster salad,
    117
radish(es)
  in kipper and tomato ring with crudités,
    226–7
  and minted cucumber salad, 20
raisins
  in apfel strudel, 168
  in plum pudding, 242
  in spiced fish, 19

raspberry/ies
  jam in queen of puddings, 22
  marshmallow pudding, 166
  meringue pyramid, 121
  in summer pudding, 191
  trifle, 293
red beet, watercress, and orange salad, 239
red, white, and black salad, 108
rhubarb
  fool, 190
  pie, 25
  pudding with strawberries, 99
rice
  in arroz con pollo, 187
  caramel pudding, 146
  in shrimp fricassee, 68
  in stuffed vine leaves, 106–7
risotto, chicken liver, 264
roast crab with ginger and scallions, 87
roast duck with chili-cherry sauce, 91
roast duck with orange and olives, 261–2
roast grouse, 139
roast pheasant and bread sauce, 209–10
roast poussin with fennel, 64
Rock Cornish hens, roast with fennel, 64
rolled seaweed Bex, 281
rose petal ice cream, 170
rum
  butter, 242
  with figs in chocolate sauce, 169
rummed maple pudding, 218
rutabaga in mixed vegetables in cheese pastry, 262–3

Sagittarius
  characteristics of, 197
  the cook, 198
  the guest, 200
  menu suggestions and recipes for, 199

salads
  avocado
    kiwi fruit, and radicchio, 33
    melon, and mozzarella, 253
  bean with lemon and yogurt dressing, 44
  black-and-white, 58
  Bute Street, 132
  chicken and asparagus, 202
  chicory with apple and bacon, 155
  crab, 133
  cucumber with yogurt and mint, 142
  fresh fig and goat cheese, 230
  grape and peach cream, 171
  Greek, 266
  jellied fruit, 267
  lentil with yogurt and parsley, 165
  lobster, 186–7
  melon, cucumber, and mango, 80
  minted cucumber and radish, 20
  mixed bean, 229–30
  red beet, watercress, and orange, 239
  red, white, and black, 108
  Saint-Tropez, 60
  salade Niçoise, 134
  spinach, cress, and water chestnut,
    291
  tropical fruit, 220
salami-cheese croissants, 155
salmon
  quiche, 233
  smoked
    fresh figs wrapped in, 278
    with scrambled eggs, 203
    tropical, 154
  tartare, 109
  wrapped in pastry, 158
sardines
  Maria's, on fried bread, 9
  in salade Niçoise, 134

sauce
  Bolognese, 234
  béchamel, 37–8
  bread, 208–9
  cheese, 69, 180
  chili-cherry, 91
  chocolate
    orange, 292
    rum, 169
  custard
    Cointreau, 97
    sherry, 194, 293
  garlic, 190
  hollandaise, 11
  mushroom, 207
  Neapolitan, 288
  parsnip, 13
  peanut, 204, 260
  shrimp, 235
  sparerib, 111
  sweet-and-sour, 65
  tartar, 205
  tomato, 85
    hot, 153
sausages
  pepperoni, hot, with pork pot, 88
  spicy garlic in Polynesian pork, 115–16
scallions and ginger with roast crab, 87
scallop(s)
  coquilles St. Jacques, 157
  in fish pie, 41–2
  and mushroom sauce with fillet steak,
    42–3
  in seafood pancakes, 83–4
Scorpio
  characteristics of, 173
  the cook, 174
  the guest, 176
  menu suggestions and recipes for, 175

scrambled eggs
  cold, tomatoes stuffed with, 256
  with smoked salmon, 203
seafood
  a mélange of, in white wine sauce, 7
  pancakes, 83–4
  zarzuela, 258
  See also under crab, fish, lobster, mussels,
      oysters, prawns, scallops, shrimp
seaweed
  Bex, rolled, 281
  as garnish for oysters with hot tomato sauce, 153
semolina gnocchi, 128
shark in spiced fish, 19
shellfish
  See under crab, lobster, mussels, oysters, prawns,
      scallops, shrimp
sherry
  custard sauce, 194, 293
  soufflé, 271
shrimp
  chicken, and zucchini tart, 92
  creole, 184–5
  in fish pie, 41–2
  fricassee, 68
  in monkfish Bombay, 105
  in salmon quiche, 233
  in seafood pancakes, 83–4
  sauce with turkey escalopes, 235
  and spinach curry, 214
  sweet-and-sour, with green pepper and cashew nuts,
      289
Singapore sole, 13
skate poached with capers and lemon, 66
smoked fish ·
  cod roe in taramosalata, 203
  haddock mousse, 62
  salmon
    fresh figs wrapped in, 278

smoked fish (*continued*)
  with scrambled eggs, 203
  tropical, 154
  trout pâté, 177
smoked shellfish
  mussels in fish chowder, 201
  oysters
    in fish chowder, 201
    and palm heart salad, 117
sole
  meunière, 232
  Singapore, 13
soufflé(s)
  artichoke heart, 255
  asparagus, 63
  chestnut, 216
  lime, 295
  Madeira, 271
  Marsala, 271
  parsnip, 137
  sherry, 271
  sweet corn, 161
soup
  almond and fennel fish, 279
  carrot, cashew nut, and dill, 57
  cauliflower and Stilton, 228–9
  chicken with vermicelli, 83
  chilled consommé Maria, 80
  corn, 131
  curried parsnip, 34
  fish chowder, 201
  gazpacho, 10
  mint and pea, 156
  onion, 181
  vichyssoise with pecans, 110
  watercress and almond, 252
soy sauce
  with creamed noodles and liver, 287
  and yogurt with quick-fried turnips, 94

spaghetti
   with mussels and garlic, 86
   with red and black caviar, 164
   with tuna fish and olives, 14
spareribs, Kaori's, oven-baked, 111
spiced eggplant, 188–9
spiced fish, 19
spiced kidneys, 211–12
spiced mixed vegetables, 21
spinach
   and chicken liver pâté, 231–2
   cooked, in lobster salad, 186–7
   creams, baked, 35–6
   cress, and water chestnut salad, 291
   leaves, young, in salad Saint-Tropez, 60
   and shrimp curry, 214
   and white Stilton tart, 259
   with yogurt and nutmeg, 239
sponge cake
   in baked Alaska, 192–3
   Victoria, in layered fruit, 98
spring chicken, 18
spring stew, 40–1
squab, roast, with fennel, 64
squid
   in a mélange of seafood in white wine sauce,
      7
   in paella formenterra, 209–10
   in zarzuela, 258
steak and kidney pie, 140
steamed asparagus with hollandaise, 11
steamed ginger pudding, 26
stew
   beef and apple, 89
   kidney, 163
   rabbit, 212–13
   spring, 40–1
Stilton
   and cauliflower soup, 228–9

Stilton (continued)
   and spinach tart, 259
stir-fried bean sprouts, 291
stir-fried beef with water chestnuts, 265
stir-fried vegetables with monkfish, 136
strawberry/ies
   banana, and kiwi fruit tart, 294
   charlotte, 272
   cream cake, 73
   with rhubarb pudding, 99
   tart, 217
stuffed cabbage leaves, 227–8
stuffed eggplant with pine nuts, 82
stuffed peppers, 178
stuffed tomatoes, 61
stuffed vine leaves, 106–7
summer pudding, 191
swede in mixed vegetables in cheese pastry, 262
sweet-and-sour
   fish, 65
   red cabbage, 93
   sauce, 65
   shrimp with green pepper and cashew nuts, 289
sweet corn soufflé, 161
Swiss potato dish, 238
swordfish in zarzuela, 258

tahini in hummus, 8
tangerines in jellied fruit salad, 268
taramosalata, 203
tart
   cheese and onion, 17
   chicken, zucchini, and shrimp, 92
   Neapolitan leek, 288
   plum, 49
   spinach and white Stilton, 259
   strawberry, 217
      banana, and kiwi fruit, 294

tart (*continued*)
    walnut, 117–18
tartar sauce with deep-fried mushrooms, 205
Taurus
    characteristics of, 29
    the cook, 30
    the guest, 32
    menu suggestions and recipes for, 31
tea in prune whip, 194
Tia Maria in coffee-hazelnut charlotte, 72
toasted apple brulée, 51
tofu in mushroom pâté, 132
tomato(es)
    in gazpacho, 10
    in Greek salad, 266
    Italian, in chili con carne, 15
    and kipper ring with crudités, 226–7
    in moussaka, 37–8
    and mozzarella sauce with celery hearts, 85
    and olives with cod, 112
    in red, white, and black salad, 108
    in salade Niçoise, 134
    sauce, 85
        hot, with oysters, 153
    in spiced eggplant, 188–9
    in spring stew, 40–1
    stuffed, 61
    in stuffed peppers, 178
    stuffed with cold scrambled eggs, 256
    in stuffed vine leaves, 106–7
torte, carrot, 144
trifle, raspberry, 293
tropical fruit salad, 220
tropical smoked salmon, 154
trout
    with mushrooms and watercress, 285
    pâté, smoked, 177
tuna fish
    in salade Niçoise, 134

tuna fish (*continued*)
    with spaghetti and olives, 14
    in stuffed peppers, 178
turbot in salmon tartare, 109
turkey escalopes with shrimp sauce, 235
turnips
    baby, in spring stew, 40–1
    in pork pot with hot pepperoni, 88
    quick-fried, with soy sauce and yogurt, 94

vanilla ice cream in baked Alaska, 192–3
vegetables
    mixed, in cheese pastry, 262–3
    mixed, spiced, 21
    stir-fried with monkfish, 136
    See also under individual names of vegetables
vermicelli with chicken soup, 83
vichyssoise with pecans, 110
Victoria sponge cake, 98
    in apple sponge, 240
    in raspberry trifle, 293
vinaigrette
    garlic, 134
    honey, 80
    hot, 133
    lemon, 117
    mint, 36
    orange, 239
vine leaves, stuffed, 106–7
Virgo
    characteristics of, 123
    the cook, 125
    the guest, 127
    menu suggestions and recipes for, 126

walnut(s)
    and crab with avocado, 278

walnut(s) (*continued*)
  tart, 117–18
water chestnut(s)
  and beef, stir-fried, 265
  spinach, and cress salad, 291
watercress
  and almond soup, 252
  in cress, spinach, and water chestnut salad,
    291
  in mushrooms with trout, 285
  in pear, cress, and chicken salad, 37
  red beet, and orange salad, 239
  See also under cress
white wine
  sauce with a mélange of seafood, 7
  in spaghetti with mussels and garlic, 86
whole wheat pastry in cheese and onion tart, 17
wine-glazed beef roll, 286

yogurt
  and lemon dressing with bean salad, 44
  and mint with cucumber salad, 142
  and nutmeg with spinach, 239
  and parsley with lentil salad, 165
  and soy sauce with quick-fried turnips, 94

zabaglione, 70
  with pears, 219
zarzuela, 258
zucchini
  all'uovo, 70
  and eggplant au gratin, 90
  chicken, and shrimp tart, 92
  in mixed vegetables in cheese pastry,
    262–3
  in stir-fried vegetables with monkfish, 136

A Note About the Author

*Lucy Ash was born in London, where she is currently
living. After completing art school, she became a
painter and exhibited some of her work in galleries in
and around London. In 1981 she began to develop
the recipes for this cookbook (portions of which have
appeared in* Gourmet*). This is her first book.*

A Note on the Type

The text of this book was composed in a film version of Optima, a typeface designed by Hermann Zapf from 1952 to 1955 and issued in 1958. In designing Optima, Zapf created a truly new typeform —a cross between the classic roman and a sans serif face. So delicate are the stresses and balances in Optima that it rivals sans serif faces in clarity and freshness and old-style faces in variety and interest.

Composed by Superior Type, Champaign, Illinois Printed and bound by Kingsport Press, Inc., Kingsport, Tennessee

Designed by Marysarah Quinn